Sept 06

All my love Dad

GENDERED PARADOXES

GENDERED PARADOXES

WOMEN'S MOVEMENTS, STATE RESTRUCTURING, AND GLOBAL DEVELOPMENT IN ECUADOR

AMY LIND

The Pennsylvania State University Press
University Park, Pennsylvania

Library of Congress Cataloging-in-Publication Data

Lind, Amy.
Gendered paradoxes : women's movements, state restructuring,
and global development in Ecuador / Amy Lind.
p.   cm.
Includes bibliographical references and index.
ISBN 0-271-02544-1 (alk. paper)
1. Women in development—Ecuador. 2. Women in politics—Ecuador.
3. Feminism—Ecuador. 4. Indian women—Ecuador. 5. Poor women—Ecuador.
6. Structural adjustment (Economic policy)—Ecuador.
7. Ecuador—Social policy.
8. Ecuador—Politics and government—1984– .
I. Title.

HQ1240.5.E2L56 2005
305.42'09866—dc22
2004015106

IN MEMORY OF MY GRANDMOTHERS,

Virginia Conger Kelsey
(1913–1982)

Marie Childers Lind
(1911–2000)

TO THE CONGER WOMEN

CONTENTS

Lynn Meisch has said, in rather ironic terms, that Ecuador had "the strongest indigenous movement and weakest economy in Latin America" at the turn of the century (Meisch 2000, 14; also quoted in Weismantel 2003, 330). Indeed, this is how most people hear about politics in Ecuador, through articles on either indigenous protests or financial collapse, if not on bananas or oil. But where are the women and how does gender shape these scenarios? With few exceptions, until very recently analysts of contemporary Ecuadorian politics, history, and economics have rarely mentioned the contributions of women to rethinking democratic governance and economic restructuring. Now, if women are mentioned, it is often as an afterthought or an aside. Likewise, gender is rarely viewed as central to the making of Ecuador as a modern nation, to struggles over national identity, or to the state's role in legislating public and private life. Through an examination of the gender dimensions of state restructuring, national identity, and global development in Ecuador, particularly as experienced through the lens of feminism and women's movements, this book places gender at the center of Ecuadorian and Latin American studies.

Like most books, this one is the result of a collective project and there are many people to whom I am indebted. I first conducted fieldwork in Quito, Ecuador, during the summer of 1989, as an intern at the Center for Planning and Social Studies (Centro de Planificación y Estudios Sociales [CEPLAES]) working on a project on collective household survival strategies of women in low-income neighborhoods in Quito. I returned in 1992–93 to conduct fourteen months of fieldwork for my dissertation. I have since returned several times for shorter periods to update my previous research, teach courses, and collaborate with Ecuadorian colleagues. Additional fieldwork in Peru (1993, 1995, 2001) and Bolivia (1995, 1999, 2001) has significantly shaped my thinking about Ecuador and Andean feminisms in general. My analysis is based on several forms of data gathering: participant observation, discourse analysis, semistructured interviews of more than seventy-five members of women's community organizations, additional interviews with professionals and activists, and secondary sources.

This book reflects the diversity of my fieldwork experiences. My ethnography is not of one site but of many; it is not a study of one type of institution but many; nor do I examine one set of discourses and practices but several. I examine a field of sites that shape and give meaning to the contemporary context of feminism, gender, and development in the Andes (Alvarez, Dagnino, and Escobar 1998a; Gowan and Ó Riain 2000). I examine women's political organizing initiatives as local and transnational networks (Keck and Sikkink 1998) and as situated within complex genealogical webs of meaning and mobilization (Alexander and Mohanty 1997).

In many ways, this book owes its existence to the extraordinary kindness of Ecuadorian women activists and others who have shared their political expertise with me and given generously to this project over the past fifteen years. Without their support, which included long conversations over coffee or tea and their hosting me in numerous ways, putting me in contact with people, helping me locate documents, and sharing with me their political histories, I could not have pieced together this analysis.

In Ecuador, I was a visiting faculty fellow at the Latin American Faculty of Social Sciences (Facultad Latinoamericana de Ciencias Sociales [FLACSO]) from September 1992 to December 1993. There I enjoyed the company and research collaboration of FLACSO colleagues, including Adrian Bonilla and Amparo Menéndez-Carrión. I thank Gioconda Herrera, who later joined FLACSO, for providing me with the opportunity to teach courses at FLACSO in 1998 and 2004 and for her personal support, including her comments on portions of this book. In Quito, I extend my deepest thanks to Rocío Rosero, a true believer in my research and an invaluable form of support over the years. Líli Rodriguez and María Arboleda also provided numerous forms of support and feedback. I thank CEPLAES for their institutional support during the summer of 1989, especially Silvia Vega, who directly oversaw my internship and who has provided invaluable feedback over the course of my research. Numerous other individuals in Ecuador have taken the time to speak with me and have made my research intellectually stimulating and rewarding: Simon Pachano, Lautaro Oveda Segovia, Rodrigo Paz, Pablo Better, Alexandra Martínez, Mario Unda, Diego Carrión, Fernando Bustamante, Magdalena León Trujillo, Dolores Padilla, Nela Meriguet, Nela Martínez, Cecilia Torres, and Patricia Palacios. Most important, I thank the many members of community women's organizations who took the time to talk to me, allowed me to interview them for this project, and, in many cases, shared their lives with me.

This book project began in graduate school. At Cornell University, first and foremost I thank Dr. Lourdes Benería, Professor of City and Regional Planning and Women's Studies, with whom I was fortunate enough to work for seven years. Her research has influenced my own in countless ways, and I thank her for that as well as for her ongoing support over the course of my career. I also owe deep gratitude to my other committee members: Dr. Susan Christopherson (City and Regional Planning), Dr. Susan Buck-Morss (Government), and Dr. Arturo Escobar (Anthropology, University of North Carolina), who served as an outside member. I also owe a special thanks to Dr. Sonia Alvarez (Politics, University of California at Santa Cruz). Not only was Dr. Alvarez the chair of my undergraduate thesis committee at UC Santa Cruz, but she also contributed in numerous ways to my later research and is an ongoing source of support and inspiration.

My early fieldwork in Ecuador was supported by grants from the Department of City and Regional Planning, Center for International Studies, Women's Studies Program, and Program on Gender and Global Change at Cornell University. My doctoral research in 1992 and 1993 was funded by the Inter-American Foundation and Fulbright-Hays. Two U.S. Department of Education Foreign Language and Area Studies (FLAS) grants allowed me to study Quechua and Andean studies at Cornell during the summer of 1990 and the 1990–91 academic year. I thank the Helen Kellogg Institute for International Studies at the University of Notre Dame for its research support during spring 1996, when I was a Visiting Faculty Fellow. At Arizona State University, I thank the Women's Studies Program for its support, including two Summer Research Grants that allowed me to work on this book. The ASU women's studies reading group provided an important intellectual space during the 2000–2002 period. I thank participants of this group for their careful reading of an earlier draft of my introduction. A 1998 Fulbright Senior Scholar Grant in Bolivia allowed me to conduct comparative research, some of which I report in this book. A 2004 Fulbright Senior Specialists Program Grant allowed me to share my findings in a course I taught at FLASCO-Ecuador. Finally, FLACSO-Ecuador has provided me with institutional and financial support, and I thank my colleagues there, especially Gioconda Herrera and Mercedes Prieto, for their generosity and collaboration.

Sandy Thatcher has been a wonderful editor and I have enjoyed working with him. From the start, he has provided invaluable feedback. I greatly appreciate his balanced insight, sense of calm, and patience. I am also grateful to Sarah Radcliffe, an anonymous reviewer, and a member of the Penn State Press editorial board for their feedback on earlier drafts.

Numerous individuals have contributed to my own thinking about development, modernity, and social change. I thank them for their intellectual presence, friendship, or both: Maddie Adelman, Vivian Arteaga, Florence Babb, Kum-Kum Bhavnani, Maruja Barrig, Mary Bernstein, Jo-Marie Burt, Carmen Diana Deere, Shohini Ghosh, Julie Graham, Jane Jaquette, Nina Laurie, Nancy Naples, Sarah Radcliffe, Helen Safa, Verónica Schild, Lynn Stephen, Virginia Vargas, and Mary Weismantel. I owe a very special thanks to Susana Wappenstein for her insight and support over the years.

Finally, I thank my mother, Carol Lind, for nurturing my intellectual pursuits and sharing with me her love for travel and passion for change, and my brother, Colby who has always been there for me. Barclay and Madison are my most loyal fans, next only to Tyler (1987–99).

I dedicate the completion of this book to Stephanie.

Portions of Chapter 1 were previously published in the chapter "Engendering Andean Politics: The Paradoxes of Women's Movements in Neoliberal Ecuador and Bolivia," in *Politics in the Andes: Identity, Conflict, Reform*, ed. Jo-Marie Burt and Philip Mauceri © 2003, reprinted by permission of the University of Pittsburgh Press. Chapter 3 includes some material previously published in my article "Making Feminist Sense of Neoliberalism: The Institutionalization of Women's Struggles for Survival in Ecuador and Bolivia," *Journal of Developing Societies* 18, nos. 2–3 (2002): 228–58, reprinted here by permission of the journal's publisher, De Sitter Publications. An earlier version of Chapter 5 was published as "Gender and Neoliberal States: Feminists Remake the Nation of Ecuador," *Latin American Perspectives* 30, no. 1: 181–207, © 2003 Latin American Perspectives, Inc., reprinted here by permission of the journal's publisher, Sage Publications, Inc.

ACRONYMS

ALAI	Agencia Lationamericana de Información
	Latin American Information Agency
ALDHU	Asociación Latinoamericana de Derechos Humanos
	Latin American Human Rights Association
AMM	Acción por el Movimiento de Mujeres
	Action for the Women's Movement
CAM	Centro para la Acción de la Mujer
	Center for Women's Action
CEAAL	Consejo de Educación de Adultos de América Latina
	Adult Education Council of Latin America
CECIM	Comité Ecuatoriano de la Comisión Interamericana de Mujeres
	Ecuadorian Committee of the Inter-American Women's Commission
CEDAW	Convention for the Elimination of All Forms of Discrimination Against Women
CEDOC	Central Ecuatoriana de Organizaciones Clasistas
	Ecuadorian Center of Class-Based Organizations[1]
CEIMME	Centro de Estudios y Investigación sobre la Mujer Maltratada del Ecuador
	Center of Research and Studies on Abused Women in Ecuador
CEOP	Corporación Ecuatoriano de Organizaciones Privadas sin Fines de Lucro
	Ecuadorian Corporation of Private Nonprofit Organizations
CEOSL	Confederación Ecuatoriana de Organizaciones Sindicales Libres
	Ecuadorian Confederation of Free Trade Unions
CEPAM	Centro Ecuatoriano para la Promoción y Acción de la Mujer
	Ecuadorian Center for Women's Promotion and Action
CEPLAES	Centro Ecuatoriano de Planificación y Estudios Sociales
	Ecuadorian Center for Planning and Social Studies

1. Formerly Confederación Ecuatoriana de Organizaciones Sindicales Cristianas, or Ecuadorian Confederation of Christian Free Trade Unions.

CEPE	Companía Estatal del Petroleo Ecuatoriano
	Ecuadorian State Petroleum Company
CIAM	Centro de Información y Apoyo de la Mujer
	Center for Women's Information and Support
CNOPM	Coordinadora Nacional de Organizaciones Populares de
	Mujeres
	National Network of Popular Women's Organizations
CONADE	Consejo Nacional del Desarrollo
	National Development Council
CONAIE	Confederación de Nacionalidades Indígenas del Ecuador
	Confederation of Indigenous Nationalities of Ecuador
CONAM	Consejo Nacional de Modernización
	National Modernization Council
CONAMU	Consejo Nacional de la Mujer
	National Women's Council
CORFEC	Corporación Femenina Ecuatoriana
	Ecuadorian Feminine Corporation
CPME	Coordinadora Política de Mujeres Ecuatorianas
	Political Network of Ecuadorian Women
CTE	Confederación de Trabajadores del Ecuador
	Confederation of Workers of Ecuador
DINAMU	Dirección Nacional de la Mujer
	National Women's Bureau
EU	European Union
FEI	Federación Ecuatoriana de Indios
	Ecuadorian Federation of Indians
FEMNYP	Federación Ecuatoriana de Mujeres de Negocios y Profesionales
	Ecuadorian Federation of Business and Professional Women
FENOC	Federación Nacional de Organizaciones Campesinas
	National Federation of Peasant Organizations
FISE	Fondo de Inversión Social de Emergencia
	Emergency Social Investment Fund
FLACSO	Facultad Latinoamericana de Ciencias Sociales
	Latin American Faculty of Social Sciences
FNMCB-BS	Federación Nacional de Mujeres Campesinas de Bolivia
	"Bartolina Sisa"
	"Bartolina Sisa" National Federation of Peasant Women of
	Bolivia

FNPME	Foro Nacional Permanente de Mujeres Ecuatorianas
	National Permanent Forum of Ecuadorian Women
FONNIN	Fondo Nacional para la Nutrición y Protección Infantil
	National Fund for Child Nutrition and Protection
FUPOCPS	Federación Unitaria Provincial de Organizaciones Campesinas y Populares del Sur
	United Federation of Provincial Southern Peasant and Popular Organizations
GAD	Gender and development
GATT	General Agreement on Tariffs and Trade
IADB	Inter-American Development Bank
ID	Izquierda Democrática
	Democratic Left
ILDIS	Instituto Latinoamericano de Investigaciones Sociales
	Latin American Institute of Social Investigation
IMF	International Monetary Fund
INECEL	Instituto Ecuatoriano de Electrificación
	Ecuadorian Institute of Electricity
INNFA	Instituto Nacional de la Niñez y la Familia
	National Institute of Children and Family
IRFEYAL	Instituto Radiofónico Fe y Alegría
	Fe y Alegría Radiophonic Institute
IULA	International Union of Local Authorities
MERCOSUR	Mercado Comun del Sur
	Common Market of the South
MNMSP	Movimiento Nacional de Mujeres de Sectores Populares
	National Movement of Women of Popular Sectors
MUPP-NP	Movimiento de Unidad Plurinacional Pachakutik Nuevo País
	Movement of Plurinational Unity Pachakutik New Country
NAFTA	North American Free Trade Agreement
NGO	Nongovernmental organization
OFNAMU	Oficina Nacional de la Mujer
	National Women's Office
PCE	Partido Comunista Ecuatoriano
	Ecuadorian Communist Party
PSE	Partido Socialista Ecuatoriano
	Ecuadorian Socialist Party
RCDI	Red Comunitario para el Desarrollo Infantil
	Community Network for Child Development

SAPS	Structural adjustment policies
SEGESVOL	Secretariado General de Servicio Voluntario
	General Secretariat of Volunteer Service
SOPM	Secretaría de Organizaciones Populares de Mujeres
	Secretariat of Popular Women's Organizations
UMT	Unión de Mujeres Trabajadoras
	Union of Women Workers
UN	United Nations
UNDP	United Nations Development Program
UNFPA	United Nations Population Fund
UNICEF	United Nations Children's Fund
UNIFEM	United Nations Development Fund for Women
UPS	Unidad de Políticas Sociales
	Social Policy Unit
USAID	United States Agency for International Development
UROCAL	Unión Regional de Organizaciones Campesinas del Litoral
	Coastal Region Union of Peasant Organizations
WAD	Women and development
WID	Women in development
WTO	World Trade Organization

Introduction

Science and expert discourses such as development create powerful truths, ways of creating and intervening in the world, including ourselves. . . .

. . . [I]nstead of searching for grand alternative models or strategies [of development], what is needed is the investigation of alternative representations and practices in concrete local settings, particularly as they exist in contexts of hybridization, collective action, and political mobilization.

—ARTURO ESCOBAR, *Encountering Development: The Making and Unmaking of the Third World*

In this book I examine one local setting in which women have politically mobilized to "encounter development" in Latin America: that of Quito, Ecuador. As I show, the political identities and strategies of women's community-based and nongovernmental organizations in Quito are neither entirely radical nor traditional, nor necessarily original. Yet they reveal much about the gendered making of modernity, national identity and politics in Ecuador, a country whose state-led modernization project has been paradoxical and inherently unequal from the start.

In the early 1980s, thousands of poor and working-class Ecuadorian women, for the first time, attended community meetings in neighbors' homes, municipal buildings, churches, or meeting halls, with the hope of addressing their economic and social circumstances. They met in poor neighborhoods in cities such as Quito, the political capital; in Guayaquil, Ecuador's industrial center; and in rural Andean provinces, El Oriente (Ecuador's Amazon region), and coastal towns. Particularly in urban areas such as Quito, where rapid rates of industrialization coupled with urban migration created higher levels of unemployment and social service needs for newly arrived migrants during the 1960s–1980s, women were faced with a new set of issues pertaining to their identities as urban dwellers, parents, workers, and national citizens.[1] In many ways, the Ecuadorian state's goals to modernize the nation during the post–World War II period, including its 1960s and 1970s industrialization policies, oil development, and maternalist social welfare strategies that "targeted" poor sectors of women as "mothers of the underdeveloped nation," coupled with its growing reliance on foreign aid and the shift toward market-led development, set the stage for women's mobilization in the early 1980s. Economically speaking, despite widespread claims by the international development community that Ecuador had "advanced" in numerous indicators (World Bank 1984; P. Beckerman 2002), many Ecuadorian families experienced ongoing, persistent poverty, which was only exacerbated by Ecuador's growing debt crisis.

In 1981, the Ecuadorian government first began to implement structural adjustment measures so that it could receive loans from the International Monetary Fund (IMF). These measures, based on World Bank– and IMF-inspired neoliberal policies, which were designed to stimulate economic growth through foreign investment, trade liberalization, privatization, state retrenchment, and the redistribution of social welfare, had some expected social consequences, such as increased unemployment and high inflation rates. Yet they also had unintended consequences for organized sectors of poor women who, by that time, had begun to receive ideological or financial support from the emerging international women in development (WID) field and from global feminist movements. During this period, many groups of women at the grass roots developed ties with feminist nongovernmental organizations (NGOs), the Ecuadorian state (including, most notably, the state women's agency), philanthropic foundations, political parties, and international development institutions such as United Nations (UN) agencies (for example, the United Nations Children's Fund [UNICEF] and the United Nations Development Fund for Women [UNIFEM]). At the time, although many women recognized the extent to which their roles as community members, mothers, and citizens had been jeopardized by the emerging economic crisis, they did not foresee how their roles would, in a sense, become integrated into the logic of development. Most attendees at the meetings mentioned earlier, for example, did not realize that their involvement as community activists would become relatively permanent, or institutionalized, as a result of neoliberal development policies (including those concerning gender) that rely on women's household and community labor as a foundation for

---

1. In 2001, 63 percent of all Ecuadorians lived in urban areas, while 37 percent lived in rural areas, in a marked shift from Ecuador's past as a primarily rural society (World Bank 2003d).

economic restructuring. In essence, these women "mothered" the Ecuadorian foreign debt crisis through their individual and collective survival strategies—a process that served more broadly as a crucial signifier for national progress and for state and global financial accountability (or lack thereof). It was a process that even global feminism could not foresee.

Ecuadorian State Restructuring and Development in Context

The Ecuadorian economic and political crises of the 1980s and 1990s must be situated within the broader context of the historical construction of the state and nation, the institutionalization of the international development field, cultural and economic globalization, and struggles for citizen rights (that is, political, social, and economic rights (Menéndez-Carrión 1989; Escobar 1995; Radcliffe and Westwood 1996; Lechner and Boli 2001). As Norman Whitten has stated, "It is essential . . . to look at Ecuador in its multifaceted particularities and to set its historical and emergent cultural systems in global dimensions" (2003, 2). The state, a crucial institution in the making of the nation, has evolved through a transnational lens in the sense that over the years it has depended on the successes and failures of the economy for its growth, including through its performance in the global market (cacao, bananas, petroleum, flowers; see Schodt 1987; Striffler 2002). From the start, ideologies of progress and modernization shaped the state's identity and goals and contributed to its identity as a modern social welfare state (a symbol far more so than a reality) in the mid-twentieth century (Clark 2001). The establishment of the post–World War II development field, which channeled bank loans and other forms of aid and assistance to the country as well as funneled ideologies of modernization to public and private sectors, has contributed to the transnational nature of the state. The state itself has relied on notions of modernization to achieve its goals of guiding the nation's development and defining citizenship (Becker 1999; North 2004). At least prior to the 1990s, Ecuador was commonly viewed by international aid institutions as "nonthreatening" and as suitable for foreign investment, because of its comparatively small population (13 million in 2004) and "low levels of social protest, geographic diversity, and relatively high political and economic stability" (Corkill and Cubitt 1988). State incentives to attract foreign investment, coupled with the discovery of oil in the 1960s, contributed to marked increases in the presence of multinational capital (Schodt 1987; North 2004). International organizations chose to house their regional offices in Quito, sometimes because of the country's romanticized image among Westerners as "safe," relatively "democratic," and open to Western ideas and values—at least prior to the 1990s (Corkill and Cubitt 1988).

Regardless or perhaps because of this exoticized Eurocentric image of Ecuador as a cultural paradise ripe for foreign investment, indigenous people, peasants, and various other political sectors have long challenged colonialism and its cultural, political, and economic legacies. By the year 2000, the Ecuadorian indigenous-rights movement was considered among the "strongest" in Latin America by many observers (Meisch 2000; Roper, Perreault, and Wilson 2003; Weismantel 2003; Sawyer 2004) and the women's movement had made comparatively significant legal and political achievements, as had the Afro-Ecuadorian movement to a lesser degree. Ecuador's move to "partyize" social movements led in part to the historically unprecedented political conjuncture in 1998, when the indigenous and women's movements helped redraft the constitution and had by then gained official representation in the formal political system, thus helping to remake party politics, and reshape the state's image, in numerous ways (Rosero, Vega, and Reyes Ávila 2000). These social movements, which gained ground in the 1980s and early 1990s, necessarily have challenged globalization and the Ecuadorian nation-state as it implements a neoliberal development project that relies on a universal notion of citizenship and uninational identity and, in so doing, have helped to inspire a rethinking of the nation-state itself. From community protests against foreign oil companies in the Amazon region to indigenous marches (Sawyer 2004), street blockades, and hunger strikes in the Andes to millions of people taking to the streets of Quito and Guayaquil in January 1997 and thereafter, Ecuadorians have not passively accepted the terms of development, globalization, and modernization, not even during periods of relatively little social movement activity, such as the 1950s and 1960s.

The so-called NGOization of social movements (Alvarez 1998b), which for women's groups coincided with the United Nations Decade for the Advancement of Women (1975–85) and the establishment of the international women in development (WID) professional field, transformed the political landscape in Ecuador. In the 1980s and 1990s, a much greater number of development organizations, particularly NGOs, received external funding in Ecuador, also a reflection of the broader trend throughout Latin America to provide support for civic organizations during the region's redemocratization period (Jaquette 1994; Jelin 1990; Alvarez 1990). Whereas prior to the 1980s there were only a handful of NGOs, by 1994 there were more than one thousand NGOs registered in the country, among them community associations and nonprofit organizations with a paid staff, all of which focused to some degree on social or economic development, including social welfare (Segarra 1994; United Nations Development Program [UNDP]/Alternativa 1992).[2] .Although they are scattered throughout the country, historically Quito has been home to the largest percentage of NGOs (UNDP/Alternativa 1992). Among the thousand NGOs in existence during the 1990s, approximately seventy of them focused on gender issues, including gender inequities in health care, literacy, income generation, land rights, and political rights (Rodríguez 1990).

The NGOization of Ecuadorian society was also spurred on by the country's new economic development strategy, which aimed (among other things) to privatize the state's social welfare functions, such as social service delivery, through establishing public-private partnerships (Sikkink 1991). The new partnerships were derived from "the purposeful attempt(s), either from NGOs or the state, to coordinate, partner, or create regular patterns of information sharing" among this newly formed "welfare network" in Ecuador (Segarra 1996, 492). Through this process, designated NGOs have been allocated new responsibilities for managing health care, welfare distribution, and other social services, areas of social and economic well-being typically gendered as "feminine." Certainly it has been true that this process, whereby the economy, social welfare, and everyday life has been privatized to some degree, has had significant gendered effects for women, in part because they are assumed to fit into the new institutional arrangements by nature of their maternal responsibilities and their perceived (voluntary) roles in community life—a topic I develop in Chapter 4. Their integration into state-sponsored projects stemming from the National Development Plan, a document that is rewritten by each new government, and into NGO projects, particularly those that operate within the logic of "free market" development, has yielded new political opportunities for women, among these increased participation in community-based, municipal, and, to some extent, national politics; the establishment of regional political networks; and the emergence of feminist public policy in Ecuador.

These factors (NGOization, globalization, developmentalism) were coupled with Ecuador's internal process of social movement formation, in which during

2. NGOs are a diverse set of organizations with a wide range of interests and goals. In this study, I draw from Monique Segarra's (1996) research on Ecuadorian NGOs and define NGOs as nonprofit organizations with a permanent paid staff and specific goals to promote economic or social development. In essence, they are organizations that compose Ecuador's civil-society-based welfare network. The NGOs cited in this study are national and do not constitute branches of international NGOs.

the 1980s many grassroots movements acquired NGO status and became professionalized as a way to advance their political agendas, much as did women's movements throughout Latin America (Alvarez 1998b). To foster this process of strengthening civil society through building the professional capacity of NGOs (that is, as part of Ecuador's redemocratization initiatives), the Ecuadorian government's laws granting NGO status were relatively lenient throughout the 1980s and early 1990s. At one point in early 1993, there were more than ten thousand organizations on a waiting list at the Ministry of Social Welfare, all of them were applying for their legal status. The ministry was unable to process so many requests and eventually froze the application process (Magdalena León, interview, October 11, 1993).[3]

The 1990s brought on a new era in Ecuador, one that shattered romanticized images of the country as subservient to foreign capital and acquiescent to global political domination. The foreign debt and neoliberalism provided the background to this, as did political and financial exigency and the escalating identity crisis of a nation-state attempting to govern individuals through a universalist lens (despite claims that the state is "plurinational" or "multicultural" [see Roper, Perrault, and Wilson 2003]) while simultaneously exacerbating important class, ethnic, racial, and gender differences among Ecuadorians. The first indigenous uprising (*levantamiento indígena*) took place in 1990; and several national strikes, protests, and uprisings of various social sectors took place in the years that followed. During the 1997–2004 period, five governments led the country and all of them implemented neoliberal policies. Their political approaches and forms of policy implementation varied, leading to entirely different neoliberalisms and distinct outcomes during each administration (Phillips 1998). Some (e.g., Burt and Mauceri [2004]) have compared the Ecuadorian neoliberal project to those of other Latin American countries and considered it incomplete and somewhat unsuccessful, to the extent that governments have not been able to implement as many reforms as they would have liked, thanks in part to the role of social movements in opposing this process. While this may be true when Ecuador is compared to countries such as Bolivia, where one of the harshest sets of structural adjustment policies [SAPs] were implemented dur-

3. All interviews in this book were conducted in Quito by the author unless otherwise noted. I have identified some people by their name and some by their generic position, at their request. In general, I opt to identify interviewees by their name, particularly those who already have a public presence in Ecuador because of their professional or political affiliations. However, all names of the members of the eight community women's organizations included in my sample are pseudonyms. All interviews were conducted in Spanish and tape recorded; my analysis is based on my notes and the formal recorded interviews, most of which were later transcribed.

ing the mid-1980s, devastating the livelihoods of tens of thousands of people (McFarren 1992), neoliberalism has been successful in Ecuador to the extent that state–civil society institutional relationships have been permanently transformed; many economic and social sectors have been dramatically restructured, some losing out more than others; and the general national development path, reinforced by the state's dependence on foreign aid, has made a marked turn toward economic liberalization (Lind 2000; North 2004).

A positive aspect of this otherwise difficult process was the increased participation of members of the women's and indigenous movements, along with that of other marginalized groups, in challenging the country to redress the financial and political corruption that culminated in the late 1990s political crisis. Although the nation was largely unmade during this period, social movement participants helped remake and transform the country, through the new public-private partnerships between the state and civic organizations; new political-participation laws; and large, national protests against government and financial corruption in the banking sector. Social movements helped renew a sense of national identity in a more inclusive way, despite the many challenges they faced. New identity claims were made by these movements, often based on ethnicity or gender, that served as a basis for Ecuador's 1998 constitution, viewed by some observers as "one of the most progressive" in the world (Jochnick 1999). Many of the legislative actions that have taken place since 1998 are based on identity claims, and these claims and their potential conflicts need to be understood in order for the reforms to truly work in the years to come (Van Cott 2002; Shachar 2001).

In 2000, Ecuador became the second Latin American country to adopt the U.S. dollar as its official currency—that is, to "dollarize."[4] *Dollarization* became an important signifier of a nation in crisis: financially, politically, and in terms of national identity. Supporters of dollarization viewed it as a necessary response to financial crisis, rather than as a symptom or cause of further conflict, although this would soon be disproved (Beckerman 2002). This governmental strategy followed a period of financial crisis that had led to bank closings, the freezing of assets, hyperinflation, and arrested social security payments. During this period,

---

4. The U.S. dollar has been the official currency of Panama since that country gained independence from Colombia, with U.S. support, a century ago. Following Ecuadorian dollarization, El Salvador introduced its own dollarization policy in 2001. Argentina has considered dollarizing following the country's severe financial crisis that reached its peak in 2001. Guatemala has legalized the dollar as a domestic currency in parallel with its own quetzal, although the country has not introduced specific dollarization legislation thus far ("El Salvador" 2000).

retired women and men lined up in front of banks, in the hope that they would be fortunate enough to receive at least a portion of their social security payments. Today, many of the children of the elderly must provide housing and financial support for their parents. Poor and middle-class women and men have been particularly hard hit; many of them have lost their entire savings. While the introduction of the U.S. dollar was meant to bring stability to Ecuador's economy, in reality, for many people it has meant lost savings, inflationary costs of living, fewer jobs, and heightened economic insecurity. According to traditional economic indicators, Ecuador's economy grew during the 2000–2002 period: in 2001 alone, it grew by 5.4 percent, the fastest rate in the region. During that same year, the national budget was balanced and inflation was 22 percent, down from 91 percent in 2000 ("Mixed Blessing" 2002). Yet it is far too soon to assume that this is a positive trend. To begin with, this growth spurt merely balanced out the economic losses from the late 1990s. And additional indicators paint a different picture of Ecuador's reality at the turn of the century: in general, real wages have declined, and in urban areas "only four in ten workers have a proper job" (1). According to government estimates, 56 percent of all Ecuadorians lived in extreme poverty in 2001, meaning that they earned less than forty-two dollars a month, the country's minimal standard for a sufficient income (1), an increase from 35 percent who lived below Ecuador's poverty line in 1994 (World Bank 2003a). Since 1999, more than one million Ecuadorians have migrated to Spain or the United States; their remittances, which totaled $1.4 billion in 2001 alone ("Mixed Blessing," 1), are now the second-largest source of foreign exchange after oil. Political protests have remained a constant in daily life throughout the country. Indeed, it is clear that the dollarization legislation has signified far more than an economic change: it reflects the growing cultural and political tensions surrounding state modernization, neoliberal development, globalization, and the ongoing struggle for national identity in Ecuador.

In this regard, Ecuador serves as an excellent example of the contradictions of modernization and development: although many large-scale economic-growth models have been introduced in the country, the fact is that income inequalities between rich and poor are higher than they were when Ecuador first established an industrial economy in the 1950s; and since the inception of SAPs in 1980, there are approximately 15 percent more Ecuadorians living in extreme poverty than prior to the introduction of SAPs and related neoliberal development policies (World Bank 2003a, 2003b).[5] Like their counterparts elsewhere, poor women

5. These figures refer to the percentage of Ecuador's total population living below the established national poverty line.

(although many men, too) have carried the heaviest burdens during this period of economic crisis and restructuring, in part because of their socialized gender roles in "reproduction"—a sphere of activities (child care, household management and budgeting, shopping) that itself has been transformed by institutional shifts and heavily questioned as conceptually appropriate or adequate (e.g., Moser 1989a, 1993; Lind 1992; Escobar 1995), and because of their marginal positions in the paid capitalist economy, including in the informal sector (Benería and Feldman 1992; Bakker 1994; Moser 1995; James 1996). Racism and Eurocentrism also factor into this situation, by shaping political and economic opportunities and more fundamentally by shaping the epistemological and ontological frameworks within which development, citizenship, and people's lives are defined, understood, experienced, felt, and lived. The nation is composed of a majority who define themselves as mestizo/a or indigenous; it contains many languages and cultures; and approximately 10 percent of its population is of African descent, with a very small population of Spanish or otherwise European origin (Whitten 2003a). Eurocentric discourses of race continue to frame social relations. Approximately 70 percent of the population live in poverty or subpoverty conditions and 7–10 percent live abroad, particularly in the United States or Spain (Weismantel 2003). Poor women who identify as mestiza, *indígena*, *chola*, or *negra* face intersecting forms of oppression that shape their everyday lives, political and economic opportunities, and visions for a future, in complex and profound yet also contradictory ways.

Women's Encounters with State Modernization and Neoliberalism

Because of how gender underscores these broad historical, structural inequalities, throughout Latin America, urban poor, peasant, and indigenous women have been among the first to make connections between global change and daily life and to politicize their "roles in development" (Benería 1992b). Sectors of poor women have responded to economic crisis and restructuring in innovative ways, often politicizing and putting into question their class positions, their racialized roles and identities as women, and their social locations as "Third World" or "underdeveloped." Although the network of Ecuadorian women's organizations and movements is small, relatively speaking, when compared with larger countries such as Brazil, Mexico, or Peru, in recent years Ecuador has had one of the most successful feminist "issue networks" in the region, one that has led to the establishment of feminist public policies and laws (Htun 2003; Herrera 2000; Rosero, Vega, and Reyes Ávila 2000). More than twenty gender-based legislative actions were made in the 1995–2000 period alone (see Appendix), including the passage of new laws against violence against women, the installation of a female quota for political participation, and the repeal of several discriminatory laws. These would not have been possible without the strong elite network of feminist policy-makers and activists, along with doctors, legislators, and state officials, who all coalesced to push for these reforms (Htun 2003, 5). Women's NGOs and networks have actively challenged the terms of neoliberal development policies in effective ways, through building national coalitions against specific government policies and through questioning the foundation of populist neoliberal governments, such as that of President Abdalá Bucaram (1996–97), that simultaneously promoted gender equality and multiculturalism on the one hand, and universal "trickle down" economic development on the other (see Chapter 5).

Feminist-issue networks have employed specific notions of gender, motherhood, sexuality, and national identity to achieve their goals—what I refer to as strategic essentialism, a term originally theorized by Judith Butler (1990). For example, members of some groups have used their traditional roles as mothers to fight for social justice or against economic imperialism; their performance of motherhood in the streets, in public protests, or at meetings may invoke a more traditional notion of motherhood than they actually live out in their own lives. *Essentialism*, a term often rejected by postmodern scholars, is what shapes their political identities and struggles. Understanding their "processes of self-essentializing" is crucial to understanding their struggles and the broader national context. "[E]ssentializing is at the heart of empowerment, pride, and alternative modernity," as Rachel Corr observes (quoted in Whitten 2003a, 13). Structural conditions such as the economic crisis and political instability were catalyzing factors for Ecuadorian women activists in their opposition to the neoliberal restructuring process, yet they were also motivated by their desire to transform broader arenas of power and to rethink fundamental concepts of democracy, citizenship, and rights. Ironically perhaps, strategic essentialism played an important role in their immediate challenges to the state and, in the long run, to the transformation of gender relations.

The challenge, though, was and continues to be how to construct political and economic strategies without selling out to the powers that be: patriarchy; the state (be it social democratic or neoliberal); or the international development arena, including the WID field. Women activists have often disagreed about whether or not they should participate in the new public-private partnerships or accept funding from international development agencies. Increasingly during the 1980s and 1990s, women began to protest the presence of foreign aid agencies and institutions in their movements, adding to their long-standing criticism and analysis of male-based forms of political power. Their notion of political autonomy was internationalized, and they began to see certain strands of feminism as part of the problem. In Quito in 1998, at an International Women's Day march, an event that takes place annually on March 8, Feminists for Autonomy (Feministas por la Autonomía) gathered at the Plaza de Independencia in Quito's historical center to pronounce their independence from the state and international development apparatus. Following years of feminist participation in policy making and the international development field, these feminists sought autonomy not only from male-based political processes but also from what they viewed as the "gender technocracy," those feminist institutions and individuals they viewed as selling out to the industrialized countries by adopting Eurocentric notions of women's liberation and modernization and by receiving funding and implementing projects that were framed through a Western lens (Mohanty 1991).[6] Feminists for Autonomy argued that this gender technocracy, including women's NGOs, UN agencies, and foreign governmental development agencies, was part of the larger international development technocracy. They referred to this web of institutions as a *technocracy* to highlight the tendency in the development field to define the realities and needs of poor countries in scientific, seemingly objective terms that, they argue, depoliticize and decontextualize the neocolonial reality of poor countries such as Ecuador (Escobar 1995).

As a way to address this set of issues, the 1998 march participants focused their attention on the political crisis following the February 1997 ousting of President Abdalá Bucaram (August 1996–February 1997) and inequalities stemming from global neoliberal restructuring in Ecuador. The autonomous feminists came on horseback, dressed as Manuela Sáenz, the lover of Simón Bolívar, liberation leader of the movement for independence against the Spanish colonial government in the eighteenth century. Recently popularized in literature,

6. To my knowledge, the term "gender technocracies" was first used systematically by the Bolivian anarchist feminist group Mujeres Creando (Kruse 2001). The two primary organizers advocate a nonhierarchical form of organization that maintains institutional autonomy from the development apparatus, and specifically from the "gender technocracy," including any feminist NGOs or research institutes funded by foreign donors. They have directly challenged "institutionalized feminists" on the basis that they are being complicit with the interests of Western imperialism. Mujeres Creando organized the first regional conference of autonomous feminism, held in Bolivia in 1998. Thus far little research has been conducted to document the struggles of autonomous feminists, despite the fact that (or perhaps because) their political platforms put into question the foundations of middle-class feminism in the region.

Sáenz is known for saving Bolívar's life on more than one occasion. As they performed Sáenz's historical image at the downtown plaza, the feminists called for a "remaking" of the Ecuadorian nation (Radcliffe and Westwood 1996).[7] This national remaking has included reforming the political system, redrafting the constitution, and challenging financial and political corruption. They invoked Sáenz, a largely unrecognized female national hero, in a challenge to the current unmaking of the nation through the government's corruption and gendered political antics and in a challenge to the global economic forces that have shaped and limited Ecuador's development agenda and sense of identity.

In this book I argue that women's political and economic struggles for survival in the neoliberal context are best understood in terms of how women negotiate, in complex ways, state modernization and global development. I examine *how* women interpret and intervene in public and private arenas, often paradoxically, and what the significance and gains have been alongside the limits of these types of gender identity politics and strategies. I foreground my primary discussion about women's movements, economic restructuring, and state modernization during the 1980–2004 period with a chapter on the historical relationship of women and the state in Ecuador. How women negotiate state modernization, including economic and social development policies, depends on their relationships to other social actors (NGO activists, development practitioners, politicians, and others who have a stake in poor women's survival strategies) and to the interventions of these other actors in the realm of development projects and frameworks that target the urban and rural poor. This broader context, after all, helps frame women's political identifications and visions from the start, along with the strategies they develop and the relationships they construct with the state and other sectors of society.

I am interested primarily in how poor Ecuadorian women's political and economic strategies, in theory and practice, have been framed (by participants themselves as well as by researchers of women's movements) within a national and global social, economic, political and discursive context.[8] As Ecuadorian

7. Radcliffe and Westwood examine the ways in which nations and national identities are historically constructed and politically negotiated. My own study focuses on how organized women have challenged the Ecuadorian nation and national identities, including constructions of gender implicit in their making (see esp. Radcliffe and Westwood 1996, chap. 6).

8. Throughout the book I define women's political practices in a broad sense, to encompass all types of women's organizing that is gender-based in nature. This includes, for example, self-defined feminist groups as well as communal kitchens, community groups, human rights organizations, rural peasant and indigenous women's associations and networks, and state feminist policy-makers. I also define *feminisms* broadly, to include the various traditions of women's political activism in Bolivia, Ecuador, and Peru that have been informed by so-called second-wave feminist thought and practice (Jaquette 1994; Saporta Sternbach et al. 1992). Many women's NGOs and community

women activists frame their struggles "in and against" global neoliberal restructuring and the nation-state (Lind 2000), they are invoking a set of assumptions
about gender, family, politics, the economy, and development. Community
women activists draw from their traditional gender roles, including their roles as
mothers, yet they do so to challenge broader structural inequalities and institutions, including the Ecuadorian state and foreign lenders (such as Citibank, the
World Bank, and the IMF). At the same time, women's community-based and
nationwide organizing has helped refashion national development and politics;
in this regard, women activists have contributed in important ways to reenvisioning neoliberal development, remaking the nation, and imagining a postdevelopment era (Escobar 1995; Saunders 2001).

As Feminists for Autonomy point out, there is a downside to becoming institutionalized and bureaucratized under the logic of neoliberal development, an
ideology and set of policies that emphasize free markets, global economic integration, and less state involvement in social welfare distribution. Neoliberal policies, especially those stemming from World Bank– and IMF-inspired structural
adjustment measures, contribute to the ideological and economic institutionalization of women's community organizing in important and unintended ways,
including through the targeting of poor women as volunteer contributors to
the development process.[9] Some women benefit from neoliberal development
policies, while others lose out; class inequalities and women's locations in this
process greatly shape the outcome of specific policies. Some women align themselves with development and progress, while others experience an "identity
crisis," as is suggested in the title of Bolivian scholar Fernando Calderón's
(1988a) essay, "Cómo vivir en la modernidad sin dejar de ser indio" (How to
live in modernity without giving up one's Indian identity).[10] Women activists

---

organizations, for example, even if they do not self-define as "feminist," have been influenced by
ideas about women's rights and roles in society and employ notions of gender equality and oppression, which have their origins in second-wave feminism. In this book I try to define organizations as
they define themselves in their literature, in meetings, at public events, and in interviews.

9. Structural adjustment measures were introduced by the IMF and World Bank as a set of
policies designed to guide poor, indebted countries and stimulate their economies. Key measure-
ments of a country's economic success include increases in gross domestic product; the lifting of
trade barriers (to stimulate foreign investment and competition); and in some cases, traditional
social indicators such as education and health. UNICEF was the first international agency to systematically address the social costs of adjustment. The so-called UNICEF approach, a term coined by
researchers after UNICEF published two important sets of studies (Cornia et al. 1987; UNICEF 1987),
addressed primarily the costs of adjustment for children and mothers. Several feminist scholars have
utilized and critiqued the UNICEF approach on the basis that it essentializes women as mothers and
as family-bound, rather than as human beings with a broader vision and set of rights comparable to
that of men (see Benería and Feldman 1992; Bakker 1994; Jackson and Pearson 1998).

10. A more recent publication, titled *Cómo sobrevivir el neoliberalismo sin dejar de ser mexicano*
(How to survive neoliberalism without giving up one's Mexican identity [no author, n.d.]) used this

have experienced this identity crisis on various levels: some feminists view the past two decades as transformative, since it has been a period of increased political visibility for women's rights; others see it as a time of economic deterioration and an erosion of women's social and political rights (Barrig 1998; Schild 1998). Some view the increased presence of WID institutions and research programs, feminist NGOs, national educational campaigns, and feminist policy-making and advocacy as a product of successful feminist organizing; others protest these very institutions, projects, and research programs on the basis that they are colonizing the realities of Latin American women, and as Westernized gender technocracies that do nothing other than reproduce and institutionalize Western forms of knowledge about women and development. A feminist achievement for some is for others a violent imposition, a negative form of gendered globalization, or a colonization of local values and forms of knowledge about women. While one can hardly divide feminists into two camps, "institutionalized" and "autonomous" (Alvarez 2000), these accusations raise much broader issues about the complexities of change associated with neoliberal development and globalization.

Hierarchies in thought and practice regarding state and international development policies (Kabeer 1994), including the power relations implicit in designating groups of people as "in need" of humanitarian assistance or loans, reflect and often reinforce the gendered, classed, and racialized social order of Ecuadorian society. During the early twentieth century, the Ecuadorian state began to see the population itself as a form of human capital, a move that had specific effects for poor women and men (Clark 2001). In conjunction with this, it began to define its role in providing social welfare as an obligation and as a citizen right. During Ecuador's first major economic crisis (1920s) and the most recent crisis (late 1990s), economic instability has produced levels of national anxiety that have crucially shaped the context in which public debates about social welfare and later, women's issues, became possible (Clark 2000; North 2004). As Mary Weismantel has stated in her research on sex and race in the Ecuadorian Andes, "Weak economies generate an even more profound threat to the nation" (2003, 330); and public debates about family and morality are often at the heart of nationalist crises (Sunder Rajan 2003).

In general, socioeconomic development frameworks that prioritize growth and posit a universal subject tend to benefit men over women, mestizos over indigenous people, industrialized countries over poor ones, and Western over

---

theme to address the cultural contradictions of modernization in the context of neoliberal policies in Mexico.

non-Western cultures. Many development frameworks assume that poor women will absorb the costs of restructuring through their unpaid household and community labor: as state social expenditures decrease, poor women are most affected, as their economic burdens tend to increase as a result of the privatization of social welfare systems (Lind 2002). Neoliberal development frameworks have exacerbated development hierarchies and inequalities by accelerating models of economic growth and liberalization and by privatizing social welfare distribution.

Paradoxically, several historically marginalized groups in Ecuador have gained some political ground during the neoliberal period, despite the fact that their economic livelihoods have eroded. The institutionalization of the international development field since the 1950s, including through funding for national governments and the efforts of the NGO sector to redistribute social welfare, has facilitated the process of social mobilization among women and indigenous sectors, for example. This is so, despite the fact that the ideas and actions of the women's and indigenous movements have at times been appropriated, ignored, or made invisible by the state and international development institutions. Ecuador's social movements have challenged state modernization and global neoliberal restructuring as exclusionary processes that place women, the poor, indigenous people, and the Ecuadorian nation-state in a contradictory position vis-à-vis the new forms of global governance.

In some ways, antineoliberal social movements in Ecuador and elsewhere are not new: many of the issue networks and coalitions that were formed during the 1990s have their foundations in earlier social movements—"old" peasant and leftist struggles and in "new" identity-based groups such as those at the heart of the women's, the indigenous, and the black movements (Slater 1985; Escobar and Alvarez 1992; Alvarez, Dagnino and Escobar 1998a). Neoliberalism is not new, either, although it heightens cultural, political, and economic tensions, because its philosophical foundations and the concrete policies that emerge from neoliberal governments promote individualism, market competition, the integration of noncapitalist labor into the capitalist economy (including women's reproductive labor and indigenous "cultural labor" (see Radcliffe, Laurie, and Andolina 2004), and globalization.

Cultural Politics and Gender

I view women's negotiations with neoliberal development as cultural-political struggles, in two important senses. First, organized women are questioning the world "out there," how we think about development, and the subjectivities of those who produce and consume images of development, including those who practice it.[11] In this regard, they are not only challenging politics and economic policies but also the cultural contexts within which these are defined, created, and translated into action. To understand this aspect of women's organizing, I examine how specific constructions of gender, family, and motherhood are produced and used strategically in women's community organizing as well as in the process of neoliberal restructuring, including in national politics, state policy making, and international institutions such as the World Bank. Second, women are struggling for access to political power and material resources as well as interpretive power, the power to interpret the reality within which they live (Franco 1989). In this regard, the power to name, to see, to identify, to make visible, is as important to their struggles as is the power to redistribute, organize a march, lead a community project, or write a policy statement. An analysis of gender politics is necessarily about culture as well, as notions of "the political" are embedded in cultural understandings of identity, power, and social change. Likewise, my analysis of cultural practice also is necessarily about politics, since knowledge production, identity production, and cultural/social institutions are embedded in and stem from political negotiations and structures of power (Alvarez, Dagnino, and Escobar 1998a).

An important aspect of my research on women's survival strategies involves rethinking "the economy" from this cultural-political perspective. While many feminist political economists and cultural studies scholars have criticized development discourse for essentializing the experiences of women in "Third World" or Latin American societies (Ong 1987; Mohanty 1991; Saunders 2002), few have analyzed the ways in which women negotiate and define their economic identities and roles from this cultural-political perspective.[12] And while many feminist scholars have turned to studies of politics and culture as a way to avoid economic essentialism, they have done so at the expense of understanding how the econ-

---

11. Here I am following the work of V. Spike Peterson (1996), in which she suggests that a critical understanding of globalization requires "relational thinking." First, she states, "this involves understanding the world 'out there' (practices, institutions, structures of social re/production), how we think (meaning systems, ideologies, paradigms) and who we are (subjectivity, agency, self and collective identities) as interacting dimensions of social reality" (185; also see Peterson 2003).

12. By *essentializing* I am referring to the tendency in Western academic research to posit "Third World women" as a largely homogenous category of women, typically characterized by their passivity, poverty, lack of education, and family-bound nature, rather than to view them in terms of the class, racial, ethnic, sexual, cultural, religious, and national differences that characterize their actual lives (see Mohanty 1991).

omy itself, and related notions of neoliberalism and globalization, are socially constructed, embedded in global power relations, and subject to negotiation by organized women. Likewise, I view policies and the arena of policy-making through the same cultural-political lens. Policies themselves are important sites of struggle and resistance (Shore and Wright 1997a, 1997b), not only in terms of how people respond to economic policy change but also in terms of how policies themselves reflect inequalities and forms of prejudice inherent in Western knowledge production. A social policy that assumes women will volunteer to distribute food or manage a day-care center, for example, posits poor women as absorbers of the crisis and transfers, in invisible and visible ways, a heavy responsibility to them to manage welfare in their communities. To the extent that this representation of women as mothers and absorbers of the crisis is translated into the institutionalization of poverty and survival in poor communities, this policy is both symbolically and materially violent for these sectors of poor women, in addition to the ways in which it constructs racial, class, and Third World difference. How people benefit or suffer from neoliberal policies depends on their material locations as well as how their lives and identities are represented in frameworks: interpretation and implementation are two sides of the same coin that reinforce societal relations of power.

Place, Transnationality, and Gender Identity Politics

As in other Latin American countries, in Ecuador social movements have developed through transnational, rather than merely local or national, networks. Globalization, a highly contested process that is at once economic, political, and cultural (Lechner and Boli 2001; Bergeron 2001), arguably has brought with it negative economic effects but also computers, e-mail, and cell phones to many activists. Through e-mail networks, an International Women's Day (March 8) march in Quito can be coordinated with marches in Brazil, Costa Rica, Mexico, and India. An idea is not formed merely from the local context but from communication across national borders, around the world. This is so despite the fact that the geopolitics of development are such that we are taught to understand not the similarities but rather the differences among nations and women's struggles within and among First World and Third World countries (Mohanty 1991; Basu 1995). As many scholars have shown, although geopolitical boundaries are very real in the sense that they shape our daily lives in powerful ways, they are also constructs or imagined communities (Anderson 1983) that discourage us from making connections, understanding the limits of nationalist ideologies (Sunder Rajan 2003), and reimagining development (Bhavnani, Foran, and Kurian 2003). Some scholars in North America have suggested that we "turn the Western lens" back on ourselves, in the West, to rethink the very concepts we use in our research on non-Western societies (e.g., Herzfeld 1992; Mohanty 1991). Indeed, this has been an important project in Western social theory and research, particularly in anthropology. However, it clearly remains important to think about, study, and rethink cultures, genders, economies, and politics around the world, in contexts different from our own. As anthropologist Orin Starn states, "The turn to 'bring it back home' is a welcome broadening of focus. Nevertheless, the persistence of Western ignorance and miscomprehension means that a role still exists for an anthropology of places like Burundi, New Guinea, Indonesia . . . Peru [or Ecuador]" (1999, 16).

In this research I examine a field of sites (Alvarez, Dagnino, and Escobar 1998a; Gowan and " Riain 2000) that shape and give meaning to women's political and economic agency in the context of state modernization, global development, and neoliberal politics in Ecuador. I situate women's community organizations and Ecuadorian feminisms within a complex web of meaning and mobilization (Alexander and Mohanty 1997), a web that is influenced by local, national, and global discourses (Freeman 2001) and networks (Keck and Sikkink 1998). Gender is both implicit and explicit in this process: on the one hand, assumptions about gender are embedded in national politics and neoliberal policies; on the other hand, organized women have challenged gender biases in Ecuadorian nationalisms and processes of globalization. I understand that what I am observing is not one process but many; not one set of easily identifiable institutions but several sites or publics (Fraser 1997); not one discourse of globalization and neoliberal development but many that travel across borders, among and within wealthy and poor regions (Grewal and Kaplan 1994; Thayer 2000). My aim in this book is to map these seemingly disparate sites and publics in order to more adequately understand the successes and limits of women's community organizing and feminism in the context of global change. The survival and political strategies I examine, while fragmented and sometimes contradictory, deserve our attention: they help us better understand how women have survived economic hardship as well as engendered and transformed public debates and global spheres of action.[13]

13. Here and throughout the book I use the terms *engendered* and *engendering* in two ways: they signify (1) adding a gender dimension to institutional practices, as in ministerial and other state institutional policy frameworks, programs, and projects; and (2) adding a presence of feminist voices and visions to (in this case) state decision-making and planning processes.

It is important to clarify that I recognize that globalization and neoliberalism (or "neoliberal globalization," as some authors have chosen to frame it [e.g., Rosero, Vega, and Reyes Ávila 2000]), are not all-encompassing and irreversible processes (Gibson-Graham 1996). To the contrary, they are historically constructed processes that have arisen through the systematization of a specific set of policies and beliefs concerning the "market," a point I elaborate on in Chapter 2. Yet we are faced with working within and advocating social change in this context. Because of this, I am less concerned about the questions of *where* women position themselves vis-à-vis the state or development field ("inside," "outside," and so on) than I am about *how* women negotiate the public/private, local/national/global boundaries of international development and globalization. In some of the cases I examine in this book, women's political struggles have brought on new public debates about much broader, seemingly gender-neutral processes and concepts such as redemocratization, citizenship, and participation. I also recognize the importance of distinguishing between different types of community women's groups and NGOs. Some women's NGOs, for example, tend to reproduce institutional and conceptual hierarchies more than others (Kabeer 1994), particularly those that have chosen to work uncritically within the framework of neoliberal development, have gained power in the new public-private partnerships, or have organized at a cost to their own survival. It is precisely these different strategies that I highlight in my study.

I situate my analysis of women's organizations in the context of the transnational circulation of finance, labor, legislation, and the production of development knowledge, demonstrating how this circulation and the associated reordering of societal institutions and hierarchies help to constitute and reconstitute specific sectors of women as constituents and targets of development (Escobar 1995; Grewal and Caplan 1994). Although since its inception the international development field's primary goal has been to alleviate Third World poverty, many women and men are worse off than they were prior to the debt crisis and SAPs. In part stemming from SAPs, many community groups must now frame their projects and goals in terms of the market in order to acquire development funding, thus limiting their political and economic possibilities. Yet how poor women are targeted by development practitioners also has positive consequences for the women involved, such as political and subjective empowerment, as many scholars have pointed out (e.g., Moser 1989a, 1993; Rodríguez 1994). If it did not, women would be less likely to work within the institutional boundaries of these neoliberal development hierarchies. I therefore emphasize the political and economic *paradoxes* of women's struggles for survival, as a way to illustrate how women and men, in Ecuador and throughout Latin America, interpret and negotiate ideas about development, state modernization, globalization, and modernity in complex ways.

One irony of the past fifteen to twenty years, since the inception of neoliberal development policies in Ecuador and throughout Latin America, is that women's movements have gained, rather than lost, institutional power. At the same time that democracy as a notion and set of practices is being challenged, and at the same time that the state is being privatized and according to some, "shrunk," women's movements have acquired important institutional spaces in the state as well as in the private realm of NGOs. Yet the question is, Which women benefit from this acquisition of institutional space—and which lose out? That is, Which women are targeted as the new constituents of development? Which women have the power to define the realm within which neoliberal development policies are designed and implemented? To what extent, if at all, does this configuration of state- and NGO-based feminist power coincide with or facilitate the broader project of neoliberal restructuring and globalization? How does neoliberalism contribute to reconfiguring gender relations and identities, and how does this, in turn, create new self-representations of the Ecuadorian nation-state? How do the new forms of gender politics themselves contribute to a restructuring of power relations among sectors of women and to refashioning national identity, development, and survival? These are some of the questions I wish to address in this book.

In Chapter 1, I address the historical trajectory of women's movements in Ecuador and their relationship to the state, beginning with early suffragist and socialist feminisms (1900–1930s), women's participation in the new labor, peasant, and indigenous struggles of the 1930s and 1940s, and their activism during the 1970s military dictatorship and the following redemocratization process. I examine the parallel process by which the Ecuadorian state made social welfare central to its modernization project, including how specific governments and ideological movements shaped the social policy field that began to develop during the mid-twentieth century. In this chapter I show how my analysis of feminism, urban poor movements, and neoliberal state restructuring will be situated in the remaining chapters.

In Chapter 2, I address the cultural politics of neoliberalism in Ecuador on two levels. First, I provide a discussion of the nature of neoliberal reforms in the country, covering the origins of the 1980s foreign debt crisis and SAPs, which importantly shaped the possibilities of state political reforms in the years to come. I pay special attention to the gender dimensions of these reforms as they have affected the urban poor and the realm of "women's work" (Benería and

Feldman 1992). Second, I discuss conceptual debates about neoliberalism and globalization, including the gendered nature of their discursive constructions in public debates and in political and economic discourse. I illustrate how policies themselves are important sites of struggle, and how and why the making of feminist public policies in Ecuador has been central to women's organizing (Shore and Wright 1997b; Rosero, Vega, and Reyes Ávila 2000).

Chapter 3 is an in-depth study of the Ecuadorian state's role in restructuring the provision of social welfare during the 1988–96 period, including through a state child welfare project that provided funding for day-care centers in poor urban communities. The child welfare project helped to strengthen local women's organizations, since they were called upon to manage the day-care centers, yet it also helped to institutionalized the women's survival struggles by requiring their participation yet paying them little and increasing their overall economic burdens. Once thought to be "temporary" participants, poor women who volunteer in community development initiatives have now become permanent players in social welfare redistribution.

In Chapter 4, I analyze the experiences of community women's organizations in southern Quito. I focus on the paradoxes of their forms of survival and struggle: the political paradoxes of utilizing specific notions of femininity (for example, their traditional gender roles as mothers) to take a stance against neoliberal state restructuring and achieve some level of political power, and the economic paradoxes that derive from the fact that they continue to be exploited laborers and second-class citizens. They, too, reinforce these paradoxes through the construction of their political identities and strategies; sometimes their use of their traditional gender roles in community development initiatives reinforce, rather than challenge, their economic exploitation and poverty.

In Chapter 5, I examine feminist politics and the gendered contradictions of neoliberal state formation in the context of the 1997 political crisis. In particular, I examine how four feminist strands responded to President Bucaram's (August 1996–February 1997) populist antics and approach to neoliberal restructuring.[14] Through their process of organizing against the Bucaram administration, a process that the entire nation participated in, the four feminist strands helped to remake the nation, both institutionally, through their participation in the constitutional reforms, and symbolically, through their challenges to political corruption.

14. By *strands* I am referring to the publicly visible, active currents of feminism in Ecuadorian society. Virginia Vargas (1992) first used this term in her research on Peruvian feminisms, in which she posits that there were three visible strands of feminism in Peru during the 1980s and 1990s: political, feminist, and popular.

In Chapter 6, I discuss the crisis of the state in Ecuador during the 2000–2004 period and its implications for feminist organizing and policies. I first discuss Ecuador's dollarization process, which began in September 2001, and illustrate the restructuring of the social welfare system. Here, too, state development strategies have been limited by the lack of sovereignty of women and indigenous people within the global financial community but the 1998 constitution has opened many new spaces for political participation of the women's and indigenous movements. The newly reformed state faces the challenge of delivering social and economic rights to these sectors in a time of economic uncertainty and heightened national anxieties. I draw out the implications of this situation for Ecuadorian politics, Latin American feminisms, and studies of neoliberalism, development, and state restructuring.

Throughout the book, I suggest that women's responses to global neoliberal restructuring and their relationships with the state are best understood as paradoxical; they participate in strategic negotiations with the state to achieve specific forms of material and interpretive power (the power to name and define policy agendas as much as the power acquired through access to the economic and social benefits of modernization and citizenship [Franco 1989]). I do not argue that women's organizations have been merely victims, be it of the state, the World Bank, their husbands, or political parties; nor do I argue that they have been entirely oppositional, as indeed they have not (Lind 2000). The historical trajectory of Ecuadorian women's organizing demonstrates that the struggle for gender-based rights (including an expanded notion of "rights" itself) has not occurred in this dualistic sense of working either in or against development and the state. This study does not portray a pure "antidevelopment" struggle nor only a reform movement; radical and reformist strands of feminism exist, however, and organizations have worked to challenge historical inequalities reinforced by the presence of international aid. Rather, this study illustrates how women's organizations in Quito work at multiple, sometimes contradictory levels and in various social spaces to achieve specific goals. Their perceived success depends on the institutional and political climate as well as the personal relationships between organizations and individuals. The paradox of urban poor women's struggles pertains to the fact that the longer the women have struggled, the worse their economic conditions have become, despite their best intentions. A broader feminist paradox is the ongoing struggle for citizen rights in a national context in which the majority lack social rights and continue to be marginalized, despite the recent political reforms.[15]

[1]

Myths of Progress:
Citizenship, Modernization, and Women's Rights
Struggles in Ecuador

Living *in* the nation today involves, also, living *with* the state.

—RAJESWARI SUNDER RAJAN, *The Scandal of the State: Women, Law, and Citizenship in Postcolonial India*

The historical relationship between women and the state in Ecuador is complex, multifaceted, and paradoxical. From the start, women's rights struggles necessarily have taken place in multiple social spaces and have cut across a range of political, economic, and geographic sectors. The state has served as an important legitimizer of women's rights struggles and has sought political accountability by granting specific rights and concessions to women, indigenous communities, the rural poor and other groups (for example, through voting and agrarian reforms). Eurocentric ideologies of womanhood, in conjunction with ideologies of progress, "whiteness," and modernity, have been central to the historical formation and implementation of Ecuadorian state policies and laws and to the broader imagining of Ecuador as a nation (Whitten 2003b). They have also shaped in important ways the boundaries of and challenges brought forth by contemporary feminist politics.

Many studies of Ecuadorian politics today focus on class- or ethnicity-based claims made by social movements to the state and pay special attention to indigenous, peasant, and labor struggles with little reference to their gender dimensions (e.g., Pachano 1996; Selverston-Scher 2001; Gerlach 2003; North and Cameron 2003; Sawyer 2004). These studies point out the important ways in which the state has developed historically and how it has promoted a self-image based on the exclusion of the (ethnic) majority of society. Studies of women's political participation, including women's grassroots organizing, participation in the Left, feminisms, and public policy making, have tended to focus on the redemocratization period (late 1970s–present) and, to a lesser degree, on the earlier period of presuffrage organizing (1900–1929; see Prieto 1987; Rosero 1988; Menéndez-Carrión 1988; Rodríguez 1992; Rosero, Vega, and Reyes Ávila 2000). Few of these studies, however, bring together, on the one hand, the processes under way within the state, which played an important role in historically constructing the professional field and discursive terrain of social welfare and, on the other, the strategies developed and used by various types of women's organizations to intervene in national decision-making and political discourse. "The family" has been at the center of struggles within both these realms of action. My examination of women's rights struggles in the context of state modernization and global development underscores the important ways in which gender was and continues to be instrumental to Ecuadorian state modernization projects and national identity. In terms of legal abstraction, women have gained important legal rights since the early twentieth century, beginning with suffrage for literate women in 1929. In practice, the extent to which these reforms benefited women has depended largely on their social location by class, region, ethnicity, race, and sexuality.

In this chapter I address the historical relationship between women and the state in Ecuador by focusing on three interrelated aspects: (1) the emergence and historical trajectory of women's movements; (2) the historical role of the state in providing social welfare, a policy framework that relied on specific notions of motherhood, citizenship, and national identity; and (3) the transnational aspects of women's movements and nation-state formation, including influences from the international development field (especially the WID field), processes and ideologies of globalization, and regional organizing efforts by women. I highlight the paradoxical consequences of this historical process for urban poor, rural peasant, and indigenous women, as they are compared to middle- and upper-class women, most of whom were mestiza, urban, and formally educated.

Before I proceed with my discussion of women's rights struggles and state modernization I would like to address some of the structural and ideological underpinnings of political movements and social reforms in the country. From the start, Ecuador was a very divided nation, geographically, politically, culturally, and economically. This had important repercussions for the historical construction of citizenship and for later citizen struggles. The coastal city of Guayaquil had already established itself as a port city and industrial center during the colonial period. The coastal region was conducive to agriculture, and by the beginning of the twentieth century it was (and it continues to be) the nation's leading export sector. Because of its connection to Europe, and later to

North America and other regions, Guayaquileños' identities were produced through a more transnational lens than were those of the people of Ecuador's Andean highlands and Amazon region (Goetschel 1999). The highland region, encompassing the nation's political capital, Quito, consisted primarily of *haciendas*, and most of the country's land was owned by large landowners until the agrarian reforms of the 1960s.[1] Many highland indigenous peasants provided the labor for these *haciendas* as *huasipungeros*, laborers who were provided with small plots of land for subsistence agriculture in lieu of wages (North 2004). The Amazon region, which constitutes more than one-third of Ecuador's total territory, was relatively unexploited by foreign capital until the early twentieth century, when oil explorers began to survey the area for a potential discovery (Schodt 1987; Martz 1987; Gerlach 2003; North 2004). These geographic differences, coupled with the extreme class, ethnic, and cultural differences, underscored the difficulty (indeed, the impossibility) of creating a cohesive national identity.

Ideologies of womanhood have always been central to Ecuador's modernization process (Weismantel 2001; Fiol-Matta 2002). Since the early days of independence (from 1830 on), the preservation of (upper-class, *criolla*, or mestiza) women's domestic roles was viewed by the state, politicians, and other elites as a crucial aspect of "civilizing" the nation (Goetschel 1999). Maintaining the image of upper-class *criolla* women as "kept" women, educated in a gender-appropriate way, and belonging to the private realm, was important for maintaining the broader social order of the new nation. Eurocentric ideologies of womanhood reinforced elite women's class and racial privileges as well as their relegation to the private realm. Paradoxically, these ideologies also opened the door for women to organize as a political sector against the very policies, laws, and cultural attitudes that oppressed them in the first place. The increasingly liberalized, secular understandings of women's roles in public life (the so-called modernization of gender), paved the way for elite women to become important political, philanthropic, and business leaders. To the extent that their class and racial interests were sustained through political domination, elite women bene-

---

1. The 1964 agrarian reform law, decreed by the 1963–67 military government (a four-man *junta*), was passed to diffuse growing political conflicts in the countryside and to organize peasants in a top-down fashion through colonization measures. Private land was transferred primarily into the hands of mestizo sectors, however (de la Torre 2000). The Institution of Agrarian Reform and Colonization (Instituto de Reforma Agraria y Colonización [IERAC]) was created at this time, "which functioned, at times for the better and at times for the worse, until 1994, when it was abolished by a neoliberal-inspired agrarian development law" (North 2004, 194; see also Saad Herrería 2000; de la Torre 2000; North and Cameron 2003).

fited from Ecuadorian nationalist political endeavors, despite their relegation to the private realm and their lack of rights.

In many important senses, both gender and race served to propel Ecuador's national identity as a postcolonial state and to defend the state's interests in this process. From the start, the state's identity as the promulgator of modernization relied on these identity constructions as part of the country's "myth of progress" (Coronil 1997). Early constitutions included categories of "citizens" and "nationals," clearly demarcating people according to race and ethnicity (M. Becker 1999). Although literate women were granted the right to vote in 1929, their vote was "optional," while literate men's vote was "obligatory," according to Ecuadorian law, until 1967 (Agencia Latinoamericana de Información [ALAI] 2004).[2] It was not until the 1980 election that the majority of Ecuadorians—including the indigenous, the poor, and women—voted during the national elections. Historically, women, indigenous, and Afro-Ecuadorians were not considered full citizens by any standards; even after they received specific legal rights, their social rights continued to be denied. Indigenous and Afro-Ecuadorians, whose identities were racialized in ways specific to each social group and who consequently suffered related yet distinct forms of racism (Cervone and Rivera 1999), were treated as inferior in all fields: law, policy, medicine, education, and the arts, to name a few. They were often subject to moral scrutiny as well as legal regulation, including through health-care reforms, prostitution laws, and morality crusades (Goetschel 1999; Clark 2000; Muteba Rahier 2003). Elite strategies over how to "civilize" Ecuador, including through citizenship, educational, and social reforms, changed significantly as the country shifted from being a religious to a secular state, and as social unrest caused elites to rethink their strategies. State transformations reflected global trends: many Latin American nations were moving in the same direction, and they often modeled their reforms after European and North American modernization projects (Miller 1991; Guy 1991).

Situating Women's Rights Struggles in Ecuador, 1900–1960s

Early twentieth-century feminists' perspectives on women's rights varied greatly according to these feminists' own identities, social locations, and political inter-

2. The 1946 constitution, for example, stated that literate men were obligated to vote but it was "optional" for literate women. Obligatory voting was extended to literate women in 1967 (ALAI 2004, 3).

ests. Although scholars have tended to contextualize Ecuadorian women's activism in two historical phases reminiscent of European and North American feminisms, "first wave" and "second wave," the historical trajectory of Ecuadorian feminism defies this type of categorization. There was indeed an important struggle for women's suffrage in Ecuador during the late 1800s and early 1900s—what some scholars might call the first wave of women's activism (Menéndez-Carrión 1988). This movement provided some impetus for the conservative state to grant literate women the right to vote in 1929. And certainly there has been enormous growth in women's activism since the redemocratization process in the late 1970s and 1980s, until the present—what has come to be known as the second wave of feminism (Rosero 1988; Rosero, Vega, and Reyes Ávila 2000). These marked waves follow the patterns of women's movements in other Latin American countries and regions, but they do not capture the depth and breadth of women's activism during the 1930–60s (Miller 1991; Vargas 1992; Jaquette 1996; León de Leal 1995). There were significant organizing efforts by women in peasant, labor, and leftist movements during this period that created a basis for later, explicitly "feminist" organizing to emerge. Urban popular movements contributed to the new gendered identities of recent settlers in Ecuador's major cities, and women have always played protagonistic roles in indigenous and rural organizing efforts, from the days of colonialism to the present. The political trajectory and engendering of these movements has not corresponded specifically with these feminist "waves" but rather with a broader range of political, cultural, discursive, and ideological factors (Rosero and Armas 1990; Rosero et al. 1991).

The available information about suffragist struggles and early feminisms is scant and undertheorized in comparison with the literature on contemporary (the 1980s on) feminisms in Ecuador (e.g., Rosero 1983, 1988; Prieto 1987; Menéndez-Carrión 1988; Rosero and Armas 1990; Rodríguez 1992, 1994; Lind 1992, 2000; Radcliffe and Westwood 1996; Herrera 2000; Roday 2002; Vega 2004), and there is some disagreement about the nature of the state's decision to grant (literate) women the right to vote in 1929 (Ecuador being the first country in the region to do so). Some scholars argue that there was not much of a women's rights "struggle" per se that led to the 1929 decision; rather, they point out, the largely conservative state granted women the right to vote as a concession, based on the then common belief held by key elites that women (presumably heterosexual women of the elite classes) would vote for the Right and would therefore be an asset to the political elites of the time (Menéndez-Carrión 1988; Ayala Marín 2004). Compared to the situation in other Latin American countries where female suffrage was granted in the aftermath of heavy feminist political organizing (for example, Argentina, Chile, and Brazil [see Miller 1991]), early feminist activity in Ecuador was limited to smaller networks, a few women's magazines and newspapers, less direct protest, and fewer visible feminist leaders in public arenas of society.

There are some explanations to support this view, including those centered on the role of religion and the nature of the state and citizen practices. The Catholic Church, a conservative stronghold in Ecuador, continued to be heavily involved in national politics and exerted great ideological and economic influence throughout the early twentieth century (Roos and van Renterghem 1997). Unlike in other countries, such as Argentina and Brazil, where the church had lost some of its influence following periods of liberalization, which emphasized the separation of church and state, in Ecuador it continued to hold relatively great political power as one of the country's largest landowners and through its conservative ideological orthodoxy.[3] The second explanation concerns the fact that, given the enormous structural inequalities, the Ecuadorian state could never espouse a cohesive national identity or adequately socialize people as "citizens." Indeed, an important result of the colonial legacy, which included insurmountable structural inequalities, was political instability. Ecuador had undergone many political-regime transitions since its independence in 1822.[4] The Liberal Period (1880–1912), which was characterized by a marked shift toward state secularization, showed more governmental stability, although this did not translate into political cohesion across social sectors. Throughout the early to mid-twentieth century, "[e]lectoral politics was a minority affair, with only about 3 percent of the population voting" (M. Becker 1999, 1). As Marc Becker has pointed out in his research on the politics of citizenship in Ecuador,

3. The "Law of the Dead Hands" (Ley de Manos Muertas), passed by the government of General Eloy Alfaro in 1908, allowed the state to claim land owned by religious institutions (namely, the Catholic Church) and allocate it for the "public benefit." In essence, it was a form of land redistribution that was a response to the fact that the church was the largest landowner in the country and underutilized its land. This was one of the largest feats of the so-called Liberal Revolution, led primarily by anticlerical Liberal Party leader Alfaro, who served two presidential terms (1897–1901 and 1907–11). Importantly, the Liberal Revolution followed President Gabriel García Moreno (1861–75), a devout Catholic and fundamentalist leader, who made many state reforms that followed Catholic orthodoxy and who did not believe in a separation between church and state. García Moreno even renamed the country República del Corazón Sagrado de Jesús (Republic of the Sacred Heart of Jesus) (Roos and van Renterghem 1997), although the name was later changed back to Ecuador.

4. For example, during the first ninety-five years of independence, there were forty presidents, dictators, and military juntas (Roos and van Renterghem 1997, 12).

it has been through literacy requirements for voting that elites have successfully "historically excluded Ecuador's large rural Indian population from political discourse" (1), and literate women were disenfranchised as well until 1929. Even within the minority voting population, there was incohesion. Voting patterns were often based on regional party affiliations. The Liberal Party came from the coast and tended to be supported by coastal residents, and the Conservative Party was based in Quito and tended to be supported by highlanders. Given this context, early female suffragists did not find it useful to work within formal political channels or to model their movements after male-based politics, as was the case in some other Latin American countries where feminist activists developed stronger political networks; at the very least, these theories need to be further explored.[5]

Yet my research supports the idea that women played important roles in transforming the national political discourse that led up to the 1929 suffrage ruling, even if there was less organizing taking place than in other Latin American countries. The emergence and integration of "feminist" ideas into Ecuadorian society occurred at levels that might be considered nonpolitical. Women played an important role in shaping the fields of social work and nursing, for example, and they became key players in education, especially at the primary level (Clark 2001). They were increasingly hired as state employees, in the emerging services sector and, as such, were integrated into the state. To the extent that this was seen as a step forward for civilized society, it also helped to refashion the state's image as modern and progressive. Feminist writers and artists contributed to creating a new popular culture, and many professional women made inroads in their professional associations, both nationally and internationally (Miller 1991). Several urban-based, educated women worked in charity and solidarity organizations with poor and indigenous people. Some formally educated women achieved entry into traditionally male professional spaces, and through their professional activities fought for women's right to vote. All these activities fall into the reform camp. They conceivably changed the elites' views of women's roles in society, as is pointed to in some studies (e.g., Menéndez-Carrión 1988; Clark 2001). Their contributions to transforming women's citizen rights need to be seen more broadly, not merely in terms of political participation in the traditional sense.

5. In more recent studies of women's voting patterns in Ecuador, it has been suggested that women vote according to their *pragmatic* interests, rather than according to ideological affiliation, which might explain why women tended to vote conservatively during the 1984 elections (Menéndez-Carrión 1989, 8). At the very least, it is important to point out the contingent nature of political opportunities such as that of female suffrage.

Zoila Ugarte de Landívar, for example, considered the founder of feminist journalism in Ecuador and one of the first self-defined feminists, edited the feminist magazine *La Mujer*, beginning in 1905 (Ayala Marín 2004). *La Mujer* played an important role in creating a public dialogue about the condition of women and their educational and legal rights. Matilde Hidalgo, who in recent times has been recognized as an important figure in Ecuador's history, was the first woman to complete secondary education (1913), the first to become a doctor (1921), and the first female elected to congress. During the 1924 elections, Hidalgo registered to vote alongside the male voting population. She argued that the 1897 constitution, which did not include any explicit explanation of why women could not vote, allowed her to vote. Although there was resistance to her case, a decision was made in her favor, making her the first woman in Ecuadorian history documented as having voted (Ayala Marín 2004). Some women's groups emerged and disappeared over periods of a few years. During the 1920s, socialist feminist groups such as the "Rosa Luxembourg Group" were politically active and played important roles in the labor protests that led up to the 1925 July Revolution (la Revolución Juliana), including the broad-based strike against the government in November 1922 that culminated in a massacre in Guayaquil (North 2004, ALAI 2004). These examples point to a more complex picture of women's activism concerning female suffrage in Ecuador. The state conceded the vote to literate women in 1929 following a period characterized by multiple discourses about womanhood, discourses that both promulgated and challenged traditional notions of gender and the family. On either side of the debate, social reformers viewed women's rights as intricately linked to the nation's quest for modernity, and ultimately, the decision to grant literate women the right to vote rested on political elites' hope and expectation that literate women would vote on their side. This concession had as much to do with race and class as it had with gender—and perhaps more so.

Changes in the international political climate greatly influenced women's political opportunities in Ecuador, affecting how they placed demands on the state and their effectiveness (or lack thereof) in obtaining rights such as to vote. Suffragists in Guayaquil and Quito, for example, were clearly in tune with regional women's networks and had kept abreast of European, North American, and Latin American intellectual currents and legal trends. Several regional conferences took place during the period that a fortunate few Ecuadorian women were able to attend. These conferences resulted in concrete platforms that women could bring home to their countries and use as organizing devices. The first International Feminine Congress (Congreso Femenino Internacional) was held in Buenos Aires, Argentina, in 1910. By the end of the meeting, the two hundred–plus delegates in attendance had put together an agreed-upon platform for addressing women's rights in the region. The platform included eight propositions that ranged from universal suffrage to divorce laws, maternity leave, and compulsory secular education for both sexes (Miller 1991, 75).[6] Delegates addressed international law and the laws of individual countries as they pertained to women's rights. The platform, although not legally binding by any means, was brought back by the delegates to their countries and disseminated. In 1924, the second Pan-American Women's Conference was held in Lima, Perú; geographically, it was now easier for Ecuadorian women to attend the conference. Like the International Feminine Congress, this conference addressed women's legal rights and allowed feminists to develop transnational networks and forms of collaboration. The transnational arena was crucial for the ideological formation of early feminist groups in Ecuador, as it generated a sense of "shared identity" among participants about their gendered social realities and provided them with legal and political tools with which to address sexism in their national legislative processes (Basu 1995).

Other structural factors shaped women's political and economic opportunities during the early twentieth century. By 1910, Ecuador had entered what would become a long period of economic crisis and the state was on a marked path toward its defined goal of modernization. World War I was beginning, causing several shock waves through the global political economy. The country's primary export at the time, cacao, was losing value in the international market; many jobs were lost in Ecuador's agricultural sector, prompting poor families to migrate to urban areas; the government was forced to take austerity measures; and the combination of rural unemployment and Ecuador's first wave of urbanization led to extremely high levels of poverty for many people (Clark 2000). The state's role in providing social welfare began to shift, leading to new forms of public assistance for sectors of the population viewed as "vulnerable" or as in need of help or social reform (more on this below).

Modern science, technology, and professional fields gave increasing impor-

6. Francesca Miller (1991) summarizes the eight propositions in the following way: (1) universal suffrage for both sexes; (2) absolute divorce; (3) an eight-hour workday for adults and a six-hour workday for children under sixteen years of age; (4) provision of a place to sit down for women workers in stores, workshops, and factories; (5) thirty-four days of leave before and after birth with full pay; (6) compulsory secular education for children of both sexes to the age of fourteen; (7) regular inspections to ensure compliance with the laws governing female and child labor; and (8) establishment of commercial schools for women, improvement of sanitary and health conditions, and promotion of the aesthetic education of the woman worker (75).

tance to the regulation of family life, and "the family" became the center of national development strategies in new, explicit ways. Regulating family life was seen by social reformists of the time as a step toward modernity. It was also a way to maintain social control in a fragile social order. During this period, new types of (gendered) political discourses emerged that reinforced a traditional Eurocentric notion of the heterosexual family as the foundation for the nation. A combination of mitigating factors contributed to this: modern medical discourses of motherhood and child development, which reinforced (in new biological ways) women's roles as mothers and their influence in child development and drew lines between "good" and "bad" families (Clark 2000); international influences from European and North American social welfare states; and politicians' concerns about voting patterns and gaining political support, especially from historically disenfranchised sectors such as the indigenous and rural poor.[7] Whereas in earlier periods elite women were viewed as belonging to the private realm, a new discourse emerged that viewed women's integration into society as a step toward progress and as a necessary aspect of the country's modernization process. Thus elite women served as a marker of national progress, while the rest of the female population remained excluded from the fruits of modernization.

Following the 1929 ruling on female suffrage, elite women's groups may have become further legitimized in the eyes of male elites, but the majority of women still lacked basic citizen rights. In addition, labor struggles came to the forefront of challenges against the state. Plantation workers on the coast were among the first to organize, and workers on *haciendas* began to view themselves increasingly in terms of their civil rights (van Renterghem and Roos 1997, 14). Ecuador did not experience an economic recovery until the end of World War II, when the banana became its leading export (rice and coffee also began to be exported during the 1920–40s), and this foreshadowed many of the labor struggles of that period. At the state level, populist president José María Velasco Ibarra was first elected to office in 1933 and his sporadic forty-year reign in politics, coupled

---

7. Kim Clark (2000) provides an interesting analysis of state regulation of family life in Ecuador during 1910–45. She focuses on specific state policies of child development and child-care and child-protective services and analyzes the intersection of gender, race, and nation in shaping national political discourse during this period. Her study provides further detail about how medical, psychological, legal, and economic discourses helped establish strict lines between "healthy," "fit," "clean," (and, I would add, heterosexual) families (and, by extension, nations) and "unhealthy," "unfit," and "dirty" individuals (who were seen on various levels as "corrupting" families and, by extension, the nation).

with his charisma and popularity, greatly influenced some of the labor reforms and social movements of that period.[8]

Many labor and peasant associations were formed during the 1930s and 1940s, often with the support of leftist political parties, and women played key, albeit underacknowledged, roles in shaping the social movements and political parties of these decades. In response to their ongoing labor exploitation, many indigenous and rural poor people organized to address their needs and create collective sets of demands. They organized regional events, networks, and congresses, leading to some important state reforms such as the establishment of the national Labor Code (Código del Trabajo) in 1938. Leftist political parties worked with peasant and indigenous groups on various levels (M. Becker 1999), and increasingly, through the 1960s, with local women's groups that sometimes became auxiliaries of the party. During this period, women's auxiliary committees (to political parties and labor and peasant associations) were instrumental in organizing protests and events that led to labor reforms and that challenged Ecuador's exclusionary citizen practices. More often than not, these committees have remained largely ignored in major studies of Ecuadorian political history, although some scholars have documented or analyzed their importance (see, e.g., Menéndez-Carrión 1988; Rosero 1983, 1988; Romo-Leroux 1997; Becker 1999; ALAI 2004).

Socialist leaders such as Nela Martínez (b. 1912) played important roles in the Ecuadorian Left and in the struggle for women's rights. Martínez, a prolific writer, was at one time a leader in the Communist Party (PC) and has been active in regional associations such as the Frente Continental de Mujeres. Martínez was a leader in the "Glorious May Revolution," the widespread rebellion that took place in Guayaquil, and then spread to many other provincial cities, on Mother's Day (May 28) 1944.[9] This rebellion ultimately led to the dismantling of the government of Carlos Arroyo del Río (1940–44). Many women participated in this rebellion and played important protagonistic roles in it and the long organizing process that led up to it (Becker 2004; ALAI 2004). Feminine Action of Pichincha (Acción Femenina de Pichincha [AFP]) was formed during this process, and women in Quito and Guayaquil organized for women's rights. Following Arroyo del Río's departure from government, Martínez assumed the role

8. Velasco served as president five times during the 1933–72 period. Several scholars have analyzed various aspects of Velasquismo; see, for example, Menéndez-Carrión 1986; Cueva 1988; de la Torre 2000.

9. Carlos de la Torre (2000) provides a detailed analysis of this rebellion in the cities of Guayaquil, Quito, Cuenca, and Riobamba. See especially chap. 2, on Velasquista populism.

of minister of government during the transition government. Indian rights activist Dolores Cacuango also actively participated in the May 1944 rebellion by leading indigenous forces in an attack on the army barracks in the northern highland town of Cayambe (Becker 2004).[10] Along with peasant leader Tránsito Amaguaña, Angelita Andrango, Rosa Cachipuela, Rosa Alba and many others, they participated in numerous uprisings and protests to bring attention to the abuse of their human rights by *hacendados* (hacienda owners) and landowners (Rodas n.d.). The presence of women in the May Revolution was significant because it was a clear shift from the earlier focus of middle- and upper-class feminists on acquiring female suffrage through diplomacy to a broader emphasis on citizen rights and social justice enacted through a multistrategy agenda that included reform as well as direct protest and revolution.[11]

Later, as women began to organize more (and be seen more) as workers, labor and peasant associations created women's secretariats. The Union of Feminine Organizations of Pichincha (Unión de Organizaciones Femeninas de Pichincha) and the Union of Women Workers (Unión de Mujeres Trabajadoras), both affiliates of the Ecuadorian Confederation of Class-Based Organizations (Confederación Ecuatoriana de Organizaciones Clasistas [CEDOC]), were established in the 1970s. Likewise, the Workers Confederation of Ecuador (Confederación de Trabajadores del Ecuador [CTE]) created its own Women's Department (Departamento de la Mujer), and the Ecuadorian Center of Free Sindicate Organizations (Central Ecuatoriana de Organizaciones Sindicales Libres [CEOSL]) created its own Women's Secretariat (Secretaría de la Mujer). These women's auxiliary groups played important roles in labor strikes, land takeovers (*tomas de tierra*), and in the neighborhood struggles that came to define the new peripheral, poor neighborhoods of Ecuador's cities. Women also played key roles in national strikes led by the major labor federations (ALAI 2004, 6).

The Developmentalist State and the Historical Construction of Social Welfare

At the same time that women joined political movements to fight against structural inequalities and struggle for a new sense of citizenship, the state experi-

---

10. Indigenous leader Dolores Cacuango (1881–1971) served as secretary general of the Ecuadorian Federation of Indians (Federación Ecuatoriana de Indios [FEI]), a national organization that she helped found in 1944 (Rodas n.d.; Rosero 1990).

11. The May Revolution led to a new, significantly revised constitution, the country's most progressive to that date, in 1945.

enced important transformations that led to new relationships between women and the state and to new configurations of power among sectors of women. Three factors contributed to changes in Ecuadorian nation-state formation. The first was the emphasis of national elites on strengthening the state's role as the benefactor of society, including in its management of social welfare and its lead role in directing the socioeconomic development of the nation. The second factor was the role of international institutions and, more broadly, the establishment of the post–World War II professional field of international development, in shaping Ecuadorian state policies, including, economic, social, and foreign relations. The third factor was the discovery in 1967 of petroleum in the Ecuadorian Amazon region, which allowed the state to directly accrue profits from the state-controlled industry like never before, thereby transforming its role in economic and social policy and its relationships with global capital, national elites, and poor communities.

Until the mid-twentieth century, the state promoted an ideology of "charity and philanthropy" and focused on providing assistance to the most in need (of help or, importantly, of social reform). Ecuador's early civil codes, which legislated family life and gender and sexual practice in important ways, were largely influenced by Catholicism and early postindependence movements. The post–World War II period brought with it new understandings of the state's role in providing social welfare. Specifically, the state began to view its role as "protector" and "defender" of society as a service, social obligation, and right, rather than a form of charity (Ojeda Segovia 1993). Although still framed paternalistically, the shift signified a move toward making the state accountable for and to its citizens, rather than it being merely a random benefactor for some of the country's unfortunate. In 1925, the Ministry of Social Prevision and Labor (Ministerio de Previsión y Trabajo), an institutional precursor of today's Ministry of Labor and Ministry of Social Welfare, was first established.[12] Several factors contributed to this new understanding of state social welfare. Velasquista populism, coupled with other ideological and structural trends stimulated by the Cuban Revolution, the Alliance for Progress, banana profits, and Ecuador's war with Peru all contributed to the new conception of social welfare and to the growing need for the state to play a more explicit, active role in protecting and managing social sectors (among them orphans, the poor, single mothers, and the unemployed) and distributing state-sponsored help (Ojeda Segovia 1993, 21). During

12. The Ministry of Social Prevision and Labor became the Ministry of Labor and Social Welfare in 1968. It later was split into two separate ministries.

the 1930s in particular, important reforms to civil and penal codes were made, such as in the 1937 Organic Law of Protective Homes (Ley Orgánica de Hogares de Protección), which provided new forms of support to orphanages and sites of other support services for children, and the 1938 Code of Minors (Código de Menores), which initiated a set of rights for minors of age with respect to Ecuador's civil and penal codes. Importantly, these codes, although slightly reformed over the following decades, remained largely the same until the 1990s legislative reforms.

Many of these early efforts to legislate family and child welfare were influenced by political and scientific discourses of motherhood. In particular, the early twentieth century brought with it new scientific appreciation for and insight into the roles that mothers play in child rearing and family welfare. Symbolically, they were seen as mothers of Ecuador's future, as mothers of the nation, and as such were targeted by the state and various professions as a central part of modernization strategies and ideologies (Clark 2000). By the 1940s, policies concerning the family and its central role in national development were well established and seen as normal and natural outcomes of social reality. Medical researchers examined the role played by "mothers" in decreasing infant mortality and life-expectancy rates. Social scientists and policy analysts examined the role of mothers in increasing opportunities for and determining the chances of literacy among school-aged children; and Ecuador's leaders—democratically elected and authoritarian alike, leaders of all ideological persuasions—tended to view women primarily in their roles as mothers and as linked to the socially perceived private realm of the family. This began to take place—to become institutionalized at the state and other levels—before the establishment of the international development field, not as a result of it, in contrast to what is assumed or argued in some of the development literature (e.g., Escobar 1995). These Eurocentric ideologies of motherhood and national identity provided the basis for the modern social policy field and helped shape the political, discursive terrain within which many contemporary feminists have formed their opposition to state power and to Eurocentric constructions of gender identity and "women's roles in development."

The state's adherence to maternalist ideologies of child welfare and development was only reinforced on a global scale by postwar development institutions such as the IMF, the World Bank, and the United Nations. In many ways these institutions helped consolidate a process already under way to define national progress in scientific, quantifiable terms and, in some cases, to reduce complex social problems to individual blame or reform. The state's framework for addressing social welfare was increasingly influenced by patterns of foreign aid and cooperation and by the international bodies of law and policy that were being created within the United Nations and in global social networks. The establishment of the international WID field in the early 1970s and of the later areas of women and development (WAD) and gender and development (GAD), created the impetus for the Ecuadorian state to revise archaic laws and introduce anti-discrimination legislation; likewise, it helped mobilize women's NGOs and grassroots organizations unlike ever before, leading eventually to the professionalization and NGOization of the feminist movement in the 1980s.[13] This process expanded the arena of social policy implementation and decision making to include civic groups and transnational networks (which could often apply pressure to the state to reforms its policies and laws). It was limited, however, by the military period of the 1970s.

Economic conditions, as seen through the lens of modernization, favored the development of the state's role as social provider through the 1960s and 1970s. Prior to the 1960s, Ecuador was widely viewed by the international development community, including institutions such as the World Bank, as one of the "poorest" countries in the hemisphere (World Bank 1984). By the 1970s, it was considered a "success story" by that same community, in part because of Ecuador's new oil industry (Schodt 1987; Martz 1987). To a large degree, petroleum changed the country's economic status and its image in the global market and international development field. A combination of policies and processes were carried out successively by governments to achieve the state goal of moderniza-

13. Many scholars have addressed the differences and similarities between WID, WAD, and GAD, among them Caroline Moser (1989b and 1993), Eva Rathgeber (1990), and Chandra Mohanty (1991). WID discourses and practices draw from modernization theory; they are situated within the original school of thought about "integrating women into development," based on Ester Boserup's book, *Woman's Role in Economic Development* (New York: St. Martin's Press, 1970). WAD scholars of the 1970s and early 1980s criticized Boserup's research on the basis that it took modernization (and sometimes Westernization) for granted and did not take class into account, including the enormous class differences between women within Third World societies and between women of First and Third World regions. WAD scholars attempted to overcome the pitfalls of Boserup's approach by addressing the relationship between "women" and "development" as categories of analysis, rather than merely by addressing "women" through the lens of modernization theory. GAD scholars, who began to emerge in the 1980s, drew from new forms of feminist theory to address gender relations, rather than merely women's issues, in their analyses of development and change. Many GAD scholars have also challenged Eurocentrism in development theory and practice, examining how feminist theory itself has been "colonized" by Western feminists (Mohanty 1991 and 2003). Despite these differences in approach and changes over time in how scholars and practitioners have approached questions of women, gender, and development, most policy continues to be framed and implemented from within the lens of WID discourse. As a result, throughout this book I refer to the WID field, although I am aware of the fact that it is not monolithic.

tion. Beginning in the 1960s and through the early 1970s, the Ecuadorian state promoted industrialization through import substitution policies as a way to strengthen the national economy. Until the 1960s, Ecuador was largely an agroexporting economy based on the production of bananas, coffee, cocoa, and sugar. A 1984 World Bank report captures the shift in Ecuador's trajectory of development as seen through the lens of modernization:

> Ecuador, once one of the poorest South American countries, became one of the middle income countries of the hemisphere; its per capita income now [in 1984] equals that of its neighbors, Colombia and Peru, and much social progress has been made. Between 1960 and 1980, more than 10 years were added to Ecuadorians' life expectancy; death and infant mortality rates dropped by more than 40 percent. School enrollment expanded rapidly. By 1980, virtually all children attended primary school; a third of the relevant cohort attended schools of higher education. Today's citizens are better educated, in better health, and better fed than at any other time in the history of Ecuador (World Bank 1984, xiii).

This newly acquired identity as "middle income" and as successfully developing (that is, achieving progress toward its goal of modernization), provided a basis for new negotiations with the state by historically marginalized groups such as women and indigenous sectors, although this would not be seen until the 1980s redemocratization process. State social spending increased during the 1970s, ironically during a period of military dictatorship.[14] It reached its highest historical peak in 1981, when the state spent almost U.S.$700 million in the area of social development—a direct result of petroleum profits (Ojeda Segovia 1993, 134). The national budget was largely dependent on oil revenues from the early 1970s on; these revenues, which came from the state's oil enterprise and were largely controlled by military interests, served as a buffer for the otherwise weak state budget and economy.[15] During the period of 1970 to 1973, real gross domestic product (GDP) rose by 15 percent annually, and the leading sector of eco-

14. The nationalist military regime was first led by General Guillermo Rodríguez Lara (1972–76) and then by the military junta (1976–78) of General Guillermo Durán (army), Admiral Alfredo Póveda (navy), and General Luis Leoro (air force).

15. By the mid-1980s, for example, oil revenues contributed to up to 60 percent of the budget; this figure fell to 41.2 percent by 1990 but it continued to represent a large percentage of the overall budget (Ojeda Segovia 1993, 131).

nomic growth shifted from agricultural exports to oil exports (de Janvry, Sadoulet, and Fargeix 1991). One reason for this tremendous growth was the fact that the state accrued profits from petroleum directly, as the owner, rather than through reliance on taxing export sectors, as it had done in the past with bananas, shrimp, and cacao. "[T]he state no longer had to rely on taxation of the private sector for revenue. With petroleum revenues accruing directly to the state, the autonomy of the public sector relative to private interest groups was greatly enhanced" (Schodt 1987, 99). This shifted economic and political control away from coastal agriculturalists to the highlands and Amazon region (to the extent that the oil industry was based there) and allowed the state to define its agenda autonomously from traditional economic elites.

The state's increased spending contributed as well to the country's industrialization and urbanization. The military, however, gambled on its oil profits and overspent. The state budget was vulnerable to drops in oil prices on the world market. By 1979, reduced petroleum exports and falling prices in the world market, coupled with rapidly rising imports (increasing by 6 percent a year), led to a growing deficit in the balance of payments. Some national industries, such as construction, transportation, and services, benefited from investments resulting from oil profits, and in general Ecuador's industrialization process accelerated as a result of state spending in these sectors. Agricultural exports, however, greatly decreased, which had multiple effects: food imports increased and, along with that, cultural practices of food consumption changed; migration to urban areas intensified; and peasant households (which at the time constituted approximately 48 percent of the population) became increasingly dependent on urban employment or incomes through temporary migration (de Janvry et. al. 1989). Urbanization rates increased significantly during this period. Guayaquil, Quito, and smaller cities all grew larger as a result of migration. In his study of Ecuador, David Schodt summarizes this set of statistics: "From 1974 to 1982, the urban portion of the population rose from 41 to just over 45 percent. Both Guayaquil and Quito, Ecuador's two largest cities, grew at rapid rates, as did many of the smaller provincial cities. Quito's growth, in particular, was stimulated by expanding public-sector employment, which grew at an annual rate of 8.8 (from 150,552 employees in 1975 to 271,966 by 1982), and by an increased tendency for industry to locate in the nations' capital" (1987, 107).

The military governments dealt with the deficit in the balance of payments by seeking foreign loans, rather than by building its nonpetroleum tax base or reducing its government expenditures (112). As it had earlier in history, the state had become reliant on a single export, although this time it had more financial legitimacy because of its petroleum riches and because international financial institutions were looking for new places to make loans. From 1976 to 1979, Ecuador's public debt increased four and one-half times; from 1979 to 1983 the rate of borrowing slowed, although the debt nevertheless almost doubled (112). The external debt grew by no less than 51 percent annually during the 1974–79 period, from U.S.$330 million in 1974 to U.S.$2.6 billion in 1979 (see Table 1, p. 53).

The economic results of the military's policies were catastrophic in the sense that there was no plan in place to address potential crises, or democratic political will or state accountability. In addition, the military governments curtailed political participation, citizen rights were greatly diminished, and some human rights abuses did occur. Although the Ecuadorian military regime's human rights record has been considered better than that of others (such as Argentina, Chile, and Bolivia [see Taylor 1997; Burt and Mauceri 2004]), comparatively speaking, it nonetheless contributed to political repression during that period. In many respects, Ecuadorians' hopes for a better quality of life, spurred on by petroleum-related national development during the 1970s, sustained citizen support during that period.

By 1981, the foreign debt had reached U.S.$5.8 billion. Although small by Latin American standards, this debt stood at twice the annual level of exports and swallowed up more than a quarter of the state budget in servicing debt payments alone. The democratic transition governments of President Jaime Roldós (1979–80) and his successor, President Osvaldo Hurtado (1980–84), were forced to find ways to curb state spending and pay back the debt.[16] In an effort to avoid the accumulation of dollar debts, in 1981 the Central Bank took responsibility for all private-sector dollar debts, allowing debtors to pay the Central Bank in fast-depreciating sucres, the country's currency at that time. This so-called sucretization of the debt essentially amounted to the Ecuadorian state's bailing out private-sector companies and transferring the debt to the public sector and society, a process that some critics at the time called "welfare for the rich" (Corkill and Cubitt 1988). This economic arrangement in the early 1980s, coupled with the redemocratization process and pressures from the international financial community to comply with debt repayment obligations (especially through structural adjustment measures), set the context for policy decisions and the shifting role of the state in governing, as well as its relationships with social sectors such as women, indigenous/peasant households, the poor, and the

16. President Roldós was killed in an unexplained airplane crash in 1981. As vice president, Osvaldo Hurtado became the new president.

middle class. Importantly, it contributed to what would become known by the international financial community as the "lost decade" of the 1980s in Ecuador (Kuczunski 1988).

The implications of these national policies and processes for contemporary feminist movements and politics are multiple. First, they constructed or shaped the political arenas within which Ecuadorians could voice their opposition to state repression, global capitalism, economic inequalities, or the lack of citizen rights. Second, they greatly affected people's livelihoods and their economic and social opportunities. Many people's livelihoods were in dire straits by the early 1980s and this greatly contributed to the emergence of grassroots community organizations and networks such as those I discuss in the following chapters of this book. Third, they contributed to new social and cultural understandings of international relations and dependency, as the country's political and economic elite became clearly reliant on foreign expertise (for example, through development assistance), aid, and capital (as in multinational oil companies). Fourth, the historical trajectory of the state as a provider of social welfare reinforced traditional notions of motherhood and introduced new concepts of gender co-opted from early feminisms, such as through the female suffrage law. Finally, despite their above-mentioned limitations, these policies opened new spaces in which women could interact with the state and, as such, allowed at least some sectors of women to negotiate or participate in state decision making and in shaping the state's agenda for national development.

Democratization and Women's Movements, 1970s–1980s

The self-defined feminist movement that was institutionalized in the 1980s emerged in the context of several overlapping processes: the redemocratization process, which opened new political spaces for women's groups; the foreign debt crisis, SAPs, and increasing economic inequalities; the professionalization of grassroots social movements; and regional organizing related to international arenas such as the United Nations Decade for the Advancement of Women (1975–85). Many social and political sectors of women in Ecuador were brought together in the context of the military governments of the 1970s. During the dictatorship, university-aged women, often of middle-class backgrounds, typically worked with leftist political parties and in social movements that focused on popular education, solidarity with rural sectors, human rights, and teachers' rights. Many of these grassroots movements were in opposition to military authoritarianism and imperialism while also having a focus on specific issues such as labor rights. According to one activist, more than 180 labor strikes or skirmishes took place in Quito alone during the course of one year in the mid-1970s (Rocío Rosero, interview, October 27, 1993). With urbanization and industrialization, more women found jobs in the manufacturing and service sectors, and they were able to organize based on their shared interests as a group of laborers. Some factory labor unions were dominated by women, such as the Iman factory labor union in Quito during the 1970s. In 1974, university students formed the Women's Committee in Solidarity of Labor Struggles (Comité de Solidaridad de las Mujeres con las Luchas Laborales). There was a concerted effort to bring sectors together, for example, on college campuses, where regional peasant federations, labor unions, and popular networks often held their meetings. One activist described this process as a "mutual appropriation of spaces" whereby otherwise unrelated groups collaborated with one another to struggle for their common political causes. "University feminine brigades" (*brigadas femeninas universitarias*) were created on campuses by groups of students. Many of the student activists graduated from college and went on to found their own organizations, direct state agencies or programs, or become political leaders.

The Revolutionary Women's Union of Ecuador (Unión Revolucionaria de Mujeres del Ecuador), a group of leftist women activists, was formed during this period, as was the Committee in Defense of Women's Rights (Comité Permanente por la Defensa de los Derechos de la Mujer). The well-known "march of pots of pans" (*marcha de las cacerolas*) that took place in Quito (and elsewhere) in April 1978 was led by women who carried their pots and pans into the streets to protest the military regime. In a markedly "female" political action based on traditional conceptions of motherhood, the participants borrowed their strategy from earlier women's protest movements in countries such as Chile (where both right-wing and leftist women had used this strategy to challenge the state at specific times [see Power 2002]).

During the transition years, women activists played important roles in Ecuador's redemocratization process. Some feminist leaders were appointed to key positions in state agencies such as the Central Bank, the Ministry of Social Welfare, and the National Women's Office (Oficina Nacional de la Mujer [OF-NAMU]), the new state women's agency. The state played a role in mobilizing women from above, through state-sponsored community initiatives (for example, child welfare projects) and the establishment of the state women's agency. This of course has had contradictory effects for women's political participation. On the one hand, women were integrated into the state: women began to head more commissions, be appointed to agencies, and direct research and policy initiatives. On the other hand, it led to the co-optation of feminist interests by the state (and to the extent that international funding was involved, by the international development community). Perhaps the most important advance at the state level was the state's recognition that gender discrimination does exist. The Ecuadorian state first signed the United Nations Convention on the Elimination of All Forms of Discrimination against Women (CEDAW) at the 1980 UN Copenhagen conference; it was ratified in 1981 (Rodríguez 1986, 323).[17] A state agency focusing on women's issues was first established in 1970 through a legislative decree but did not receive institutional support until 1980, when First Lady Martha Bucaram de Roldós took action to activate OFNAMU, located in the Ministry of Social Welfare.[18] Her action was not isolated; it represented the changing national context in which "women's issues" had entered public discourse and the imaginations of politicians (Menéndez-Carrión 1988). The United Nations Decade for the Advancement of Women had begun five years earlier, funding became increasingly available for development projects that targeted women as a social group or class, international as well as local women's groups were pushing for institutional reform, and it was the year in which President Roldós led the country through a democratic transition. Women, along with indigenous, poor, and other marginalized sectors, were able to play roles in transition politics like never before.

Knowledge about women's issues became part of the political culture of the state to the extent that women's issues had to be incorporated into documents such as the National Development Plan and into specific social policies in the Ministry of Social Welfare. A feminist leader prepared OFNAMU's first plan of action in 1980. This did not mean that all state employees had an understanding of women's or gender issues, but the integration of these issues in specific agencies did lead to the wider dissemination of knowledge about gender. The historical integration of women's issues into the state helped women achieve some political goals, such as the ratification of CEDAW, and it also helped the state maintain its accountability, vis-à-vis Ecuadorian society, by demonstrating its commitment to expanding citizen rights.

17. CEDAW was used as a mechanism to pressure governments to repeal anachronistic and discriminatory laws based on gender.

18. OFNAMU later became the National Women's Bureau (Dirección Nacional de la Mujer [DINAMU]), when in 1986 the agency acquired higher status within the Ministry of Social Welfare. In 1997, the state agency was moved from the Ministry of Social Welfare to the Office of the President; hence its current name, the National Women's Council (Consejo Nacional de la Mujer [CONAMU]).

At least four strands of women's rights activism began to emerge through the redemocratization process: the working-class/popular struggles that were continued from the 1970s and that flourished in the 1980s; the growing sector of feminist bureaucrats and planners, based primarily in Quito; the professional women (the "damas") who worked in philanthropy or as volunteers, the "wives of the engineers, agronomists, the Red Cross doctors," as one interviewee described them (Rocío Rosero, interview, October 27, 1993); and women's NGOs (for example, advocacy, policy, resource, and research centers). Feminist ideologies influenced all these strands, although feminism was an integral part of some groups and movements whereas in others it only served to legitimize their entry into traditional male spaces such as the state or business sector. For example, the increased presence of women working in the state led to them organize their own workers' associations. By most standards they were not political in nature, but they transformed the state's image, so to speak, vis-à-vis society. Feminine associations (*asociaciones femeninas*) were established in most of the ministries, including the Finance and Defense Ministries, and in state entities such as the State Oil Corporation of Ecuador (Corporación Estatal de Petróleo del Ecuador [CEPE]) and the Ecuadorian Institute of Electricity (Instituto Ecuatoriano de Electrificación [INECEL]).

From the professional strand came gender-based reforms to the sector of social welfare and social work; these reforms were maternalist in nature and largely converged with (or explicitly supported) the state's interests as protector of the nation. They contributed to a "ladyization" of the state rather than helping to engender it from within a feminist framework. Their efforts were similar to those of early elite women who worked in the suffrage and social reform movements. For example, the General Secretariat of Volunteer Service (Secretariado General de Servicio Voluntario [SEGESVOL]), an autonomous organization founded in 1971 to coordinate public- and private-sector social welfare projects, began to address women's issues in its projects in the 1980s as a result of the participation of specific professional women who had been exposed to feminist ideas. SEGESVOL projects included day-care centers and communal markets in new poor neighborhoods on Quito's outskirts; and training poor women in traditional skills such as child care (presumably to prepare them to be domestic servants) and home economics, that is, cooking, beauty, and manual arts (Rodríguez 1990). Some of these elite women also participated in the Ecuadorian Federation of Business and Professional Women (Federación Ecuatoriana de Mujeres de Negocios y Profesionales [FEMNYP]), founded in 1970 and housed in the Ministry of Social Welfare. FEMNYP is a member organization of the United

Nations. A group of women from this professional association, along with feminists working in NGOs and in the state, collaborated in the early 1980s to create the Ecuadorian Feminine Corporation (Corporación Femenina Ecuatoriana [CORFEC]). CORFEC was founded in 1983 and was one of the first organizations in the country to work in the area of WID. Its mission and objectives were written entirely from the liberal perspective of WID, which promoted the integration of women into what was viewed as an otherwise benevolent process of development (read: modernization), and it focused on rural and urban issues throughout the country (Rathgeber 1990; Kabeer 1994). It was designed as a "women's institution" that would serve the interests of diverse sectors of women and support capacity-building for community-based feminine organizations (*organizaciones femeninas*) around the country (Rodríguez 1990).

Religious institutions also played a role in shaping women's gender consciousness during the early 1980s, and they continue to do so. Some were influenced by radical liberation theology and focused on women's issues as a way to empower a marginalized group in society; others provided assistance to women because of their traditional perspective on charity and helping the poor; yet others capitalized on the historical moment to increase the size of their congregations. Quito-based Pastoral Social, for example, originally established in the early 1970s, had several projects targeting women during the 1980s that were integral to their mission to espouse "Christian living" (*vivencia cristiana*; Rodríguez 1990, 42). They provided skill-building workshops (*capacitación*), a mothers'-milk program (*programa de leche materno infantil*), and popular medical programs (for example, how to dispense medicine, how to address family emergencies). The Fe y Alegría Radiophonic Institute (Instituto Radiofónico Fe y Alegría [IRFEYAL]) has been extremely popular (and controversial) in Ecuador since it became one of the nation's most powerful radio stations in the late 1970s. IRFEYAL has several radio programs that focus on popular education, including those on literacy and skill-building knowledge (for example, sewing and dressmaking, electricity). It has women's programming that targets the sector of domestic servants by addressing their needs, lifestyles, and legal rights. Brethren and United Foundations of Ecuador (Fundaciones Brethren y Unida del Ecuador) is a Christian NGO that provides technical and financial support to rural communities in areas such as popular education, capacity building, leadership training, communications, and health. The organization has provided support for projects that address peasant women's leadership training and rural women's maternal health, especially pregnancy and child care. These types of Christian NGO projects have helped to organize some sectors of women, but they have also reinforced women's traditional gender roles; their ability to transform gender relations has depended greatly on the specific NGO's approach to religion, gender identity and roles, family life, and politics in general.

Explicitly identified feminist groups emerged in separate, parallel spaces, beginning in the late 1970s. Most, although not all, of these groups were based in Quito. Quito continues to be the nation's center of feminist political activity, for several reasons. First, it is the political capital and as such houses many of the government branches, ministries, and offices. The capital city has a unique political climate because of Quiteños' proximity to politicians, public meetings, state enterprises, and, generally speaking, the center of political power. Partly because of this, the second reason for its uniqueness concerns the fact that Quito is home to many international organizations and as such is the city that connects the nation to international political and financial institutions. When IMF and World Bank officials make visits to Ecuador, they go to the Central Bank in Quito and to political administrative offices, also in Quito. Many UN offices are based in Quito (among them UNIFEM, UNICEF, and the United Nations Population Fund [UNFPA]) as are the regional offices of international organizations such as Oxfam and the International Union of Local Authorities (IULA), which housed the United States Agency for International Development [USAID]–sponsored regional project on women and decentralization in eight countries (IULA/CELCADEL/RHUDO -USAID 1992, 1996, 1997). There are, of course, UN offices and chapters of international organizations and NGOs in Guayaquil and occasionally in provincial cities such as Cuenca and Riobamba. Historical and geographic factors also play into the vast differences in NGOization present in Quito versus in other regions, and into women's organizing being centralized in the capitol.

One of the first feminist groups of this period was Colectivo Eva de la Manzana, a Quito-based group composed of women from various social and political backgrounds that existed in 1980–81 (Rosero, Vega, and Reyes Ávila 1991; Rocío Rosero, interview, October 27, 1993). Many women's groups sought NGO status in the 1980s, as a result of several factors: the desire to professionalize or to create a stronger institutional basis for their social movement activism; increased development assistance and aid; global feminist solidarity movements; the need to shift their focus from antiauthoritarian, grassroots, underground movements to institutions working within a formal democratic context; and the widening of the movement to include new generations of feminist activists. Several key women's NGOs were formed during this period. The Center of Women's Information and Support (Centro de Información y Apoyo de la Mujer [CIAM]) was founded in Quito in 1981. CIAM's objectives included "developing a research agenda about issues pertaining to women, children and the elderly," and "supporting women in the areas of education, legal advice, economic and political empowerment" [Rodríguez 1990, 74]). It specialized in communications and had a radio program for several years. The Ecuadorian Center for the Promotion and Action of Women (Centro Ecuatoriano para la Promoción y Acción de la Mujer [CEPAM]), an NGO that focuses on women's economic, social and legal empowerment, was founded in Quito in 1982 and continues to provide social services to women (domestic violence shelter, legal advice) and serve as an advocacy- and policy-oriented research center. Centro Cultural Pájara Pinta was a women's resource center that had a café, small bookstore, and reading room and was based in north-central Quito for several years during the 1980s, before its leader left the country for personal reasons. The center held workshops and public events and housed a feminist collective (Colectivo Identidad). Its motto, "A space for us [women]; a place for everyone" (Un espacio para nosotras, un sitio para todos), conjured the image of woman-identified space that was open to all people.

Feminist groups were emerging in urban poor, or popular, sectors as well. The Secretariat of Popular Women's Organizations (Secretaría de Organizaciones Populares de Mujeres [SOPM]) was formed in the mid-1980s, following the UN women's conference in Nairobi, Kenya, as a way to bring together these grassroots groups, and many other networks have been developed since then that have waxed and waned in size and strength. In Quito, women's participation was crucial in the well-organized neighborhood of Comité del Pueblo, which was centrally involved in a series of protests in 1978 against the increased public transportation rates, known as the "Guerra de los cuatro reales" (Rosero and Armas 1990, 23). Women's visible presence in these protests led to the realization among the male leadership of urban popular movements that women were central to the movement's success and needed their own auxiliary groups. At the same time, women from leftist parties began to forge ties with urban popular activists as a form of solidarity and a way to learn, and also as a way to create stronger institutional ties (Rosero 1987). This helped shape and in some cases solidify the institutional relationships that were being developed among leftist political parties and community women's organizations, and that paralleled the same process occurring among middle-class NGOs and community women's organizations during the 1980s and continuing into the 1990s. These relationships were and continue to be based on a combination of assistentialism and paternalism, on the one hand, and solidarity and networking on the other.

Women's NGOs were formed in other cities as well. In Guayaquil, the Women's Action Center (Centro Acción de la Mujer [CAM]) was founded in the early 1980s with the explicitly feminist mission of addressing women's needs and "increasing the capacity of women to recognize themselves as social subjects and integrate their interests into popular movements" (Rodríguez 1990, 30). CAM provided educational outreach and capacity-building skills to community-based women's organizations in the Guayaquil area; generally speaking, it was a professional NGO that worked in solidarity with women's organizations in urban poor sectors. CAM's leaders helped organize the First and Second National Feminist Theory Conferences (Primer y Segundo Encuentro Nacional de Teoría Feminista), held in Ballenita (Guayas province) in 1986 and 1987 (CAM/CIAM 1988). CECIM opened a chapter in Guayaquil beginning in 1986. As NGOs received funding for gender-related projects, they too created areas of research dedicated to women's issues. The Social and Peasant Education Corporation (Corporación de Educación Social y Campesina), with offices in Guayaquil and Quito, focused on women's empowerment in urban poor and rural areas. The Center for Social Studies (Centro de Estudios Sociales [CES]) was founded in Guayaquil in 1970 and emanated from the urban popular movement of that time, a result of Guayaquil's urbanization process. CES originally worked with labor and neighborhood movements and later began to work with urban popular women's organizations as well (Rodríguez 1990).

Organizations were established throughout the country; one study estimates that as many as eight hundred grassroots groups existed during the 1980s, although this figure is difficult to prove given the informal nature of these groups (Centro María Quilla 1990). Several more established NGOs were formed as well, along with regional associations and federations of peasant and indigenous women. Most major peasant and indigenous associations had established women's auxiliaries by that time, and splinter groups were also formed. Some groups that held importance included the Women's Committee of the Coastal Regional Union of Peasant Organizations (Comité de Mujeres de la Unión Regional de Organizaciones Campesinas del Litoral [UROCAL]); the Women Workers Union of Vinces-Baba (Unión de Mujeres Trabajadoras de Vinces-Baba [UMT]); the indigenous organization Lorenza Abimañay, which is part of the Chimborazo Indigenous Movement (Movimiento Indígena de Chimborazo); and the Women's Secretariat of the United Provincial Federation of Southern Peasant and Popular Organizations (Secretaría de la Mujer, Federación Unitaria Provincial de Organizaciones Campesinas y Populares del Sur [FUPOCPS]; Rosero and Armas 1990). National conferences were held, including the two national conferences of women belonging to the Federation of Peasant Organizations (Federación de Organizaciones Campesinas [FENOC]) in 1986 and 1987. Many women began to see their organizing efforts "not only in terms of supporting the peasant struggle, but also as a complement to it" (quoted in Rosero and Armas 1990, 22). Many began to see their struggle in terms of gender as well, as a participant in the Organization of the Women's Popular Union of Loja (Organización de la Unión Popular de Mujeres de Loja) describes it for a researcher:

> We [peasant women] see the many common aspects that unite us and that make our histories similar. We were in our homes, we went out to support something that wasn't ours, and once we got there and became involved things no longer functioned well . . . once we arrived there [at the peasant organization], we [women] looked at each other and discovered that we had the same problems and that we trusted each other, but the men wanted us to go home . . . [in the end] we found a space of our own that we enjoy. (Quoted in Rosero and Armas 1990, 22).

Another participant describes it in the following way: "In the beginning we organized as a form of support [for the men], not for ourselves but for our compañeros or for circumstances that didn't really pertain to us; later we became aware that it was important to prepare ourselves better for the house, to sew, and to lose fear" (23). These narratives speak to the process by which many peasant women's organizations were formed. Although rural women have played important roles in peasant and indigenous organizations, they still represent a small fraction of the leadership. One study indicates that in the late 1980s, of a total of 4,623 rural organizations legally registered with the Ministry of Agriculture and Livestock, only 31 were led by women: 8 in the sierra and 23 on the coast (Cuvi 1992, 48).

Many movement events took place throughout the country during the 1980s, and umbrella organizations were formed that crossed social, geographic, and class sectors. In 1986, an international conference on women's political participation was held in Quito, an event sponsored by Latin American Human Rights Association (Asociación Latinoamericana de Derechos Humanos [ALDHU]) and the Latin American Institute of Social Investigation (Instituto Latinoamericano de Investigación Social [ILDIS]). Leaders such as Rigoberta Menchú (Guatemala) were invited to speak at the conference, which led to increased dialogue in national newspapers, magazines, and networks about gender and politics.

The political opinion magazine *Revista Nueva* helped publish the results of the conference. In 1984, feminist activists created the political action network Women for Democracy (Mujeres por la Democracia) as a way to push for political reforms and further democratization. In 1986, a broad-based feminist network was established, Action for the Women's Movement (Acción por el Movimiento de Mujeres [AMM]). AMM was founded to coordinate women's (especially feminist) groups and to "create new, distinct forms of dialogue" about women's issues (Lilia Rodríguez, interview, October 29, 1993). Many struggles took place within this group to define itself and its purpose. One feminist leader worked closely with the wife of President León Febres-Cordero and was chastised for her tie to male/state power. There was general disagreement over the issue of political autonomy, particularly regarding the relationship of AMM to political parties. Part of the conflict arose from the fact that several of the participants were also members of political parties and wanted AMM to echo the structure of those parties; others wanted AMM to be structured in a new, less hierarchical way. One participant described this dilemma as arising from the fact that "there was no strong proposal for the women's movement"; rather, there were women from several political sectors who believed that they needed to maintain their status or roles in those institutional places more than they needed to create their own new space "for women." A related issue concerned three AMM participants (Zonia Palán, Carmen Gangotena, and Teresa Minuche), all leaders in their own right, who ran for political offices.[19] AMM could not decide whether to support them and what the nature of the support would be; in the end, AMM did not support the candidates as a group, although some individual members did.

Conclusion: Myths of Progress

The changing nature of women's participation within the state, in its agencies and offices, and with the state, from their locations in civic and business sectors, demonstrates how the state itself is a historical construction. It has been shaped over time through a set of actions that were set into place by various social actors; for example, national political leaders, agricultural and industrial elites, the mil-

19. Zonia Palán ran for a seat as representative (*diputada*) of the Broad Leftist Front (Frente Amplio de la Izquierda [FADI]); Carmen Gangotena ran for a seat as *diputada* of the Socialist Party of Ecuador (Partido Socialista del Ecuador [PSE]); and Teresa Minuche, a member of Concentration of Popular Forces (Concentración de Fuerzas Populares [CFP]), ran for president.

itary, international organizations, the church, organized social movements, the media, and popular culture. The state has never been monolithic: it is fluid, subject to multiple identities and positions, and to negotiation and conflict, even during periods of military rule (Radcliffe and Westwood 1996; Htun 2003). The changing relationship(s) between women and the state had positive outcomes for Ecuadorian feminism, since important legal and political gains were made during certain periods and women's entry into public life, facilitated in part by state modernization, helped shape the new gendered identities of urban-poor and middle-class sectors. This new awareness of gender provided ontological and institutional bases for postdemocratization feminisms to come into being (Vargas 1992; Olea 1995). The state's role in modernizing gender by establishing a new model of social welfare brought societal validation to its modernization project and changed its self-image over time. "Ladies' spaces" in the state, such as auxiliary groups and committees, and in social work and philanthropy sectors were important for engendering the state modernization process by virtue of their increased presence in public life (viewed traditionally as the realm of white or mestizo men). They also helped to consolidate women's interests as a category of workers.

But ladies' spaces were not enough to transform gender relations and other structural inequalities that resulted from Ecuador's colonial legacy, as feminist groups have long pointed out (Rosero 1988; Rosero, Vega, and Reyes Ávila 2000). Furthermore, many urban settlers began to recognize the fragmented and unequal nature of the modernization process itself, particularly since new structural inequalities were developing in the nation's cities. Post–World War II global restructuring; the channeling of international aid; global feminisms; and later, NGOization all contributed to the construction of a feminist political identity that necessarily questioned the nature of state power, including its implementation of social welfare projects, its role in antipoverty struggles, and its interests in maintaining a limited notion of citizenship. And this was necessarily tied up with the state's positioning in the global political economy, including its dependency on foreign aid, and with specific sectors of elites within Ecuador and their interests in maintaining or transforming the national social and political order.

Neoliberalism transformed the Ecuadorian state and dismantled some of these earlier processes. The historical development of the social welfare state (never a clear or complete project, by any means) began to be dismantled when the state adhered to the first World Bank– and IMF-inspired austerity measures in 1980. Struggles for citizen rights were brought into the fold of national development in new ways, for example, through popular participation and decentral-ization measures that were separate from but converged with the goals of neoliberal modernization (Arboleda 1994). Neoliberal governments used dual strategies of seeking the increased participation of civil society, on the one hand, and on the other, limiting the access of traditional political and economic elites to state decision making (Conaghan 1988; North and Cameron 2003; Mario Unda, interview, July 28, 1993; Diego Carrión, interview, July 26, 1993). Urban poor sectors began to feel the effects of these policies and to develop growing dissatisfaction for their deteriorating economic conditions and lack of citizen rights. It was through this process that women began to challenge neoliberal modernization on the basis of its contradictory and exclusive nature, a topic I address in the remaining chapters.

[2]

Ecuadorian Neoliberalisms and Gender Politics in Context

In 2000–2001, Ecuador's foreign debt of U.S.$16 billion was the highest per capita debt in Latin America (see Table 1; World Bank 2001; Latin American Bureau 2001). At the time, Ecuadorians faced higher levels of unemployment and income inequality than they did prior to the introduction of SAPs. The number of people living in extreme poverty (insufficient income for a minimum food basket) climbed from 15 to 17 percent between 1995 and 1998 and jumped to 34 percent of the population in 1999 (World Bank 2001, 2). In 2002, about 88 percent of the rural population was living in extreme poverty, compared with 69 percent in 1999 and 54 percent in 1995 (World Bank 2002). Poverty rates increased in urban areas as well. At the same time, inequalities between Ecuador's rich and poor continued to be among the highest in the world. In 1995, for example, the lowest 20 percent of the population earned 7.6 percent of the reported national income while the wealthiest 20 percent earned 49.7 percent (World Bank 2003a). Although this figure does not take into account informal-sector employment, in which many people make their livelihood, it nevertheless reveals a disparity in the concentration of wealth.

Some of this can be attributed to environmental and natural disasters in recent years—to earthquakes and volcanic eruptions, not the least of which were the reactivated Pichincha volcano, upon which lies the city of Quito, and the nearby Reventador volcano, which erupted in November 2002, seriously stopping business and daily life in the capital city.[1] Yet this contemporary political economic process is foregrounded by colonialist images of Ecuador as "back-

Table 1 Ecuador's total external debt, 1974–2002 (U.S.$ billions)

Year	1974	1979	1981	1984	1990	1999	2002
External Debt	330*	2.6	5.8	8.6	12.1	14.5	18.1

SOURCE: World Bank 1984, 2001, 2004; IADB 1994.

NOTE: *U.S.$ millions

1. Quito is a long, narrow city that lies on a plateau. Its widest point is just more than one mile long. Its length spans more than twelve miles. The west side of Quito lies at the foot of the Pichincha volcano; some poor neighborhoods are built on the side of the volcano, closer to the rim. To the east of the city lie lower valleys, some of which have become middle- and upper-class bedroom

ward" and "uncivilized," images that have been largely reinforced by contemporary development discourse and practice (Escobar 1995; Weismantel 2003). This
Eurocentric view of Ecuadorian reality as problematic, as a country in need of
foreign humanitarian intervention and aid, is in many ways what led members
of the international aid community to consider Ecuador's foreign debt crisis as
"an internal matter" that Ecuador should "handle on its own." This was so
despite the fact that Ecuador's large foreign debt can be attributed to the international aid community itself, including development, lending, and philanthropic institutions, insofar as they view the problem as separate from Ecuador's
dependent relationship on Spain, Britain, and later the United States, rather
than as stemming directly from these historical relationships. In this context,
both discourses and practices of development contribute to Ecuador's contemporary reality. And the transnational web of international relations, gender politics, and social movement networks greatly shape the successes, limitations, and
gender effects of Ecuador's neoliberal development model.

In this chapter I examine the political, economic, and discursive context of
neoliberalism and gender politics in Ecuador. First, I discuss the beginning of
the contemporary foreign debt crisis and state restructuring in the 1980–88 period, emphasizing how women in urban poor sectors have developed individual
and collective survival strategies to endure the crisis. Through this process, I
argue, these sectors of women have emerged as new political actors. Second,
I address discourses and practices of neoliberalisms in Ecuador, noting how
materiality and discourse together shape the cultural meanings assigned to neoliberal development and to antineoliberal social movements. Third, I analyze
the political strategies adopted by community-based women's organizations to
oppose neoliberal policies. I situate my study in the broader, regional context of
women's movements in the late twentieth century, noting some similarities and
differences among Ecuadorian and other Latin American women's survival
strategies and political struggles. Finally, I examine how policies themselves are
important sites of cultural-political struggle and resistance and serve as concrete
examples of how women negotiate development and modernity through their
everyday interactions and forms of resistance. This chapter acts as a framework
for understanding the specific transformations in state practices and policies
brought on by neoliberalism, and women's organizations' responses to these
transformations, that I address in later chapters.

---

communities, while others remain largely agricultural and rural. At a far distance lies a portion of
the Andean mountain range.

Gendering the Foreign-Debt Crisis

The transition team of Jaime Roldós and Osvaldo Hurtado led the first institutional response to Ecuador's debt crisis in 1980, when the country was attempting to rebuild the economy following the former military government's heavy spending and the pending budget problem. The first World Bank and IMF loans were taken out during this period; those loans held specific criteria for adjusting Ecuador's economy, including how the state budget was to be spent on social and economic programs. Faced with the legacy of military rule and the country's redemocratization agenda, the Hurtado government was overburdened and limited from the start, despite Hurtado's own role in redrafting party and election laws and in democratizing the political system.[2]

The subsequent administration of President León Febres-Cordero (1984–88) saw the implementation of the first harsh set of neoliberal reforms, which led to inflation, currency devaluation, job layoffs, and a general rise in the cost of living. During this period, the first massive labor strikes took place, in protest of high prices, Febres-Cordero's plan to privatize some state enterprises, and his general rhetoric that Ecuadorians needed to "tighten their bootstraps" and "sacrifice for the country" in order to keep the national development priority on track (Conaghan 1988). Like other neoliberal presidents in the region, Febres-Cordero promoted a "trickle down" program in which his administration claimed that broad macroeconomic changes in the export and industrial sectors would eventually raise the standards of livings of all Ecuadorians, including the poorest of the poor—an adoption of a traditional modernization approach to national development.

During the 1980s, numerous sectors of women began to feel specific, gendered effects of these policies, among them changes in household expenditures and consumption patterns; changes in family structure; continuing lack of access to basic resources such as water, electricity, and paved roads; inflationary costs of food, transportation, and education; and generally, increased workloads in the household as a result of the more "invisible" aspects of privatization, marketization, and globalization (Moser 1989b; Lind 1992, 2000; León Trujillo 1992; Rodríguez 1994). Caroline Moser (1989b), for example, has shown how women in poor sectors in Guayaquil endured the economic crisis and related reforms in the 1980s through a variety of survival mechanisms, including indi-

2. Hurtado helped redraft Ecuadorian party and election laws as part of the transition to democracy. These laws, among others, were designed to prevent populist and "caciquist" phenomena such as that of Velasco Ibarra's becoming a five-time president (Bonilla 1992; Hurtado 1977).

vidual strategies within their households and increased participation in community networks and organizations (that is, collective survival strategies). In her study she found that the women who had relatively heavy domestic burdens and did not have the time or energy to seek community forms of support were the most at risk. Unable to seek support, they became further isolated and poor. In contrast, women who found creative strategies for survival at the household level, and women who participated in informal "safety networks" or community-based women's organizations were better off to the extent that they had access to more forms of support. Moser (1989a, 1993) refers to three roles that women play in community development: reproductive (child care, household management), productive (paid labor, in either the informal or the formal sector), and community management (participation in safety networks, community associations, local political or decision-making processes).

In Quito, as in Guayaquil and elsewhere throughout the region, poor sectors of women have always relied on strategizing among family members, to some degree, to make ends meet. From the beginning of the debt crisis, many began to pool resources, combine families into one household, have multiple members working, increase the number of members working, or seek more than one job, often in the informal sector. Those who participate in community women's organizations have access to additional resources, forms of knowledge, and support. Although there are no studies that compare the livelihoods of women who organize collectively and those of women who do not during the neoliberal period (1980–present), studies of community organizing suggest that women who participate are better off not only for economic reasons but also because of an increased sense of economic security, a greater degree of emotional and material support, and an ability to make sense of the macrolevel, societal issues contributing to their family's situation (Moser 1989b and Rodríguez 1992).

While it has been shown that women have created interesting projects in their communities and have organized politically to address their economic burdens, it is also true that development institutions and policies reinforce women's individual and collective participation in voluntary survival strategies in two important ways. First, they reinforce such participation through women's invisibility as contributors to community and national development initiatives, including in an assumed divide between "formal" and "informal" planning, whereby only formal planning is recognized as true development (Sandercock 1998a, 1998b). This is true despite the fact that women and local communities have had to develop themselves for decades, since the beginning of urban migration in the 1950s. This scenario renders women's economic and political participation invisible, an issue at debate now in the context of Ecuador's decentralization process, in which some women are finally being recognized for their community leadership, a realm in which women have participated for decades (Arboleda 1994). Second, they reinforce participation in voluntary strategies through development policies that assume women have "endless amounts of time" to participate, on a volunteer basis, in their communities (Elson 1992, 1998), sometimes even targeting them as project participants during the project design period.

In this context, one important policy conclusion has been that neoliberal development frameworks that target women as volunteers in the newly privatized welfare distribution schemes, which include communal kitchens, food-for-work programs, day-care centers, and women's community organizations, tend to exacerbate the workloads of poor women, rather than alleviate them, regardless of the intentions of development planners. In Lima, Peru, for example, the large soup kitchen movement (*cocinas comunales* or *cocinas populares*) largely has been viewed as successful by the international development community: in the mid-1980s and -1990s, there existed as many as two thousand kitchens where forty thousand women volunteered to prepare and distribute food to more than two hundred thousand people on a daily basis (Barrig 1989; Delpino 1991; Lind 1997). Yet seen from the perspective of the women who "mother" this movement, the communal kitchens are a development failure to the extent that twenty years later women continue to work in them for little or no pay, while the larger context of poverty continues to exist. This has occurred despite the fact that women's participation in the kitchens was seen as "temporary," and the kitchens themselves were seen as a temporary solution to Peru's economic crisis (Barrig 1996). What these studies show is that women's participation in Lima's communal kitchens actually became a permanent aspect of Peru's neoliberal development project, whereby the state relied increasingly on civic organizations to manage social services such as food distribution. The strategy to organize kitchens in the midst of poverty was institutionalized and integrated into the logic of neoliberalism, despite participants' own perspectives on state development policies, which tended to be critical.

Neoliberalisms in Context

While women have organized against neoliberalism in Ecuador and globally, including in the Americas, the Caribbean, Africa, and Asia (Basu 1995; Lind 1997; Naples and Desai 2002), their motivations vary as much as the neoliberal policies themselves. Indeed, until now, neoliberalism has been widely seen as universal, omnipresent, and homogenizing. Given the fact that people around the world have challenged globalization and neoliberal development policies, from Quito to Johannesburg to Seattle to Prague, it would appear that these processes are the same around the world and irreversible or immutable. Yet like *globalization* (Bergeron 2001), *neoliberalism* has multiple definitions and meanings. Here I examine some of the meanings ascribed to the latter term, as a way to explain why it has acquired so much political salience among Latin American social movements, including in Ecuador. But it is also true that these meanings, often collapsed into overly simplified, purportedly easy-to-absorb labels, can "obscure as much as [they] reveal," as Lesley Gill points out in her study of globalization politics in El Alto, Bolivia (2000, 12).

Some see neoliberalism as a set of economic policies, strategies, or beliefs about the (capitalist) economy; others as a political strategy that relies on an ideology of the market and the implementation of a certain set of economic and social policies. Certainly neoliberal economic policies themselves are not new, in several important senses: international trade and comparative advantage, for example, have been theorized and practiced for centuries (Benía and Lind 1995); privatization and economic liberalization are strategies that had been used in many countries and regions well before the 1980s; and modernization theory, including the notion that economic growth will trickle down to the poorest sectors of society, has provided the conceptual foundation of the development field since its inception in the 1950s and 1960s (Escobar 1995; Phillips 1998; Lefeber 2003). And as Lynne Phillips (1998, xii) points out, "the objectives of many aspects of neoliberalism have been around for some time under guises."

Many speak of the homogenizing effects and globalizing tendencies of neoliberalism (Fisher and Kling 1993; Phillips 1998; Veltmeyer and O'Malley 2001; Babb 2001). A defining feature of neoliberalism is the push to introduce a specific set of policies (privatization, economic liberalization measures, regional trade initiatives such as the Southern Cone Common Market [Mercado Común del Sur (MERCOSUR)] and the Pacto Andino, and decreased state spending) in order to integrate (and "globalize") national economies, cultures, communication, and ideas at a historically unprecedented pace. With the advent of information and communication technologies (ICTs)—entailing the fact that television stations such as CNN can now bring us live stories from towns and rural villages on the other side of the world—the neoliberal push toward market integration, coupled with a new global, multilanguage, consumer culture, is occurring more rapidly than ever.[3] Neoliberal policies help to crystallize what George Ritzer (1993) has called the "McDonaldization" of society; what Benjamin Barber (1995) describes as the new "McWorld"; and what John Comaroff and Jean Comaroff (2001) view as nothing less than a redrawing of capital-labor relations and of capitalism itself: "Neoliberalism aspires, in its ideology and practice, to intensify the abstractions inherent in capitalism itself: to separate labor power from its human context, to replace society with the market, to build a universe out of aggregated transactions. . . . Once-legible processes—the workings of power, the distribution of wealth, the meaning of politics and national belonging—have become opaque, even spectral" (14–15). As suggested in this quote, whereas at one time the boundaries of the nation-state were clear, they no longer are. Current events reflect this process. For example, we can no longer trace the amount of capital that electronically crosses national borders on a daily, an hourly, basis. And whereas previously labor, as a social class, was seen as cohesive and unified (in the age of mass factory production, of Fordism [see Piore and Sabel 1984; Scott and Storper 1986]); we now must turn our attention to labor's fragmented and transnational nature, evidenced in the displacement of workers around the world and associated changes in post-Fordist family structures (creating, for example, "transnational motherhood" [see Hondagneu-Sotelo 1991; Chang 2000]), and the ways in which women's historically invisible reproductive labor and "cultural labor" is newly commodified and seen as productive for the neoliberal market.

For example, women's volunteer contributions in their communities, including through their roles in day-care centers (see Chapter 3) and food distribution (Barrig 1996), are now seen as viable development strategies by international organizations. Another example concerns so-called social capital and cultural labor. Until recently, women's contributions to cultural preservation were seen largely as noneconomic. Now, the subfield of ethnodevelopment addresses women's (and men's) contributions to capital formation through what planners call their cultural labor; that is, their noncapitalist roles in preserving their cultures and communities. In these new frameworks, embraced by institutions such as the World Bank, the IMF, and USAID, *social capital* has been redefined so as to incorporate traditional, nonmarket roles and responsibilities into the modern market economy. Whereas previously women's participation in cultural prac-

3. For an analysis of the role of CNN in shaping the new world international communication order, see Friedland 2000.

tices was viewed as "outside" the realm of economic development, it is now seen as central to the success of such development. Traditional social activities and cultural practices, such as preserving the cultural heritage of indigenous families and communities through rituals and customs, are considered beneficial, rather than detrimental, to the modern market economy.

One obvious problem with ethnodevelopment is its central tendency to view non-Western (that is, indigenous) cultures as "ethnic," while European cultures remain the unmarked norm. Thus in social-capital frameworks, indigenous women, because they are seen as the primary transmitters of culture in their families and communities—another Western gender bias (Crain 1996)—are essentially linked to culture but now seen as a virtue rather than an impediment to progress. As a result, indigenous women are now viewed as central to making development more "efficient" and "profitable" and as an economic asset, through the integration of their newly defined labor into the modern market economy (Radcliffe et al. 2004).

In Latin American and Third World studies, neoliberalism also appears all-encompassing, similar to how capitalism and globalization have been viewed conventionally by neoclassical economists and Marxians alike.[4] It seems to be a given, as when (even postmodern) scholars naturalize the economy, despite their denaturalization of just about everything else (culture, community, citizenship, nation, language, and so on [see Gibson Graham 1996; Escobar 1995]). For better or worse, neoliberalism has become the dominant model, displacing all others; this is highlighted even more, some would argue, by the demise of state socialism and the so-called end of the Cold War era (Phillips 1998). Some view neoliberalism as the answer to Latin America's debt problems; others as an overarching evil contributing to Latin America's highest levels of inequality in the twentieth century (George 1997; Petras and Morley 1992; Conaghan and Malloy 1994; Phillips 1998). Among the Left, some argue that we would be best served by negating neoliberalism altogether and finding a postneoliberal alternative; others, such as cultural critic Nestor García Canclini (2001), argue that we must necessarily negotiate, rather than entirely reject, neoliberalism, as this is the reality within which we live, regardless of one's views on postmodern-

4. In their study of globalization discourse and "capitalocentrism" (a privileging and centering of capitalism in economic discourse), J. K. Gibson-Graham (1996) argues that neoclassical economic traditions as well as socialist and Marxian traditions essentialize and naturalize capitalism. In many leftist accounts of development, they argue, capitalism is assumed to be ever present, powerful, expansive, penetrating, systematic, self-reproducing, dynamic, victorious, and capable of conferring identity and meaning.

ism and the meaning of "reality" itself (see Rodríguez 2001). In both supportive and oppositional stances on neoliberalism, none provide satisfying definitions of what neoliberalism is and is not.

In various academic fields, including political science, urban planning, geography, economics, anthropology, and sociology, scholars often define neoliberalism based on its characteristics. These characteristics often include the following: emphasis on market-based economic growth; establishment of new markets, especially regional and global markets; economic integration initiatives, including the establishment of the World Trade Organization (WTO) in 1995 and free trade initiatives such as the North American Free Trade Agreement (NAFTA), the European Union (EU), and MERCOSUR; structural adjustment policies, at least in debt-ridden poor countries; state retrenchment, including massive layoffs of state employees; privatization; and the liberalization of domestic economies (Conaghan and Malloy 1994; Benería 1992; Phillips 1998; Petras and Morley 1992; Smith, Acuña, and Gamarra 1994).[5] Some scholars, in their research on the political implications of neoliberalism, have argued that the "neoliberal period" in specific countries has brought with it new forms of organizing, new political identities, and a new emphasis on social justice. For example, in her study of postrevolution politics in Nicaragua, Florence Babb (2001) cautiously argues that the post-Sandinista, neoliberal period has brought with it new political opportunities for groups such as women and gays and lesbians and for environmental organizations.

Some argue that neoliberalism is a clear example of postmodernity in Latin America because the neoliberal context reflects a further fragmentation of political and cultural identities and a wider gap between rich and poor (Fernández-Alemany 2000). Others argue that since the region has barely reached modernity, it can hardly be postmodern.[6] Yet others argue that Latin America should not be viewed in Western terms, as "premodern, modern or postmodern," but rather in its own terms, as eclectic, nonlinear, and hybrid (Klor de Alva, 1995).

Despite one's theoretical perspective on neoliberalism, it can hardly be viewed as homogenous, even when its presence is acknowledged throughout the

5. The WTO is the successor of the General Agreement on Tariffs and Trade (GATT) and is composed of approximately 142 member countries, China being the newest member (since December 2001). For further discussion of the role of the WTO in global governance, see Sampson 2001. NAFTA members are Canada, the United States, and Mexico. Established in 1991, MERCOSUR core members are Argentina, Brazil, Uruguay, and Paraguay. (Chile, Peru, Bolivia, and Venezuela are associate members; as of 2004, Ecuador and Colombia have requested associate membership.)

6. For an overview of the debates on postmodernism in Latin America, see Beverley and Oviedo 1993 and Rodríguez 2001.

world. Neoliberalism represents much more than just a standard set of policies with a standard set of economic and social outcomes, although indeed this characterizes the international financial community's (World Bank, IMF, WTO) approach to addressing the debt problem in poor countries. Policies introduced by states or by international financial institutions have been and continue to be challenged, contested, ideologically supported or dismissed, and negotiated. Their cultural effects are widespread, yet they vary geographically, historically, and politically from country to country, region to region. Neoliberal policies are "subject to transformation" and therefore fluid, changeable, and negotiable (Phillips 1998, xii).

This resonates with recent comparative research in Latin America that emphasizes different neoliberalisms (xvii). Linda Green (1998), for example, argues that neoliberalism in Guatemala is a "militarized neoliberalism," since Guatemala's long history of violence has been a central component of neoliberalism's success in that country. Similarly, Peruvian president Alberto Fujimori's (1990–2000) perceived economic success depended largely on his control of Shining Path–induced political violence. There, too, militarization was required to successfully implement harsh neoliberal reforms. Hans Buechler and colleagues (1998) argue that Bolivia has experienced a form of "experimental neoliberalism" since the 1990s because neoliberal governments have given some attention to sectors of the population (in the case of their study, small-scale enterprises) that have previously been overlooked. However, it is also true that Bolivia in the mid-1980s underwent the harshest set of adjustment measures ever faced by a Latin American country, when President Victor Paz Estensoro (1985–89) introduced Decree 21060, a set of SAPs that led to hyperinflation, the privatization of Bolivia's state mining enterprise, and the layoff of more than twenty-seven thousand miners (see McFarren 1992).[7] One consequence of this was that mining families were displaced from their communities and forced to migrate to one of Bolivia's cities or its Amazon region, leading also to rising homelessness rates in cities such as Cochabamba, where many miners relocated.

In Ecuador, neoliberal policies have been implemented in a less orthodox fashion and at a slower pace. Nonetheless, they have had dramatic effects on the organization of the economy, the state, and civil society. This has varied from government to government and has been coupled with growing political instability and a general distrust of the democratic system. Particularly in the

7. Following the introduction of Decree 21060, hyperinflation reached 20,000 percent in 1986. At one point, miners and other laborers brought home their weekly earnings in large flour sacks, and a loaf of bread cost the equivalent of one flour sack worth of deflated bolivianos.

1990s, Ecuadorian administrations have relied on a combination of conventional neoliberal policies and political populism; perhaps characterizing Ecuador's process as a form of "populist neoliberalism," which has been somewhat unsuccessful from the perspective of the IMF and World Bank, yet largely successful from the perspective of most Ecuadorians in the sense that institutions have been dismantled, institutional relationships have been transformed, and many people have suffered negative consequences from these policies.

Although clearly neoliberal development policies have concrete gender effects, most neoliberal development policies are written in a gender-neutral language, making them appear unbiased. One result of this is that it appears that these policies will benefit everyone, regardless of gender, ethnicity, class, or geographic location. It appears, for example, that "women" and "the market" are two separate entities, far removed from each other. Likewise, noncapitalist forms of economic exchange (an idea already based on specific assumptions about people's roles in the economy and about the economy itself) such as those found in nonmonetary markets are often considered "outside" the modern market economy and removed from modern society; the racialized effects of this conjure up an image of communities in the indigenous/rural/informal sector as separate from or not yet integrated into the modern market. As Marianne Marchand and Anne Sisson Runyan (2000) have observed, "[I]t is nowadays increasingly recognized that the 'world of political economy' and the daily lives of women are no longer (and never have been) two separate worlds" (1). One need only stroll through one of Quito's street markets, where many women work, to see these overlapping and intertwined "worlds." Furthermore, neoliberal restructuring itself "depends heavily on gendered discourse and gender ideology for its own construction" (1). SAPs, the backbone of neoliberal restructuring in Latin American nations, take as given the idea that families can "absorb" the effects of restructuring and privatization without considering the disproportionate amount of work that women do to maintain their families and communities during periods of economic crisis (Benería and Feldman 1992; Bakker 1994). As Latin American states abide by the terms set forth in their IMF-inspired loan packages, including cutting state social expenditures, it is assumed that families will and can survive on their own or seek help from civic organizations such as NGOs. Because neoliberal frameworks assume that economic growth and liberalization will lead to social development, they help exacerbate the inequalities that arise from the public/private dimensions of Western development models, including the fact that so-called informal labor, such as women's domestic labor and informal-sector employment, are seen as outside the development model or remain invisible, rather than being seen as an integral part of the modern economy; the "other" to the capitalist economy, one that gives meaning to capitalism itself. Through this privileging of the "public" and the "formal" in neoliberal development discourse, the assumption that families and especially women can absorb the costs of restructuring appears "natural and inevitable" (Marchand and Sisson Runyan 2000, 18). The so-called male bias in political economy analysis may make gender invisible in neoliberal development frameworks, yet in actuality, "gender is everywhere" (Marchand and Sisson Runyan 2000), and poor women in particular tend to lose out as a result of this conceptual and structural bias.[8]

Women's Antineoliberal Protest

There are two general stories that researchers have told about neoliberalism in Ecuador. On the one hand, as seen from the eyes of policy makers and social movement analysts, Ecuador's neoliberal project has been relatively unsuccessful compared to those of other Latin American countries (e.g., Burt and Mauceri 2004). On the other hand, when seen through the eyes of poor and middle-class men and women (the majority), the restructuring process has been quite successful to the extent that political, economic, and cultural institutions have been irreversibly transformed, as has the social welfare structure of the state. It is true that the opposition to neoliberal policies since the late 1980s has obstructed the successful implementation of structural adjustment measures in Ecuador, perhaps more so than in the neighboring countries of Peru or Bolivia. National mobilizations against neoliberalism and political corruption have greatly challenged the ability of policy makers to effectively carry out state neoliberal restructuring. The effects of globalization, including Ecuador's relationship to donors and wealthy governments, has reinforced this pattern of instability by exacerbating tensions between the rise of global governance, on the one hand, and the assertion of local/national cultural identity on the other.

Yet, clearly, women's antineoliberal protest, along with that of members of other social movements, began in the first place because of the living conditions that women faced. Sectors of poor women opposed to neoliberalism have been

8. Diane Elson first introduced the term "male bias" in feminist economics as a way to indicate how " gender neutral" policies (i.e., macro- and microeconomic policies that do not explicitly address gender issues, including structural adjustment policies) have implicit gender biases that privilege men's economic roles and identities over women's. See Elson 1992 and 1998.

concerned about their increased poverty and have addressed inflation, currency devaluation, unemployment, and the rising costs of previously state-owned services such as electricity and gas. In a discussion about the governments of León Febres-Cordero and Sixto Durán-Ballén during a 1993 interview, one community activist stated, "The government is implementing privatizations that affect us poor people . . . we want the World Bank to forgive our debt so we can get out of this crisis that is killing us all" (Diana, interview, March 15, 1993).[9] Another organization member said, "Neoliberalism is an idea from the powerful countries. Why can't they forgive our debt?" (María, interview, March 16, 1993). In reference to the harsh adjustment measures of the Durán-Ballén administration (see Chapter 3), a third female member summed it up as follows:

> [W]e thought that Sixto was going to bring us forward but of course there was little time to judge; even after a month [of Durán-Ballén's presidency] he gave us tremendous economic shock measures, which almost sank us poor people because you know that the rich have their properties, their businesses, and they don't feel the hunger. But for one that has children and a home to take care of [these measures] were harsh. Later it will only become worse because they're preparing another adjustment package. (Alejandra, member of women's organization, March 10, 1993)

From this perspective poor communities are suffering at the hands of the state, although many acknowledge the powerlessness of the "underdeveloped nation" itself. These three women, all members of a community women's organization in southern Quito, are referring to the contradictory role of the nation-state in regulating the lives of poor people while simultaneously itself being regulated by international financial institutions and the governments of industrialized nations.

Because women of poor and working-class backgrounds in countries around the world share similar daily experiences of poverty, unemployment, and often racism, having a shared identity in this regard, they often choose similar issues to protest and similar political strategies (Basu 1995). For example, neoliberalism has led to locally organized protests against the establishment of McDonald's and other businesses in several Latin American countries, including Bolivia, Peru, Mexico, and Brazil. In many cases, women are the first to protest against foreign corporations. In Porto Alegre, Brazil, on International Women's Day

9. All names of interviewees of community women's organizations are pseudonyms.

(March 8) in 2001, approximately one hundred women occupied a local Mc-
Donald's restaurant and called the Brazilian government a "vassal of world neoliberalism" (*Arizona Republic*, March 9, 2001). The so-called IMF riots are
another example: in some countries such as Argentina and Venezuela, women
have been involved in supermarket riots as a spontaneous mobilization against
the cost of living and overnight inflation (Walton and Seddon 1994).

Yet it is also true that political-protest strategies work better in some country
contexts than others. Communal kitchens such as those found in Lima, Peru,
may not be as successful in environments characterized more by individualistic
competition than by cooperation (as was the case in one study of women's survival strategies in Mexico City in the 1980s [see Benería 1992b]). Protesting a
local McDonald's may not be effective in Ecuadorian cities, where fast-food
franchises are easily found and incredibly popular. Demanding to play a formal
role in drafting a new constitution may not be a feasible strategy in countries
with strong or authoritarian governments, although this also depends on the
nature of the regime transition and the ability of women's organizations to create
a public-policy presence in the democratization negotiations. In this regard,
neoliberal policies, although apparently uniform across countries, offer distinct
strategic interventions in national political economies, diverse consequences,
and therefore unique local political responses and survival strategies.

Feminism and Neoliberalism: Struggles over Policy

Women activists, too, have been divided over how to view the overall process of
neoliberal restructuring as it relates to the lives of the marginalized sectors, a
result of class, ethnic, geographic, and ideological differences between them. In
the 1980s there was much skepticism among women's NGOs about participating
in government meetings to address the new public-private partnerships, including in committees and umbrella organizations set up to institutionalize the partnerships. Particularly women's NGOs that were prepared to retool for the market
economy were more willing to participate and perhaps less skeptical than NGOs
that clearly would not have interpretive power in the meetings. Some NGO professionals viewed their participation as a form of co-optation or as acquiescing
to the neoliberal model; others saw participation as important and valuable. Yet
others felt that such involvement was a necessary evil, a way to engender the
discussions and policies. Most agreed that allowing the participation of NGOs, as
representatives of civil society, in the national decision-making process about

development was a marked shift in government philosophy and conceivably a democratic opening for traditionally marginalized groups such as women. Yet as some observers have pointed out, "[I]t is important to keep in mind that a strengthened civil society is also on the neoliberal agenda"; while civil society is a "familiar terrain" for feminists and NGO activists, it is "also the terrain where religious and nationalist fundamentalist groups, business networks, and other groups with 'less-than-progressive' agendas are active" (Marchand and Sisson Runyan 2000, 20). In this regard, there is a convergence between, on the one hand, the globally inspired, neoliberal goal in Ecuador to transfer responsibilities to the private sector, and on the other, the Ecuadorian women's movement goals of strengthening civil society and engendering national politics.

Yet despite the possibility of political and discursive co-optation, it is precisely the members of Ecuadorian social movements that have shown agency and opposition through their participation in national political and policy arenas. In essence, it is their negotiations with governments and international agencies that give meaning to Ecuador's restructuring process. The Political Network of Ecuadorian Women (Coordinadora Política de Mujeres Ecuatorianas [CPME], the National Permanent Forum of Ecuadorian Women (Foro Nacional Permanente de Mujeres Ecuatorianas [FNPME]), and the National Women's Council (Consejo Nacional de la Mujer [CONAMU]) have intervened and engendered Ecuadorian laws, policies, and political spaces. They have negotiated the terms of neoliberal policies and politics, not merely accepted them as givens, or entirely negated them. This is not a romanticization of their political strategies but rather an understanding of them as contradictory, complex, and engaged with current forms and relations of power in their society.

One important aspect of negotiating the terms of neoliberal development concerns how women view policies themselves. Policies, too, are negotiated and contested, rather than merely implemented in a technocratic manner, as earlier development studies have suggested.[10] Increasingly, scholars have acknowledged the importance of a feminist presence in public advocacy and policy (Alvarez 2000). Indeed, how development policies get framed has important consequences for who benefits from them and how; a shift in language in a policy document can translate into an alternative distribution of resources throughout

10. James Ferguson's (1994) ethnography of developing planning in Lesotho is perhaps the most thorough empirical study to date on development discourse, including its technocratic nature and the economic, cultural, and psychic consequences of Western development logic in a postcolonial society.

the country. When neoliberal policies are viewed this way, people's protests against them reflect much broader cultural struggles over modernization, modernity, social inclusion, and citizenship. As Cris Shore and Susan Wright (1997a) point out, policy "has become an increasingly central concept and instrument in the organization of contemporary societies," including "the way individuals construct themselves as citizens" (4). They continue: "Through policy, the individual is categorized and given such statuses and roles as 'subject,' 'citizen,' 'professional,' 'national,' 'criminal,' and 'deviant.' From the cradle to the grave, people are classified, shaped and ordered according to policies, but they may have little consciousness of or control over the processes at work" (4). Thus how women's organizations viewed their participation in the state-civil society meetings that began in the late 1980s depended also on how they viewed their role(s) in state policy making and planning. As in countries throughout the region and world, the strategies used by Ecuadorian women's organizations to oppose neoliberalism have consisted of two interrelated factors. First, their strategies typically depend on the long-term visions and goals of the particular group, which in turn are related to group members' social locations (such as working class or middle class) and political ideologies. Second, their strategies depend on conjunctural issues such as what the current administration is like, who is in power, what the internal dynamics of the women's movement are, and how the economy is affecting their personal or professional lives, to name only a few. In essence, the institutionalization of the neoliberal development model in Ecuador and women's political responses to it are negotiated encounters that take shape according to Ecuador's historical, political, cultural, geographic, and economic location in the world; to women's perceived places within that world; and to the discourses that shape and give meaning to scholars' and activists' perceptions of reality (neoliberalism, identity, power, the state, democracy, citizenship, globalization, gender). Thus, materiality and discourse are inseparable. In the following chapter I examine the 1988–96 period, in which neoliberal reforms were further institutionalized. During these years, women's struggles for access to material resources were directly linked to broader struggles over policy, in this case, policies of social welfare redistribution.

[3]

Neoliberal Encounters:
State Restructuring and the Institutionalization of
Women's Struggles for Survival

Citibank go home!
—Women protesters outside Citibank in Quito, May 1992

In May 1992, several neighborhood women's organizations participated in a protest outside the Citibank office in Quito. Following a dispute regarding loan-repayment guidelines, Citibank–New York, the bank that headed the group of foreign lenders to the Ecuadorian government, had frozen U.S.$80 million of the Central Bank's assets, claiming that the Ecuadorian government had defaulted on its loan payments. The following day, a group of approximately one hundred women gathered outside Citibank's office to protest. Their participation in this protest was an important public response to the economic crisis that the country faced. It was a public statement against what they viewed as Ecuador's dependency on foreign aid, especially from the United States, and it represented a challenge to the "development establishment" as the women involved in the protest saw it. Acting primarily as mothers, they felt compelled to protest the role of foreign aid—in this case, Citibank—in exerting power over the Ecuadorian government. But while critical of what they perceived as economic and cultural imperialism in their nation, they also challenged the Ecuadorian government to redistribute wealth and socialize state-led welfare activities. Thus, they on one level acted as mothers of families—and by extension, as mothers of the "underdeveloped" Ecuadorian nation vis-à-vis First World states—and on another level positioned themselves in opposition to the Ecuadorian state and placed demands on it for further access to their rights as consumers and citizens, that is, to their social, economic, and political rights. At the time, this type of protest was unprecedented in Ecuadorian history.[1] Participants in the protest

1. Several antidebt protests have occurred since then, attended by members of women's organizations as well as of other political sectors such as the indigenous movement, labor, peasants, and

publicly invoked a politicized notion of reproduction based on women's roles as mothers and consumers, as those most affected by the changes in consumer prices that accompany adjustment measures. In addition, by acting as mothers of the nation, they presented themselves and their "national family" as produc-ers: they pointed out that the Ecuadorian nation's role has been to provide First World countries with natural resources, agriculture, and labor (Lind 1992).

Members of women's organizations from Chillogallo and other adjacent neighborhoods were among the first to directly protest international banks and lenders for their roles in the debt crisis, particularly as these institutions affect women's work in their communities and families. Although in the early 1980s many political sectors were not yet prepared to challenge these international institutions, these women did. What neoliberal policies were implemented that led to organized women's awareness of the international financial community? What was the local process of organizing and identity formation that led up to this and subsequent protests against globalization? In this chapter I address these questions by analyzing the process by which women's community-based strug-gles for survival in Quito became permanent and institutionalized, rather than temporary, during the period 1980–96.

Institutionalizing Women's Struggles for Survival, 1988–1996

The women who arrived at the doors of Citibank in May 1992 had interacted in a number of arenas prior to their participation in the protest. They had direct experience with state agencies and the municipality of Quito, having registered to gain legal status as an organization; met with the mayor's office to discuss neighborhood problems that arose; and requested funding from city and state offices for small projects, including the establishment of a local police station, inaugurated in Chillogallo in the early 1990s. In addition, many of them already had relationships with middle-class feminists by that time. The community women activists did not organize the protest purely by themselves; rather, they organized it in conjunction with a broader network of feminists and NGO activ-ists who knew one another through their activism and jobs. In this sense, the protest reflected their shared identity as community activists; a shared identity

the urban poor. Other protests of this kind, led by women, have occurred throughout Latin America, such as the so-called IMF riots in Venezuela and Argentina, and the food riots in Brazil. For a comparative analysis of women's roles in food riots and protests against the IMF and World Bank, see Daines and Seddon 1994.

that they defined through their organizational process and their interactions with development practitioners, politicians, neighbors, feminists, NGO activists, and male community leaders. In addition, many of the protesters had learned about the daily effects of economic crisis and the foreign-debt burden in Ecuador through a wide range of sources: newspapers, magazines, and television; conversations with neighbors; notice of weekly, even daily, changes in the cost of food, transportation, and gas; and workshops in their organizations. An important aspect of their shared perspectives on globalization and neoliberal development concerned their own experiences in their families and in their organizations: specifically, the institutionalization of their struggles and the privatization of their "everyday lives" (Benería 1992b). In the following two sections I discuss the state and international development policies that were implemented during the governments of Rodrigo Borja (1988–92) and Sixto Durán-Ballén (1992–96).

The Rodrigo Borja Administration, 1988–1992

President Rodrigo Borja's social democratic leadership extended certain benefits and rights to community women's organizations yet also helped to institutionalize women's so-called survival strategies. I examine the Borja administration in terms of its policies and of how the administration itself was influenced by the international development field, especially its institutions the World Bank and the IMF. My analysis is based on the idea that Latin American nation-states do not and, for the most part, cannot act autonomously, but rather negotiate policy decisions within a transnational context of power and globalization. Indeed, the Citibank protest raises this issue: on the one hand, the Ecuadorian government has "power over" Ecuadorians and "power to" produce a certain kind of citizen; on the other hand, the government is confined by the boundaries of World Bank and IMF prerogatives and the logic of development. As a result, politically, they are viewed by women's organizations has potentially oppressive but also as victims of First World imperialism. The Borja administration is an important example of how one government attempted to work outside the logic of the World Bank and IMF (to some degree), yet was confined by the broader global, neoliberal development project.

In 1988, President Rodrigo Borja was inaugurated. A social democrat and member of the party the Democratic Left (Izquierda Democrática), President Borja took a different approach to economic and social policy than did his predecessor, León Febres-Cordero (1984–88), who was influenced by Reaganomics and British Thatcherism, then two dominant neoliberal models, and by the Chilean neoliberal model of economic development imposed by the regime of Augusto Pinochet (1973–90). In this regard, Febres-Cordero was one of the first democratically elected leaders to implement harsh economic liberalization measures, which previously had existed only under military authoritarian rule (see Schodt 1987, especially chapter 8). Borja reversed Febres-Cordero's conservative trend and aimed to address poverty through an interventionist framework, similar to Hurtado's, which integrated social and economic policy concerns at both conceptual and institutional levels. Rhetorically speaking, in Borja's political discourse, the "social" was given central importance, versus the additive approach of Febres-Cordero, who addressed social needs as an afterthought to economic development. Along with his team of policy advisors, Borja designed a national development plan in an attempt to integrate once historically separated economic and social policy approaches and institutions and establish a stronger basis for self-sufficiency and popular support among poor communities. Perhaps the most successful aspect of Borja's reforms were not the reforms themselves, but the political reemergence of an intellectual community that not only gave priority to social concerns but also generated a proliferation of academic literature and debates within intellectual and activist circles on these issues.

On the economic front, beginning in 1988 there was a shift toward more state control of the economy specifically through increased control of the foreign-exchange market, including through regulated interest rates. Also, there was an attempt to increase savings and domestic investment by establishing (positive) real interest rates and by encouraging the repatriation of Ecuadorian capital that was invested outside the country. Essentially, the government shifted resources away from the production of nontradable goods and services toward the production of tradable goods and services, combined with import substitution. The first step toward achieving this goal oriented toward the export sector was to devalue the real exchange rate by more than 50 percent in the first two years of Borja's term (1988–90). Borja's mixed-economy model was designed to encourage manufactured exports and boost agriculture primarily through publicly financed infrastructure improvements and moderate land reform (de Janvry et al. 1994). His policy approach was aided by the fact that in national polls, "most Ecuadorians had come to realize that austerity was indispensable for dealing with an economic crisis as severe as their own" (74). His model was also supported to some degree by the conciliatory tone of his proposed tripartite *concertación nacional* (national agreement, or consensus) among business, labor, and government, and by his campaign promise to not change the ownership of companies through nationalization or privatization.

In addition, Borja's approach included an intent, however rhetorical, to "pay back the social debt" to the Ecuadorian people. Borja was elected, in part, because of his liberal platform and his political discourse of socially aware national development. Components of his policy to pay back the social debt were a move to formalize the informal economy through increased funding for the creation and legalization of small businesses (especially in the agricultural sector);[2] a strategy to restructure and more closely align the Finance Ministry with the social ministries concerned with public health, social welfare, education and culture, and labor and human resources; an educational campaign aimed at eliminating illiteracy throughout the country; and a political promise to make poor, marginalized sectors agents of change in the policies that targeted them. This promise entailed a proposal to establish popular kitchens and grassroots networks, a strategy to eliminate intermediaries in the market provision of basic food items, and the establishment of popular-action cells (*juntas de acción popular*) to gain further political support for the Democratic Left (Izquierda Democrática), Borja's political party (more on this below).

At the time, Borja was faced with the worst inflationary pressures in Ecuador's history up to that point. Thus although he differed ideologically from his predecessor, when it came to addressing the economy this did not matter; what mattered was the Ecuadorian state's relationship to the international development community, especially to the World Bank and the IMF. Before Borja entered office, Febres-Cordero had artificially held down inflation as well as real prices (particularly in the service sector). This was done by taking loans out of the Central Bank and artificially pumping money into the economy. Consequently, higher inflation rates were generated during the Borja years: inflation rose from 33 percent at the end of 1987 to 85 percent at the end of 1988, reaching its peak at 99 percent in March 1989 (*El Comercio*, August 16, 1989, A-7). While the Borja administration regulated inflation by decreasing money supply (*agregados monetarios*), real prices continued to increase. Despite these price increases, the administration's intent was to control prices, particularly those held down artificially by the previous government. From the perspective of most Ecuadorians, however, the price rises were interpreted as government initiated (namely, Borja initiated).

2. At the time, Peruvian economist Hernando de Soto's (1989) widely circulated publication, *El otro sendero* (The Other Path), influenced many policy makers to formalize the informal economy rather than try to suppress it.

In the political discourse of the Borja years, the debt was called an "integral debt" (*deuda integral*), and not an "economic" or "foreign" debt. Rhetorically, the debt was viewed as not just financial, as having not only economic conse-quences. Rather, the debt crisis was posed explicitly as a structural situation that had economic as well as social, political, and cultural consequences for the majority of Ecuadorians. This resonated well with many women's organizations whose members had viewed the debt in broader cultural and historical terms from the beginning. From this ideological perspective, social policy was priori-tized rhetorically and mildly reflected in the state budget: By 1990, the Ministry of Social Welfare's percentage of the total fiscal budget rose to 3.3 percent; while a small percentage of the overall budget, this figure contrasted sharply with the previous average of 1.0 percent during the 1980–88 period (Ojeda Segovia, 1993). A former finance minister stated in a personal interview that "in Borja's govern-ment social policy was not secondary . . . not in the mind of the president or in the minds of the people that had the most influence in the government. Social policy was always important and central. Economic policy was a necessary evil, I would say, and Borja said this many times" (Pablo Better, interview, August, 19, 1993). The Borja administration operated under the pretext that social policy must play a central role in the national development plan and that while struc-tural adjustment was necessary for continuing debt renegotiations with foreign lenders, it was not the only strategy that the government would take to seek further economic and social equality. An increase to 3.3 percent in state spend-ing on social services still represents a minute portion of the total state budget. This mixed-economy approach was Borja's both success and failure; on the one hand, through his political rhetoric he captured the support of sectors frustrated with the earlier austerity and adjustment measures of Febres-Cordero and Hur-tado; on the other hand, his socially aware approach to liberalization led to a set of incoherent policies, which according to one study, "provoked less conflict [than during earlier governments] yet inspired little strong support either. The picture that emerges is one of a government willing to listen to business and labour organisations, and desiring to use concerted action as a way out of the crisis, yet unable to reconcile the differing demands of these groups. Borja real-ised that the socialist agenda to which he felt morally committed was impractical given the current economic situation" (de Janvry et al. 1994, 77).

This resulted in initial widespread support for Borja's plans, although it di-minished over the years as Borja was forced to further prioritize debt repayment over social-sector spending and take a stronger stance against public-sector labor strikes. The labor strikes were a response to his policies to reduce public-sector spending and wages, and his public opposition to them ruined his public image as a "consensus-builder" (de Janvry et al., 1994). Borja's policy framework therefore must be viewed both in terms of its approach to addressing social concerns and in its incoherence in addressing the "integral debt" in its entirety, particularly given the structural limitations that exist during economic adjustment.

Since the military years of the 1970s, the government was divided by *frentes* (fronts): the Frente Económico (Economic Front), the Frente Social (Social Front), the Frente Interno (National Front), and the Frente Externo (Foreign Front). During the Borja years, the Social Front was given priority, and institutional relationships between it and the Economic Front were strengthened.[3] President Borja established instruments to coordinate action within the social sector; namely, between the Ministries of Social Welfare, Education and Culture, Labor and Human Resources, and Health, and later, the National Housing Board (Junta Nacional de la Vivienda). In effect, the minister of social welfare, Raúl Baca, was coordinator of social policies (Pablo Better, interview, August 19, 1993; Simon Pachano, interview, July 6, 1993). The Economic Front at that time consisted of the Central Bank and the ministries of finance, agriculture, industry, and public works. A representative from the Economic Front, often the finance minister, was present at meetings of the Social Front; likewise, a representative of the Social Front, often the minister of social welfare, was present at meetings of the Economic Front. This allowed for further coordination among the social and economic sectors of the government than had previously existed.

Central to Borja's policies was the long-term goal to reform and decentralize the social ministries in order to address more effectively the state's role in social and economic development—particularly for urban and rural poor sectors. The restructuring of the state was being further institutionalized, despite Borja's rhetoric to the contrary. During this time, Borja created the Social Policy Unit (Unidad de Política Social [UPS]), located at the National Development Council (Consejo Nacional de Desarrollo [CONADE]), the principle state planning agency. The UPS was designed with the goal of mainstreaming and rationalizing state bureaucracy, and with the specific goal of initiating a social-investment

3. Some claim that the Social Front was invented rather than reinstated during this period (see Ojeda Segovia 1993; Delgado Ribadeneira 1992). Pablo Better, finance minister for the Borja administration (1988–90) and advisor to the military government in the 1970s, explained in an interview that the fronts were officially established during the military period, although they have changed dramatically, and have played roles to varying degrees of importance under subsequent governments.

fund in the country. Thus, beginning in 1989 during the Borja administration, negotiations were already under way for the state to become a recipient of the World Bank– and IMF-sponsored Emergency Social Investment Fund (Fondo de Inversión Social de Emergencia [FISE]), designed to address the negative consequences of SAPs and other policies related to the country's adjustment process and its debt-repayment obligation, as defined by the international financial community. The fund was officially inaugurated in 1993, during the administration of President Sixto Durán-Ballén (1992–96).

Many factors contributed to the inability of the FISE to take off during Borja's term, although there are contending views on what occurred. Some argue that because of internal conflicts between Borja's appointees in the Ministries of Labor and Social Welfare, the administration was never able to present a coherent, unified fund proposal to the World Bank. In this view, it is implied that the Borja administration did, in fact, want to inaugurate the fund and that it was simply a misfortune that the government itself could not "get its act together" to present an adequate proposal (Segarra 1996). By contrast, other Borja political appointees who did not work directly in the UPS but who worked in other ministries or offices were reluctant to inaugurate a social policy framework that would restrict the government to tighter controls by the World Bank and that would be focused almost exclusively on ameliorating the impacts of "shock treatments" induced through IMF/World Bank–inspired structural adjustment measures. A former finance minister discusses differences in social policy initiatives during the Borja and Durán-Ballén administrations:

> [T]he FISE was created by pressures from the World Bank. . . . the Bank says to the [Durán-Ballén] government, "Sir, you don't have social policies . . . we aren't going to give credit to Ecuador." For that reason, the FISE was created. [The Borja administration] always struggled with the IMF and the World Bank because according to them, we wanted to emphasize social policy too much. In the end we had to address the economic part. Now the World Bank is saying something quite different. (Pablo Better, interview, August 19, 1993)

Other policy advisors agree that the Borja administration was reluctant to inaugurate such a fund (Simon Pachano, interview, September 25, 1993; Lautaro Ojeda, interview, October 28, 1993). Similarly, the Borja administration's economic policy, which emphasized gradual reform rather than shock treatments, did not require the same type of "emergency" fund that the Bank proposed as a method to address "social resistance" to structural adjustment measures (Segarra 1994b). All these factors contribute to a larger question about the extent to which the Borja administration could initiate social reforms independent of the World Bank framework, particularly because the Ecuadorian state was dependent on foreign loans to carry out its project.

Borja's Social Front initiated a series of programs and policies that targeted urban and rural poor sectors and that aimed at strengthening the welfare state. Originally, this included the initiation of two general areas of emphasis: the promotion of popular participation, and child development (*desarrollo infantil*). In terms of promoting popular participation, there were four areas of emphasis: open markets (*ferias libres*), communal kitchens, community stores, and popular-action cells (*juntas de acción popular*), although these programs were only marginally successful.[4] In terms of child development, the most successful and widely known program was the Community Network for Child Development, a program that targeted young children and their mothers and fell within the lines of conventional scientific and political knowledge about social welfare and motherhood.

Community Network for Child Development

The Community Network for Child Development (Red Comunitaria para el Desarrollo Infantil [RCDI]) became a central focus of governmental strategy during the Borja years.[5] It is an example of one governmental program that drew

4. Although Borja's Promotion of Popular Participation program included four components, only three of them were actually initiated: open markets, community stores, and popular-action cells. Among these, the only project that had any success was the project to develop open markets, which was initiated in 1989 with the idea that central producers would sell directly to consumers, thus eliminating the role of the intermediaries and lowering consumer prices (CONADE 1989). Pilot-project markets were established in rural and urban areas throughout the country. Government-sponsored community stores were initiated, although they did not last long and were very limited in their success. Popular-action cells, the educational aspect of the proposal, were organized alongside the other initiatives to promote political support and grassroots participation for governmental policies and reform. The fourth part of Borja's proposal, the establishment of communal kitchens, was based on the comparatively successful model of food distribution in Peru (Barrig 1996; Lind 1997). They were never actually tested. I gained this information through interviews with members of the Borja administration.

5. The Community Network for Child Development (RCDI) stemmed from an earlier child-development project, Modalidades No Convencionales de Atención Integral del Niño, initiated in 1979 (Delgado Ribadeneira 1992).

from conventional, Eurocentric notions of motherhood as a way to improve children's lives, but it can also be seen in the broader context of the Ecuadorian state's goal of modernization. Raúl Baca, then minister of social welfare, was the principal promoter who gave new life to the RCDI. The RCDI was viewed as serving the purpose of paying back the social debt, particularly to sectors of children under the age of six and to their mothers, who had been most severely affected by the negative consequences of structural adjustment and the foreign-debt burden. In 1990 it was estimated that from a total population of 12,000,000, there were 1,900,000 children under the age of six. Of this 1,900,000, it was estimated that 1,400,000 children, along with their families, needed direct social assistance. Based on average figures, the average poor family had two children under the age of six, in which case the program targeted approximately 570,000 poor households (Delgado Ribadeneira 1992).

To support this endeavor, the National Fund for Child Nutrition and Protection (Fondo Nacional para la Nutrición y Protección Infantil [FONNIN]) was established in February 1989 as the investment plan that would give financial life to the project. Economically speaking, the central focus was to "dynamize" the social and economic conditions of the families who used the services of the RCDI, primarily through investing to "activate the economies of the poorest sectors" (Ojeda Segovia 1993, 194). This included the idea that all projects initiated would have productive components that could become self-sustaining in the long term. Significantly, the fund was set up independently from renegotiation plans scheduled by the Ecuadorian state and the World Bank. It therefore represented a break from Febres-Cordero's policies, derived from IMF/World Bank frameworks, and as will be discussed below, is also quite distinct from the later IMF/World Bank–inspired Emergency Social Investment Fund. If anything, the Borja administration was criticized by the World Bank for emphasizing social policy "too much," and for not adhering to IMF/World Bank guidelines for debt repayments (Pablo Better, interview, August 19, 1993). It is not a coincidence, then, that Ecuador was placed in contempt by the World Bank during this period and that frictions between the Ecuadorian state and foreign-bank lenders increased, culminating, perhaps, in the 1992 Citibank crisis. This dispute between the Ecuadorian Central Bank and Citibank, in which Citibank froze the state's assets (U.S.$80 million) until Ecuador agreed to make its scheduled payments, ended when pressure was placed on Citibank by Ecuadorian political and economic elites (especially the financial sector) and by popular sectors, through direct protest. In the end, Citibank agreed to revise the Ecuadorian state's loan-repayment schedule, under better terms than those of Ecuador's original plan.

RCDI's main objective was to organize day-care networks, with the participation of local communities in both urban and rural areas. At its peak, it reached approximately between 140,000 and 200,000 children daily, in both rural and urban areas, through contracts between the state and more than three hundred popular organizations.[6] The concept of "child development" was central to the program's philosophy: it emphasized not only "evolutionary development," but also the "influences from community, environment and family" that affect children's development in poor sectors (Delgado Ribadeneira 1992, 1–2). RCDI was meant not only to improve direct living conditions for poor children, based on indicators of health and nutrition, but also to "initiate interinstitutional activities oriented to improve the economic and social bases of the children's families" (2). Thus the program was linked to other efforts taken by the government to improve health conditions, education, and the mobilization of parents in local communities (under the rhetoric of "popular participation").

In theory, RCDI offered much, and it focused on traditional welfare as much as on generating productive work for the poor. The program included the establishment of day-care centers, which provided productive work, particularly for the mothers who worked at the centers, and a parallel educational project to "empower" the people who worked at the day-care center, used the service for their children, or both. Central to the program's success was the idea that social development requires a collaborative effort by the state and popular sectors: "The [Community] Network presupposes . . . an innovative conception of social development, in a coordinated effort between the state and popular sectors. It is innovative in the sense that services are organized in an integral, interrelated way. Popular and community participation are articulated as the crux of development, and it views community development in relation to the [broader] economic and social environment" (Ojeda Segovia 1993, 197, my translation). This project relied on parents in the communities to provide the labor for the day-care centers, including the small percentage who were employed by the centers, and the parents who were asked to voluntarily participate in community meetings to organize and maintain the centers as efficient community services. Their participation, it was viewed, would help to generate the "participation of civil

6. This number has been disputed: official reports of the RCDI, based on information provided by the participant organizations, estimates that 200,000 children were served daily. Ernesto Delgado Ribadeneira, ex-director of the RCDI, contends that the figures used to arrive at this estimate were probably conflated, and in his own estimation the program supported 140,000 children on a daily basis (see Delgado Ribadeneira 1992). In terms of the number of popular organizations involved, unfortunately I do not have specific figures, besides the figure of "300 organizations" that Delgado himself relies on.

society." By asking people to actively participate in their own welfare, the Borja administration claimed, it had overcome paternalistic and top-down ways of providing welfare.

In practice, however, many problems arose. In terms of reaching its goal of targeting 570,000 households, even the ex-director of the program, Ernesto Delgado Ribadeneira, has stated that by 1992, the program probably reached only about 120,000 households, as opposed to the original estimate of 570,000 (Delgado Ribadeneira 1992). And despite the rise in the fiscal-budget share of the Ministry of Social Welfare (that is, despite the redistribution of public social spending), a World Bank report claims that the redistribution has had "limited effects" and that the sectors who have benefited most are not the poorest but rather those of the "middle class" (quoted in Ojeda Segovia 1993, 199). Additionally, the report argues, public spending has "contributed to a regional concentration of goods and services" (Ojeda Segovia 1993, 199). While there are ideological disparities between the World Bank's official position on social policy and reform and the stance of Borja administration, causing uncertainty about the validity of the report, it nevertheless raises important questions about the extent to which Borja's social policies successfully reached sectors of society that had not been reached in the past or that had been most severely affected by the economic crisis.

Problems arose, as well, with the implementation of the day-care centers. In particular, it was assumed that women, targeted as mothers of the preschool children, would play central roles both in the centers' productive work and in the voluntary parents' associations that served as informal boards for the centers in the respective neighborhoods. Several issues arose from this situation. The centers provided employment for some women, however small a percentage. At a center that provided day care for fifty children, for example, five or six women were employed on either a full-time or part-time basis. Typically, two women worked on a full-time basis, and the rest worked on a part-time basis. This depended, largely, on decisions made within the popular organization that was responsible, locally, for the day-care center's success.[7] Furthermore, the women employees were paid little ("not enough for the vital minimum"), and they tended to "lose their rights in terms of stable employment, work promotion, salary raises, and participation in unions" (Costales, quoted in Ojeda Segovia 1993, 209).

7. A fundamental strategy of the program was the following: "To optimize the social networks of popular organizations, parents' committees, cooperatives, interest groups, and youth and feminine organizations, to fortalize participation and integration of services, with the purpose of improving child development" (Delgado Ribadeneira 1992, 3).

During the 1992–94 period, one such day-care center operated in southern Quito. It was located on property that had been the *hacienda* of ex-president Velasco Ibarra and abandoned during the 1960s, following Ecuador's 1964 agrarian reforms. By the 1990s, this area of the city had become an incorporated district and had begun to take on the appearance of a shantytown, with its unpaved roads and self-built houses, despite the majestic road, lined by trees that were remnants of the old *hacienda*, leading into the area. Interestingly, the district's official name is Cooperativa de Vendedores Ambulantes (Cooperative of Street Vendors), reflecting the local residents' background in this cooperative movement to establish rights for street vendors, many of whom came from families who once worked on ex-president Velasco Ibarra's ranch. When I conducted interviews with members of the women's organizations in this district in 1992 and 1993, many of the approximately two hundred homes did not have running water or electricity. It was a poor neighborhood by many standards: the average monthly household incomes of the women I interviewed were significantly lower than those of women from other districts whom I interviewed: S/119,500, or U.S.$66 a month, compared with S/179,375 or almost U.S.$100 per month across the sample. Many of them worked in the informal sector, as street vendors or domestic servants. Some provided services such as ironing and washing clothes; some did piecework for local factories, such as a local bra manufacturer.

The small women's organization in this district, with an approximate membership of twenty-five women, had received funding from the RCDI and had established a day-care center in 1992. The day-care center itself was located in a building made of cement blocks and mortar, an austere structure with basic supplies and sleeping arrangements for approximately forty to fifty young babies and children. Bunk beds for eight children were crammed into one small room. Often, at least two children shared one mattress. There were two long, low tables in the dining room where the children sat to eat soup or bread for lunch. The floors were primarily made of dirt. The five to six women who worked there were members of the local women's organization, one of the three groups organized by the Chillogallo women's organization Centro Femenino "8 de Marzo" ("March 8" Women's Center). For those who received a wage for their work, salaries were minimal (approximately S/5,000, or U.S.$2.80, a week) and were not designed to promote self-sustainability among the women workers. The RCDI funding provided small salaries to day-care center employees but generally was based on the assumption that women would be available and willing to volunteer or to accept a low wage.

According to results of an RCDI pilot project, evaluated by CONADE, the project was viewed differently by state bureaucrats and by the mothers and community residents who participated in it.[8] On the one hand, the project was designed to promote "integral child development" as opposed to being an "alternative strategy for child day care." The mothers who participated in it, however, viewed it as an "alternative form of assistance for immediate subsistence, given the critical situation in which they live" (Ojeda Segovia 1993, 208). Neighborhood women's organizations that provided local support for the day-care centers therefore took advantage of the government's support and spent exhaustive amounts of time and energy in an effort to make the centers a success, mainly because they and their families needed them. In this sense, the establishment of the day-care centers had both positive and negative effects for the neighborhood organizations that supported them, as well as for local families who relied on the service. The local community and the neighborhood organizations themselves were in desperate need not only of day care, but also of forms of subsistence and, generally speaking, of funds that would give further meaning and life to the organizations in a decade when funding had thus far been extremely limited and when there was little economic hope for poor families. Thus during this period, many neighborhood organizations were enthusiastic about establishing day-care centers in their neighborhoods, many of which had had no such service beforehand.

On the other hand, many critics of the RCDI are quick to point out that the originally proposed "interinstitutional relationships" and "state-popular sector relationships" did not pan out, in part because of the age-old problem of excessive bureaucracy, characterized specifically by the lack of a "culture of coordination" between ministries and state agencies to foster a genuinely collaborative effort. In particular, the Ministry of Social Welfare and of Public Health, and the National Institute of Children and Family (Instituto Nacional de la Niñez y la Familia [INNFA]) had "political differences," and the Social Front and the general secretary of planning (the head of CONADE) were "weak" in establishing the much-needed institutional links and systems of communication (Ojeda Segovia 1993, 209). This therefore created policy inaction and a lack of concern on behalf of state bureaucrats for the pilot project's outcome in local communities.

These critiques of RCDI raised issues concerning the Borja administration's overall social reform strategy, which he called the "democratization of the grassroots." Many insiders and critics alike questioned the extent to which Borja's social policy reforms, which, under the banner of "democratization through

8. The pilot project took place in two locations: in a rural village in the Pichincha Province, and in a poor neighborhood in Guayaquil. The results of this study were published in 1991 (see CONADE/UNPD/UNESCO/UNICEF/Ministerio de Bienestar Social 1991; also see Ojeda Segovia 1993).

decentralization," included popular sectors and local governments in the national development process, did more than rely on the voluntary or cheap labor of sectors of poor people to carry out the administration's proposed projects (Ojeda Segovia 1993; Delgado Ribadeneira 1992; CONADE/UNDP/UNESCO/UNICEF/Ministerio de Bienestar Social 1991). For example, his strategy helped to institutionalize poverty and women's struggles for survival, and to the extent that it shifted public attention to private-led development (be it nonprofit or for profit, at informal or formal institutional levels), it set the stage for the Durán-Ballén administration's neoliberal reforms. In this regard, all the above-mentioned projects, both in the areas of promotion of popular participation and of child development, are characterized by the state's implicit assumption that poor women (and men, to some degree) have endless time to participate in and supposedly benefit from community development projects. This is reminiscent of the more general trend followed by Latin American states, with the support of international development institutions, to co-opt women's political support through providing them with (typically volunteer) opportunities to participate in development initiatives and sometimes receive, in exchange, food, some kind of political support, small remuneration, or a combination of these, in a trend now inherent in neoliberal policies (see Barrig 1996; Ochsendorf 1998).

In 1992, upon Durán-Ballén's entry into the presidential office, RCDI was left inactive and Borja's Social Front was dismantled and replaced by the FISE. The initial impact of putting this program "on hold" (which ended up being indefinitely) was devastating for the day-care centers and community women's organizations involved in the centers. Those centers that continued to exist did so because of the efforts of women's, parents', and children's groups that pushed for these centers to remain active, even when no funding was available. They therefore operated through other voluntary efforts to raise funds, and most of them had extremely limited funding to continue the centers' main tasks of caring for up to approximately fifty children a day, five days a week; providing the children with lunches; and providing salaries (however limited) for the women who managed the centers.

The Borja administration's policies continued the institutionalization of neoliberal reform initiated in the early 1980s in Ecuador. Given Borja's emphasis on social policy and issues, including women's rights and roles in development, women's struggles for survival were targeted more explicitly, with women as participants in state-initiated local development practices. While Borja's policies served to make women's roles in community development more visible, they also helped institutionalize women's struggles for survival. The administration that followed further institutionalized these struggles by transferring the state's role in providing child care to the private sector, by excluding communities from state development planning, and through the privatization of everyday life.

The Sixto Durán-Ballén Administration, 1992–1996

The government of President Sixto Durán-Ballén accelerated the process of restructuring through its modernization plan, alienating key economic and political sectors in order to achieve his goals. This strategy has been common among governments that suspend some democratic rights in order to implement adjustment measures, as was the case in the earlier Febres-Cordero government (León 2000), the Bolivian president Victor Paz Estensoro's "new economic policies" and the repression of mining labor in the mid-1980s (McFarren 1992), and President Fujimori's "Fujishocks" in Peru in the early 1990s (Barrig 1996). Durán-Ballén's reforms included economic liberalization, the privatization of key state enterprises, state modernization and decentralization, and, generally speaking, integrating Ecuador into the global economy.

The Durán-Ballén administration viewed social policy primarily through the lens of the World Bank and the IMF, as a series of reforms needed primarily, if not exclusively, to respond to the drastic shock treatments induced to stabilize the economy and to bring about desired long-term economic growth. Its social reforms were combined with the government's relatively stringent plan to service the foreign debt, which by 1994 had reached U.S.$13.2 billion. In Durán-Ballén's attempts to modernize the state, it was deemed unnecessary and costly to appropriate such a high percentage of the state budget for social spending (as during the Borja years), in part because it was assumed that economic growth would trickle down and lead to better social conditions, and in part because cuts in social spending were seen as a necessary component of the short-term economic reforms that would purportedly bring eventual wealth and other fruits of modernization—the "tighten our bootstraps" approach to development. (Of course, this all depends on one's perspective and location in this process.)

Initially, Durán-Ballén achieved this by restructuring the state bureaucracy. His administration dismantled Borja's Social Front, gave greater power to the UPS, still located at CONADE, and centralized (and made semiautonomous from the state bureaucracy) social policy concerns in the President's Office, again under the framework of IMF/World Bank social-investment funds.[9] He also gave

9. Durán-Ballén assigned the UPS the task of managing and implementing the overall FISE project framework; thus it was primarily technocratic power that he gave the office. Because the

great importance to the National Modernization Council (Consejo Nacional de Modernización [CONAM]), the state agency directly in charge of the rationalization of the state sector and privatizations. The Durán-Ballén administration's neoliberal reform initiatives were crystallized in its so-called modernization plan, described in the *1993–1996 National Development Plan* (*Plan nacional del desarrollo, 1993–1996* [see CONADE 1993]).

Durán-Ballén's modernization plan closely followed IMF–World Bank guidelines for Ecuador's foreign-debt obligations. Above all, it mandated decreasing inflation; eliminating excessive state social spending; and making the state more efficient, primarily through privatizations and through bureaucratic retrenchment. During the first two years of his administration, more than twenty thousand state employees were laid off, contributing to an overall 4 percent decrease in the public payroll (Inter-American Development Bank [IADB] 1994).[10] Also during this time, Durán-Ballén semiprivatized the management of the Pension Fund (Fondo de Pensión) as well as medical benefits for pensioners and state employees. In addition, he initiated the privatization of state-owned, or semi-state-owned, enterprises such as Aztra, a sugar-processing firm; Cemento Nacional, a cement company; and the telecommunications and electricity sectors. Perhaps the most important reform in this third area was the Petroleum and Natural Gas Law, which authorized privatization in the areas of distribution and marketing and allowed the government to establish more flexible rules for determining the domestic prices of fuels. This permitted more flexibility in domestic prices of fuels: beginning in January 1995, the domestic price of gasoline was to be determined by the exchange rate, the international price, and taxes. Essentially, the government quit subsidizing this sector and let the market determine the price of gasoline. At that time the price of gasoline rose by an initial 70 percent, and it has remained at relatively high levels ever since. The government sought this measure in part to counterbalance a late 1993 fiscal crisis, the effects of the Ecuador-Peru border war (which led to Ecuador's inability to stick to its stand-by agreement with the IMF), and the extremely low currency reserve

---

FISE has been the primary social policy tool used during this administration, the UPS has relatively more power than it did during the Borja years, when it was a separate entity from state institutions that handled the Program of Popular Participation and the RCDI, among others.

10. In Durán-Ballén's plan to buy out workers, employees were given the option of accepting a lump sum of money (often the equivalent of sixteen paychecks [a year's salary in Ecuador]) plus a bonus, if they agreed to retire from their current position and not seek future employment in the state sector. This plan cost the government a hefty sum; the idea was that the initial cost for the government will provide long-term relief by making the state bureaucracy more efficient.

that resulted from the financial market's fear of the effects of Ecuador's wartime economy (see IADB 1994).[11]

In addition, the Durán-Ballén administration subcontracted private firms and NGOs for work that traditionally was carried out by the state, in the name of "efficiency" and cost reduction. This subcontracting strategy involved operating and construction concessions for roads, ports, and airports, as in the international competition for the operation of the Quito and Guayaquil airports, scheduled in 1995. Importantly, it also encompassed the subcontracting of private (both for-profit and nonprofit) organizations, among them NGOs, that focus on issues of poverty and welfare as well as networks of doctors, lawyers, and policy makers. Many of these newly formed policy advocate groups played key roles in the liberalization of trade law, medicines, and medical support and in welfare reform and poverty reduction in the country. Ironically, one result of the Durán-Ballén administration's modernization plan was that, ultimately, it reached out more successfully to the NGO sector and local municipalities. Indeed, decentralization measures, including the shifting of resources, knowledge, and decision-making powers to some NGOs and to municipalities, occurred more systematically under his government than under Borja's, despite the striking ideological differences in their rhetorical appeal to these very sectors (more on this below). What many activists, policy makers, and intellectuals have now been debating for years—the role of women's organizations and movements in the new state-civil society arrangements—was institutionalized through policies such as these during the 1990s in Ecuador.

During the same decade in which U.S. president George H. W. Bush (1988–92) launched his "thousand points of light" campaign and asked both private and voluntary sectors of civil society to take responsibility for what had previously been viewed as state activities, the Durán-Ballén administration called for NGOs to take over specific development tasks and transferred many of the state's welfare and community-development responsibilities to local institutions and civic and community groups. In the political discourse of the Durán-Ballén administration, it was argued that the private sector was more efficient, the state was overburdened, and civil society could provide the thousand points of light

11. Ecuador and Peru have disputed seventy-eight kilometers of frontier, along the southeast border of Ecuador and northeast border of Peru, which was never determined after the Rio Protocol ended a short war between the two countries in 1941. The border area has been a point of contention in Peruvian-Ecuadorian relations ever since, erupting in a dispute in January 1995 in which at least one hundred soldiers were killed as well as in several later skirmishes (see Economist Intelligence Unit 1995b).

that were needed to confront Ecuador's foreign-debt and economic crisis. Interestingly, the thousand points of light were gendered: during this period, local municipalities continued to employ more men than women for pay, whereas volunteer efforts throughout the country tended to be managed and run by women (María Arboleda, interview, February 17, 1993).

In terms of social policy, the administration's initial goal was to further integrate the four principal programs of the RCDI: the Program of Child Nutrition and Day Care (Programa de Nutrición Infantil y Cuidado Diario) of the Ministry of Social Welfare, the Preschool Education and Recreation program (Educación Preescolar y Recreación) of the Ministry of Education and Culture, the Child Nutrition and Integrated Health program (Nutrición Infantil y Salud Integral) of the Ministry of Public Health, and the Popular Capacitation program (Capacitación Popular) of the Ministry of Labor and Human Resources (CONADE 1993). The *1993–1996 National Development Plan* emphasizes the "strengthening of community service networks, through actions promoted by the State, that bring together the participation of community base organizations and of groups from civil society and local governments such as NGOs and Municipalities" (CONADE 1993; see also Ojeda Segovia 1993). Central to this plan was the strategy to "decentralize [RCDI's] administrative activities and program execution, through processes of subcontracting with entities and organizations from civil society and local government that are accredited for such activities" (Ojeda Segovia 1993, 214). In the end, RCDI was disbanded and defunded; the Durán-Ballén administration chose to shift its focus to the establishment of the FISE, in a World Bank– and IMF-inspired social policy framework that focuses exclusively on the social costs of structural adjustment policies.

The Emergency Social Investment Fund (FISE)

The final version of the FISE, announced by presidential decree on March 13, 1993, differed sharply from its original design.[12] The Durán-Ballén administration's plan to induce economic shock treatment made it politically imperative to develop a structure for absorbing "social unrest" (Segarra 1996). Indeed, the FISE was rapidly inaugurated in order to preempt further disorder following an indigenous rebellion and series of indigenous and labor strikes in the early

---

12. For further discussion of the history and political negotiations that led up to the inauguration of the Ecuadorian FISE, see Segarra 1994.

1990s.[13] During preparation for the FISE project under the Borja administration, many NGOs, particularly those that were more professionally oriented, were motivated to participate in the new public/private development "partnerships," a term popularized in World Bank studies of civil society and citizen participation (e.g., World Bank 2001).

When CONADE originally proposed its fund to the World Bank in November 1992, the FISE's general goals included (1) constructing a mechanism to channel the needs of the poor to the government and a means to deliver the services demanded outside the traditional administrative model; (2) encouraging the participation of popular organizations, cooperatives, private enterprises, and NGOs in program and project development; (3) decentralizing poverty reduction programs by involving local organizations; (4) prioritizing social spending in order to address the most serious instances of poverty; and (5) providing a greater understanding and appreciation of poverty which would serve to focus state poverty-reduction initiatives (Lautaro Ojeda Segovia, interview, October 28, 1993).

To operationalize these goals, a technical program was proposed that would (1) target funds for aiding in the institutional strengthening of CONADE itself by providing computers, technical training, and support; (2) provide state planners with training in running the FISE and coordinating the fund's implementation with NGOs; (3) hire a NGO-CONADE liaison officer who would work solely on incorporating NGOs into the management and implementation of the FISE; and (4) systematize the new NGO-state relationship through workshops and seminars focused on institutional strengthening of the NGO community (ibid.). Thus, the technical component created a formal mechanism to facilitate linkages between the state and NGOs. These steps to formalize the FISE and delegate traditional state responsibilities to the private sector helped to institutionalize the state's new technocratic order, always with the understanding that the state continued to play the central role in defining social policy outcomes.

Later, when Durán-Ballén placed the fund in his Presidential Office, and therefore gave it more autonomous status than had it been located at CONADE, the role of NGOs became even less clear. In the end, specific NGOs such as the Ecuadorian Corporation of Private Nonprofit Organizations (Corporación Ecuatoriana de Organizaciones Privadas sin Fines de Lucro [CEOP]) and Alternative (Alternativa, a national intermediary NGO) played pivotal roles in organiz-

13. The Durán-Ballén administration anticipated further protests by labor and indigenous sectors to its modernization plan. In this context, the FISE was viewed as one way to preempt resistance by incorporating (and co-opting) NGOs, which often represented marginalized groups of people, into the development process.

ing the NGO community and in representing that community in the state negotiations. Nevertheless, under the final agreement, formal representation by NGOs remained in the form of two NGO representatives on the administrative council overlooking the fund (Segarra 1994). In essence, the fund was primarily controlled by the President's Office,[14] administered according to World Bank guidelines, and did little to truly incorporate NGOs' visions, concerns, and methodologies into national development planning.

At the beginning, the FISE's funding came from USAID; since then funding has also been secured by the World Bank and by state donor agencies in Germany, Spain, and other countries. In general, the Durán-Ballén administration emphasized physical infrastructure (roads, bridges, buildings) rather than social welfare, despite the fund's social purpose and goals. In the early 1990s, people often explained this to me as resulting from the fact that "the president is a trained architect." Women rarely benefited from physical infrastructure projects, except through their increased access to roads and transportation; the relatively small proportion of FISE projects that addressed social welfare needs did reach women, although primarily in their capacity as volunteers, rather than paid staff members (CONADE staff member, interview, April 23, 1998).

Conclusion: Engendering Neoliberalism

The day-care centers that were institutionalized through Borja's social policies also served to institutionalize women's struggles for survival, for better or worse. On the one hand, some local women's groups benefited from policies that provided funding for projects and activities that they managed. As the neoliberal state is privatized, women have become the bearers of what were previously state welfare responsibilities: they are now service providers in the realms of community development, family, health care, day care, and local produce markets. Through development policies and practices, including those of both international agencies and nation-states, these sectors of women have been brought into the visible fold of development. In conjunction with this, they have become models of the new market citizen[15] and of "modern economic woman,"[16] the

14. To illustrate this point, the FISE director was directly appointed by the president, with little input from the NGO sector.

15. Verónica Schild (2000a and b) theorizes about the new gendered market citizenship in her study of women's movements and neoliberal state formation in Chile.

16. I thank Lourdes Benería (1996) for her insight on the notion of "modern economic woman" in economic discourse.

latter a representation that draws on notions of "modern economic man" in neoclassical economics and that is a model institutionalized through development practices operating on the assumption that women's and men's identities, and their racialization,[17] are defined in terms of their economic functions and their roles in the modern global market.

This process was further institutionalized outside the state, at the community and household levels, through Duran-Ballén's reforms. Most of the day-care centers were dismantled as Duran-Ballén emphasized the FISE over other social policies. The staff of many day-care centers were faced with the reality that they had to continue operating the centers privately or close them. Those running the day-care center in Hacienda Ibarra, for example, chose to continue their work without funding. Indeed, this is a choice many women's organizations in Ecuador and throughout the Andes and Latin America in general have had to make. The institutionalization of women's struggles, coupled with the privatization of everyday life, has led to increased work for many women of poor backgrounds and increased inequalities between the rich and poor. For poor women, neoliberal development is not working as it should, hence their readiness to participate in antineoliberal protests.

Indeed, both administrations discussed above have had to operate within a severe set of economic and political constraints. Borja's policy framework, considered economically and politically moderate, encompassed converging the Social and Economic Fronts and presenting an integrated framework for addressing the social and economic effects of foreign-debt and economic restructuring in Ecuador. Rhetorical notions of "participation" and "popular organization" were invoked and sometimes translated into practice, as was the case for the Program on Popular Participation and the Program on Child Development, which included RCDI. His social democratic agenda reflected both the success and the failure of his administration: on the one hand, his administration gained support from many economic and political sectors whose members felt marginalized by earlier governments; on the other hand, his mixed-model approach lent itself to criticism, and ultimately Borja, like previous presidents, was forced by the World Bank and business sectors to prioritize structural adjust-

17. The more recent social-capital approach, in which indigenous cultural labor is viewed as productive for the capitalist economy and in which there is an attempt to integrate indigenous women's and men's nonmonetary labor (e.g., crafts production, subsistence agriculture) into capitalist development on this basis, is one example of how development frameworks racialize indigenous identity and Westernize forms of labor that fall out of the conventional realm of a monetary economy (Laurie and Radcliffe 2001).

ment over other social policy concerns. The contradictions that arose became increasingly evident, especially to sectors of workers, among them public-sector employees, and to members of poor sectors who felt no relief from Borja's gradualist approach to restructuring the economy.

Durán-Ballén's reforms fall much in line with the more general project of neoliberal reform in Latin America in the 1980s and 1990s. In this sense, his neoliberal approach, both in rhetoric and in practice, was different from Borja's: the two administrative approaches to development reflect the different neoliberalisms we witness in Ecuador (Phillips 1998). Durán-Ballén institutionalized the World Bank–inspired Emergency Social Investment Fund, which helped him gain political support from the development community, both nonprofit and for-profit organizations that reaped the benefits from their increased involvement in development planning. His reforms, however, also have evoked negative reactions, particularly from poor sectors, including participants in neighborhood women's organizations, who have felt the immediate effects of job layoffs, price rises, decreased provision of state social services, and the institutionalization of their struggles for survival.

The Citibank protest and many subsequent protests, marches, rallies, and other organizing efforts by women reveal the contradictions of neoliberal development in Ecuador. In the following years, heightened political crisis and financial crisis only worsened the situation for the majority of Ecuadorians. Despite government attempts to further integrate Ecuador into the global economy, poor and middle-class women continued to protest against the reforms as they affected their daily lives and influenced their political perspectives. Interestingly, these crises opened up new political opportunities for women in community and national realms, one of the paradoxes of women's activism during this period. Their political activism and community participation necessarily had to shift in order to address their agenda in the context of the new public-private partnerships and the general reordering of civil society. As Janine Brodie (1994) notes, "the current round of restructuring entails a fundamental redrawing of the familiar boundaries between the international and the national, the state and the economy, and the so-called 'public' and 'private.' This realignment, in turn, undermines both the assumptions and sites of contemporary feminist politics and invites new strategic thinking about the boundaries of the political" (46).

The women at Citibank addressed this "redrawing of boundaries" to some degree. They questioned Citibank's role in the foreign debt and challenged the Ecuadorian state to take responsibility for its own role in reproducing poverty and oppression. They made use of conventional gender roles by invoking their status as mothers of families and of the nation, thus conveying that this type of development did not benefit them. Effectively they questioned the role of global economics in restructuring their communities, the public/private dimensions of social life, and their roles and identities as women.

Yet their roles in the day-care centers and in social service delivery in general beg further inquiry into the extent to which their claims are actually being heard. The international development field has heralded women's "roles in development" since the 1970s, yet their integration into state and international development projects have been enacted on a clientelistic, often paternalistic basis. Neoliberal restructuring has exacerbated this situation by shifting the perceived responsibility of welfare distribution from the state to civil society, and specifically to the realm of women's work at the household and community levels—one of the hidden dimensions of macroeconomic and social welfare policies that claim to be gender neutral (Elson 1992). In the following chapter I examine more closely how gender identity formation foregrounds women's community activism and contributes to the paradoxical outcomes of women's survival strategies and political struggles. A broader issue that I continue to examine concerns how to integrate women's visions into the country's economic development and democratization processes, all the while rethinking the very concepts of citizenship and national identity that underscore contemporary political processes.

[4]

Women's Community Organizing in Quito:
The Paradoxes of Survival and Struggle

[W]e vest great hopes in the "resistance" everywhere in evidence in women's daily lives, household survival strategies, and collective struggles. Yet we too often ignore the less glorious, more contradictory, more paradoxical dimensions and sometimes ephemeral qualities of those struggles.

—SONIA ALVAREZ, "Concluding Reflections: Redrawing the Parameters of Gender Struggle"

Since the inception of the restructuring process in the early 1980s, Ecuadorian civil society has been increasingly called upon to provide essential services for poor families. In many ways, it was poor families themselves—particularly women—who became the new civil society actors, a phenomena exemplified in the Borja and Durán-Ballén administrations' child development policies in 1988–96. Either explicitly or implicitly, it was expected that components of civil society, including community associations and for-profit and nonprofit organizations (such as NGOs), would pick up where the state left off. In general, a new model for social service delivery was being proposed, one that relied on the traditional gendered division of labor and assumed that women and families would "absorb" the costs of restructuring and take on the new market-related responsibilities (Fisher and Kling 1993). The once-familiar public/private boundaries of the state, economy, and civil society were being redrawn (Brodie 1994), leading not only to shifts in the broader economy but also to the restructuring of everyday life (Benería 1992b): the organization of paid-labor sectors, the intensification of domestic work (both paid and unpaid), changes in family structure (as in male migration to the United States and Spain, an associated rise in female-headed households, and an increase in household size) and social relations, an evolution in cultural notions of play or vacation (such as fewer days off, fewer holiday get-togethers), and alterations in community development strategies or initiatives. As a result of this restructuring, Ecuadorian businesses, NGOs, and newly formed public-private partnerships began to play important roles in defining the country's social development agenda; this required, among other things, reenvisioning social policy and community development, two important areas of concern for poor neighborhoods.

During this same period, somewhere between five hundred and eight hundred grassroots women's groups were established during the 1980s, as a way for women to address the needs of their communities and families (Centro María Quilla/CEPAL 1990). While many scholars have acknowledged that business and NGO sectors have retooled to meet the demands of the Ecuadorian state's neoliberal agenda (e.g., Segarra 1996; Conaghan 2000; Bretón Solo de Zaldívar 2003), in many ways it was these grassroots women who "mothered" the crisis, both individually and collectively. Through the process, they have gained some political visibility and have helped strengthen feminist demands for women's rights, although, I argue, often at a cost to their own survival. Constructions of femininity, particularly constructions of motherhood, have been central to their organizing strategies, just as they have been to the external actors and institutions that have helped mediate the women's forms of survival and struggle.

In this chapter I address the paradoxes that emerge through the process of women's community organizing, including the paradox of gender identity formation in the politically mediated context of poverty alleviation and, more broadly, Ecuador's modernization project. First I discuss Ecuadorian women's responses to the foreign-debt crisis and neoliberal restructuring in relation to how feminists, NGO activists, and development professionals intervened in the sphere of women's community organizing. Next I analyze how women's gender identity formation, especially their urbanized roles and identities as mothers, has been shaped in the broader context of collective action and has influenced their forms of organizing and perceptions of poverty itself. I then address the political and economic paradoxes of women's struggles for survival, including the successes and limits of this type of women's community-based organizing in the neoliberal era. Organized women have gained some political power, visibility, and recognition as public actors. Yet in many ways their activism has been reduced to a new form of clientelism among their organizations and the developmentalist state, particularly in light of this neoliberal shift toward positioning poor women explicitly as clients (Schild 2002b).

Organized women have been heralded as acquiring some economic "empowerment" through their activism, yet overall it is clear that their livelihoods have eroded since the inception of neoliberal development policies, leading to

the institutionalization of women's struggles for survival (to "mothering the crisis") rather than to poverty alleviation or a significant transformation of gender
relations. By *mothering the crisis*, I am referring to the multiple material and
symbolic ways in which women have used their traditional gender roles in community activism, whether it be to survive economically; to take care of their
family; to preserve a tradition, set of values, role, or activity; or to challenge
traditions, values, and societal inequalities. Scholars of women's movements
have seen women's community organizing as conservative or nontransformative
at times, and at other times as radical and transformative; some have highlighted
the contradictions of this process (Barrig 1989, 1996; Jetter, Orleck, and Taylor
1997; Molyneux 1998; Bayard de Volo 2001; Power 2002). What interests me
in this chapter is how organization members invoke specific constructions of
femininity in their political organizing, as expressed through their conversations,
group meetings and activities, newsletters, and public marches and protests.
How they express their gender identities is a result of their complex relationships
with one another and their families, as well as with their organizations and with
external political actors such as middle-class feminists, development practitioners, politicians, male community leaders, and church leaders. In other
words, context is everything. In this chapter I find that members of community
women's organizations in southern Quito negotiate their socially ascribed gender roles in a variety of ways, both reinforcing and challenging gender relations
(Bayard de Volo 2001). One way they do this is through a performance of motherhood as a way to acquire their essential material needs and challenge what
they define as globalization and neoliberalism (Taylor 1996). Self-fulfillment,
or subjective "empowerment," has been somewhat of a by-product, albeit an
important one, that was "directed" to some degree by the interventions of external actors such as feminist NGOs and neighborhood movements (Alvarez 1996;
Bayard de Volo 2001). Their experiences of "empowerment" have depended on
these interventions, as scholars such as Sonia Alvarez (1996) have observed:
"The interventions or mediations by the state, the church, political parties,
NGOs, and international and national development and philanthropic agencies
have many implications for women's 'empowerment.' These multiple actors
hold agendas and stakes in poor women's struggles which can significantly reconfigure, redimension, and even redirect those struggles" (141). Their collective
political identity has emerged through this broader history of neighborhood organizing in Quito and through influences from the contemporary women's,
popular education, liberation theology, and labor movements. In the following
section I describe these community women's organizations, offering a closer

examination of one organization in Chillogallo (Centro Femenino "8 de Marzo") whose members have had significant experience working with feminists, NGO activists, and development practitioners and that is perceived as having acquired some political visibility in urban Ecuador.

Community Women's Organizing in Quito

In Quito, where earlier decades of industrialization and urban migration greatly outweighed the new, rising demand for municipal and state services, women from poor sectors were motivated to organize around the growing economic crisis as it was manifested in the already overburdened city. Although many of them had never organized before, they worked together, with their neighbors, family members, and friends, to build houses, stake out pieces of land, buy food in bulk and share costs, establish community cooperatives or stores, develop a business (for example, selling goods), or simply to meet and discuss their lives as new urban settlers. They were organizing not to explicitly challenge or criticize gender relations per se but rather to improve the gendered conditions of their daily lives—two very different things. The possibility for their existence emerged historically through at least two processes and sets of discourses: that of neighborhood organizing and urbanization and that of WID. The institutionalization of the WID field paved the way for organized groups of women around the world to receive funding and ideological support for their struggles, which were often perceived by Western feminists as necessary and important challenges to entrenched forms of sexism, colonialism, class exploitation, and sometimes racism in poor countries (Kabeer 1994). Grassroots women's groups received legitimacy for their organizing efforts in a way they never would have a decade earlier, even from organized women in industrialized countries. WID discourses of "integrating women into development" also allowed local middle-class feminists to articulate their political agenda in a new way that was viewed as more legitimate by the state, political parties, and male-based institutions in general. Money is power, and funding provided the impetus for many institutions to engender their organizational frameworks and projects as a means to receive legitimacy, support, and funding from international organizations and, later, from the state as well. The state itself was bound by this paradox. Middle-class feminists employed WID discourse in various, complex ways: some endorsed it and made it their own ideology; others criticized it, yet used it to advance their own political agendas; most found ways to negotiate it in one way or another to advance their own causes and institutionalize their organizations (the "NGOization" of the movement).

WID discourse, as contested as it was and continues to be (Mohanty 1991), allowed sectors of poor women to articulate their identities in ways that were actually heard by political institutions. It provided the framework for integrating women into various kinds of projects, including income generation, microenterprise, rural agriculture, and education. Those who directed poor women's struggles were products of this context; they also negotiated its terms and reinvented it in their own practices and relationships. Ideas about gender and women's "gender needs," a concept that has been operationalized in many World Bank and UN projects, is now a well-known signifier among various strands of women activists throughout the country and region (Moser 1989a, 1993; Anderson 1990).

Community women's organizations came into being through these discourses and lived histories. Women began to develop their own organizations rather than work within mixed neighborhood organizations as a result of this history. Their organizations differed in many ways from mixed organizations. They became even more distinguished over time as their own collective construction of politics and history took place. In Chillogallo, some women organized educational workshops, to which they invited outside speakers to discuss topics such as women's small-business ownership, alternative gardening, gender needs, herbal medicinal remedies, and the foreign-debt crisis. The ideas for these types of workshops were often introduced by feminist NGOs influenced by WID discourse and funding. Even now, some of these groups organize their own workshops or hold weekly meetings at which they discuss community issues such as the need for paved roads, neighborhood security, local leadership, and water and plumbing, to name only a few. Most of these organizations have participated in marches, planned protests, and national mobilizations, such actions including the annual International Women's Day march in downtown Quito; protests against the government's adjustment measures; marches against political corruption; and protests against foreign banks, among them Citibank and the World Bank. Typically, the women do not work very closely with mixed neighborhood organizations, although they have done so for specific events or occasions. Today, many of the original groups continue to exist; others have been discontinued because of lack of interest, energy, or funding, and yet other, new groups have emerged.

These groups have learned from the experiences of women in land, housing, and social justice struggles in earlier decades, including in Comité del Pueblo (Mario Unda, interview, July 28, 1993; Diego Carrión, personal interview, July

26, 1993). Often by acting in their roles as family members, neighbors, caretakers, and mothers, the women have secured much of the socially and culturally defined necessities for their families and loved ones at the household and community levels. City of Quito planners and politicians have necessarily had to address these groups of women as part of their citizen- or popular-participation initiatives over the years; Quito mayors have typically considered the voluntary involvement of urban poor women as crucial to the survival of poor immigrant households, although their organizations have not always been recognized by political administrations (Rodrigo Paz, interview, August 2, 1993). During the mid- to late 1980s, a combination of factors contributed to the increased politicization of urban poor women; these factors revolve around changes in the cost of living, including decreased state subsidies for infrastructure (roads, electricity, water, gas), higher transportation fares, higher costs of school books and supplies, lower wages because of inflation, the unavailability of well-paying jobs, informalization and "flexibilization" of the labor market, higher food costs, and heavier domestic burdens for women (Lind 1997).[1]

In central and southern Quito, where approximately twenty organizations existed during this period,[2] I interviewed fifty-five members of eight organizations to find out about their backgrounds and reasons for participating during the 1989–93 period.[3] Organizations varied in size, from eight members to eighty-one, partly reflecting the size of each district and the stage of each group's organizational development.[4] Participants came from a wide variety of backgrounds: from northern provinces on the Ecuador-Colombia border, from southern provinces, the coast and sierra, from former ranches and from dilapidated neighbor-

1. *Flexibilization (flexibilización)*, a term used widely in some Latin American countries, refers to the fragmented nature of global production processes, in which workers increasingly are hired as temporary or part-time employees, on a piecework basis, or in small workshops where labor conditions are less than optimal and pay is lower than in more formalized business or factory settings. Labor flexibilization has increased in Ecuador particularly in sectors where employees are working indirectly for large regional or foreign corporations (e.g., Brazilian, Argentine, U.S., and Japanese industries). For further information, see Lawson 1991; Gill 2000. On the broader process of global industrial restructuring, see Piore and Sabel 1984; Scott and Storper 1986; Peet 1987).

2. This figure and the data that follow are based on two studies I conducted in 1990 and 1992–93 on community women's organizations in central and south Quito (Lind 1990, 1992, and 1995). One study shows that fifty community women's organizations existed throughout the Quito metropolitan area during this period (Centro María Quilla 1991).

3. The eight organizations had a total membership of 214 members. Centro Femenino "8 de Marzo" had 81 members.

4. Centro Femenino "8 de Marzo" was the largest. It was also the oldest and most established organization.

hoods in Quito's *centro historico*.[5] They ranged in age from fifteen to more than sixty years old, although the most active participants typically were in their thirties or forties. Most women were married, two were divorced or separated, and nine were single mothers. Some had finished high school, others only the fourth grade; some speak Quichua as their first language, most speak Spanish. The majority identified as Catholic, and a small group identified as Christian, Mormon, or Jehovah's Witness. Average income was S/144,000, or U.S.$80, a month. Each household spent an average of S/125,480, or almost U.S.$70, a month on "household purchases," which included food, household maintenance items, clothing, and school materials.[6] Some reported that their monthly household expenditures were higher than their monthly incomes; this could be the result of a few factors. First, some women did not know what their husbands' incomes were. Second, their responses are estimates, not precise amounts. And third, they simply may not have made enough income to cover their household expenses. A few women lived in extreme poverty, with virtually no monthly income; the highest-earning household made approximately S/250,000, or U.S.$139, a month. Nine of the single women were mothers; all of them spoke about the difficulties of simultaneously raising children and earning an income to support them. All the single mothers worked in the informal sector, either as street vendors or domestic servants, usually six or six and a half days a week. Often, their oldest daughter (who, in one family, was as young as nine years old), took care of her younger siblings. Some mothers who were street vendors brought their youngest children with them to work. Some expressed relative contentment or perhaps resolution about their life situations, despite the fact that they had little money; others, often the women in their twenties, described feeling hopeless and dreamed about "making it" in college or finding a way to get to the United States. In this regard, their age and generation greatly shaped their perspectives on their current life situation and their ambitions, hopes, or cynicism.

5. In recent decades, many families have left Ecuador's northern border provinces to escape violence induced by the military, paramilitary groups, guerrilla movements, and crime related to the drug trade in Colombia. Most of the families have migrated to Quito and surrounding provinces.

6. At the time of the study, the sucre was valued at S/1,800 to one U.S. dollar. The average for monthly purchases is based on a weekly average of S/31,370. I multiplied it by four to arrive at an estimated monthly average, although during most months this average would be higher. My estimate, then, is low. "Household purchases" is defined as "household expenses, including food, clothing, and school supplies" (gastos para la casa, incluyendo comida, ropa y útiles escolares). However, many responded only in terms of what they spend on food. Again, this indicates that my estimate is low.

The largest group, Centro Femenino "8 de Marzo," named after International Women's Day, had acquired a building on the district's central plaza. It was donated by the municipality of Chillogallo with the support of the municipality of Quito.[7] Approximately twenty-five members were actively involved with remodeling the house and preparing it for meetings and social events. This donation, along with a small grant from a Spanish foundation and external support from NGOs and feminists, including one feminist who helped organize women at an earlier stage in the early-mid 1980s, significantly helped the group establish itself and strengthen its identity.[8]

While the experiences of members of the Centro Femenino "8 de Marzo" cannot be summarily described, as the women come from a wide variety of backgrounds, they do share some experiences that make their sense of daily life and globalization a shared identity, a concept Amrita Basu (1995) describes as characterizing many Third World women's movements. This shared identity is something they have created internally through their organizing and open discussions about their personal experiences, in relation to others whom they view as somehow different from themselves.

One aspect of their shared identity concerns their socioeconomic location in Chillogallo and, more broadly speaking, in the Quito metropolitan area. When approaching Chillogallo from the north, one sees rich, green agricultural fields that look like a patchwork quilt spread across the foot of the Pichincha mountain. Because of the location, it is relatively easy for a family to rely on subsistence agriculture while also living within city limits. Once a village during Spanish colonial rule, Chillogallo became incorporated as a city neighborhood in 1972. There is an intact central plaza and a local market. Traditionally, the small municipality has been led by members of locally prominent ranch families dating back decades and even centuries (B., member of Chillogallo women's organization, interview, Quito, July, 2, 1989). Chillogallo is not a wealthy neighborhood by any standard, although neither is it the poorest of the poor. Families that have lived in the area for more than a century coexist with recently arrived migrants from rural provinces or Quito's historical *centro*.

In contrast, in northern Quito, where most international organizations and private businesses have their offices, skyscrapers line the horizon. Many wealthy

---

7. Although Chillogallo has its own municipality, it also falls within the domain of the larger municipality of Quito; hence both municipalities were involved with this donation. By this time, Centro Femenino "8 de Marzo" already had acquired its legal status (*personería jurídica*).

8. This feminist activist, Silvia Vega, lived in Chillogallo for several years and inspired women to create the group. I discuss this further in the later section on Ecuadorian feminisms.

neighborhoods are located in this area. Quito's guardian angel, a monument of the Virgin Mary that one can see from almost any point in the city, marks Quito's historical center, composed of colonial buildings and narrow streets. Locals call this monument the "panecillo" because Mary rests on a small, round base that looks like a dinner roll. She faces the north and her back is turned toward the south—oddly reflecting Quito's built environment, in which developers have made large investments in the north and much less so in the south. When standing at the foot of the *panecillo*, one has a view of nearly the entire length of the city. The north's landscape is decorated with high-rise buildings, many new ones having been built in the past ten years, including the new "World Trade Center" on Avenida 12 de Octubre. The World Trade Center, whose name is spelled and pronounced in English, was clearly built to symbolize the growth of Ecuador's market economy. The north of Quito continues to grow (upward) at an amazing pace. Just in the past five years several hotels and large buildings have been constructed. Some remain half empty, a testament to the fact that Ecuador's economy is not doing as well as the image of world trade might suggest.

The south is a horizontal, rather than a vertical, landscape. A handful of four-story buildings are scattered close to the *centro*, although farther south most neighborhoods are composed of one- or two-story dwellings, reflecting the informal planning and building traditions of poorer communities (Sandercock 1998). The Panamerican Highway weaves together the three general sectors of the city, bringing urban life to the southernmost districts, which were once rural villages or agricultural land and offered country picnic getaways for Quito's rich. Members of the women's organization share this sense of urban space and history, in which they are at once part of the metropolitan area yet very removed from the center of urban activity and political power (despite their location in the nation's capital city). Their identification with urban space is based on their gendered, classed, and racialized locations in Quito and the nation. Their community's categorization as a city neighborhood was (literally and figuratively) mapped onto the old colonial organization of society, with its corresponding taxonomy of gender, race, and class difference (Moallem and Boal 1999).

One aspect of daily life they all share concerns the roles and responsibilities they have in their households and, related to this, their self-perceptions as mothers. Several expressed feeling tired and worn out or feeling frustrated with their maternal/family roles and angry about the economic situation; these feelings were something that most of them identified with and shared as a group. In one interview, a woman told me about her daily life:

I get up at around 4:30 A.M. I go to the local market to buy some eggs and possibly some meat. I return to prepare breakfast and wake the children. I help dress the children and prepare them for school. I bring the children to the bus stop. I return home to clean the house. I iron the clothing for my family and for other families (I get paid to do that). I clean the yard. I prepare lunch. I go to the local cooperative store in the afternoon. I prepare dinner. On Friday afternoons I attend the women's organization meeting (Alejandra, interview, Quito, July 2, 1989).

This description captures only a portion of her day, as I later found out. She also works on some afternoons, selling shoes in a public kiosk on a busy street in the *centro*, and she exchanges services with her neighbors or family or organization members. The majority of the women in Chillogallo whom I interviewed (thirty-three out of fifty-five) depend on some type of exchange such as ironing, washing, or tailoring clothes. Another common activity was taking turns going to the market, buying food in bulk and distributing it among organization members. Their organization had developed a program to distribute food in bulk among the members' families; other neighbors became interested in participating as well. They all spoke of having less time and more household responsibilities, a situation that researchers have reported on in several countries undergoing adjustment measures (Dwyer and Bruce 1988; Benería and Feldman 1992; Menjívar 2002). They devoted more time to household chores, their daily routines had become longer; they worked longer days as a result of not being able to pay for outside resources such as transportation, hiring someone to iron clothes, and affordable groceries (Lind 1990).

In relation to this, Centro Femenino "8 de Marzo" members perceived changes in their gender identities and roles in the context of the economic crisis. At one general meeting of the organization, a member mentioned that "she doesn't feel like a good mother." Another member disagrees, saying that "it's difficult to get everything done." Another states that she "gets up at 4:00 A.M. and stops working at 9:00 P.M." (María, member of Chillogallo women's organization, interview, Quito, February 16, 1993). A common theme that emerges is that they can no longer provide for their families as they could before. In a sense, their elevated status as "mothers"—a status ascribed to them through religious, cultural, and political discourses of motherhood and family, sometimes described as "marianismo"—was being challenged; the power they perceived to have in the private, reproductive sphere was under scrutiny and they felt marginalized from the public sphere of politics and decision making.[9] In this sense, recalling mothers' movements in other countries (Jetter, Orleck, and Taylor 1997; Power 2002), in Ecuador motherhood became an important mobilizing metaphor for women throughout the country, as it did for the politicians and leaders who defended the purpose behind economic restructuring and the need for families to "sacrifice" for the nation under distress. As before in Ecuadorian history, gender continued to be central to discourses of national identity and state modernization. Now, partly as a result of development discourse, it had become central to discourses of poverty and survival as well. Neoliberal discourse brought with it an emphasis on poor women as clients of and volunteers for the free market.

Because motherhood was linked to family survival, national development, and women's societal status in neoliberal discourse, Centro Femenino "8 de Marzo" members made use of their maternal roles to struggle for access to resources, raising a challenge to development policies. In this regard, it was not out of sheer economic necessity that women organized in their so-called reproductive roles; rather, a combination of cultural, political, and discursive factors played into their motivations for participating. They questioned their "supposedly natural maternal traits" (Bayard de Volo 2001, 239) as they were shaped by their social environments. They addressed the double bind they faced as women: on the one hand, they were socialized to perform traditional gender roles in the division of labor within their households, including serving as the

9. According to some scholars, *marianismo* is the female corollary to *machismo* and is a cultural and religious concept "where the ideal of womanhood is self-abnegating motherhood . . . [t]his is very much reinforced by the iconography of the Virgin Mary that is central to Catholicism" (Craske 1999, 12). The virgin mother is "an impossible role model to follow," as Nikki Craske points out, yet *marianismo*, with its emphasis on motherhood, has significantly shaped women's involvement in Latin American politics (12). See also Elsa Chaney's (1979) earlier work on Latin American female politicians who act as "supermadres" and Margaret Power's (2002) more recent research on *marianismo* in relation to right-wing women's politics in Chile during the 1960s and 1970s.

Marysa Navarro argues that *marianismo* is a "seriously flawed" concept based on "an extrapolation [of] impressionistic data that has been mistakenly used to account for the gender arrangements of an entire continent" (2002, 257). Her critique challenges Eurocentric academic frameworks of women's political participation in Latin America on the basis that they essentialize "Latin American women" as a homogenous group of women born into a culturally given dichotomous context of *marianismo* and machismo. In this book I examine *marianismo* as a type of religious/cultural/political discourse about womanhood and gender that is politically negotiated by women through their activism and their performance of identity. Thus while I agree that the dualistic framework of *marianismo*/machismo has been applied uncritically, through a "Western lens" (or a northern lens, as the case may be [Mohanty 1991]), in studies of women's political participation in Latin America, *marianismo* as a discourse that holds specific types of gendered (and other) meanings in women's and men's daily lives and in academic studies, and that is politically negotiated, deserves further academic attention.

primary caretakers of their children. They faced discrimination in society as a result of their location within structures of gender, race, and class. Yet they also acknowledged that they had a certain status, as women, in their homes and communities, by virtue of being mothers. One way this was made clear was through comments made by women who could not have children and who felt marginalized in the community as a result of this. With motherhood came certain benefits and forms of respect. This elevated status is the flip side of gender discrimination; the two occur hand in hand, an important aspect of constructions of femininity (and masculinity) in cultural contexts in which motherhood and normative heterosexuality are glorified (Jetter, Orleck, and Taylor 1997; Kaplan, Alarcón, and Moallem 1999; Lind and Share 2003).

Thus, on the other hand, when the economic crisis began to affect women's domestic labor, it called into question the only type of status Chillogallo women felt they had in their community. As a result, they were propelled into action unlike before, since the restructuring process had, in a sense, called into question the entire meaning system of their household gender relations and identities. It was unclear not only how they would survive economically, but also how resources would be distributed and managed within their families and how they would present themselves to the world. In this regard, their reasons for collectively organizing emerged from a combination of factors (for example, changes in household structure, economy, management, and changes in identity perception) and included the struggle to conserve certain aspects of their gender identities and roles (that is, their maternal status), even when they were challenging the broader gendered system within which their self-perceived forms of motherhood have been historically produced, interpreted, and negotiated. Their self-empowerment emerged through a reessentializing of their identities (Corr 2003; Whitten 2003), rather than strictly by their being put into question or challenged. Their presence as a group and as part of a broader social movement may have contributed to transforming gender relations but only in this contradictory way. Many external factors, as well, contributed to their understanding of their gender roles and identities, including their interactions with feminist professionals and NGO activists.

Gender Identity Politics and Feminism

The reessentialization of identity is central to feminism, despite the fact that feminist scholars have long challenged hierarchical forms of essentialism (Butler

1990; Butler and Scott 1992; Moallem 1999). *Feminism* has multiple meanings in the context of community women's organizing. How it is interpreted within small, grassroots women's groups that have little access to political and economic power and relatively little training in Western philosophy and history depends on the group members' own learning processes and the terrain within which they relate to and negotiate with actors and institutions outside their own neighborhoods. Their own forms of identification with feminism depend more on these relationships than on their individual "readings" of feminist thought or activism. Within the same organization, some women identify as "feminist" while others do not. Just as Alejandra calls herself a feminist, other members, such as Nina, a hairdresser who organized women in adjacent neighborhoods, says, "No, I'm not a feminist . . . I don't like politics" (Alejandra, interview; Nina, interview). After working with these organizations for several years, I cannot easily camp them into categories of "feminist" versus "nonfeminist," although I can provide a discussion of how they have developed as a strand of the broader terrain of women's activism in the country.

Ecuadorian feminisms have played an enormous role in supporting community struggles and in providing an ideological and discursive framework for understanding the identities and strategies of poor sectors of women. Clearly, power relations are involved in this process of community organizing and education, a subject that many scholars of Latin American women's movements have addressed over the years (Radcliffe and Westwood 1993; Jaquette 1994; León de Leal 1995; Stephen 1997). Importantly, and this has been much less acknowledged in the literature, the act of an individual or group adopting a political ideology directed or promoted by an outside group does not automatically imply an unhealthy power imbalance; rather the nature of power in this context depends upon how social relations are constructed and negotiated. Some members of Centro Femenino "8 de Marzo" employed feminist ideas about gender to organize other groups themselves. In the early 1990s, members organized three groups in surrounding neighborhoods. While the new organizations never grew in size and number, as the Chillogallo organization did, they provided significant support for women from poorer, less developed districts. It was a period of growth for community organizing during a time of ongoing economic restructuring in this area. Women drew from various political and cultural traditions to create their organizational strategies, making use of their connections with feminists as well as with local churches, participants in labor struggles, male community leaders, municipal officials, and NGO activists.

Part of the organization's success was attributable to the fact that it was aided by a middle-class feminist. This activist, who had a background in leftist party politics and feminism, played a pivotal role in teaching members how to mobilize themselves and others. During this period in Quito, many community women's organizations had relationships with middle-class feminist groups. The feminist NGOs CEPAM, Women's Communication Workshop (Taller de Comunicación Mujer), and the Center for Planning and Social Studies (Centro de Planificación y Estudios Sociales [CEPLAES]) all had established ties or conducted research projects on community women's organizations in central and south Quito. Typically, such relationships were hierarchical, between the middle-class group and the community group, rather than horizontal, among community groups themselves, although feminists originally organized in poor districts out of solidarity rather than paternalism. There have, however, been some attempts to organize at the horizontal level, although often with the assistance of NGOs: in the early 1990s the first national conference of popular (that is, community-based, working-class, peasant) women's organizations was held, and several other meetings and conferences have taken place over the years to bring together rural and urban women from poor and working-class backgrounds. In this regard, community-based activists envision their goals and strategize within this web of social relations; their struggle is best described as emerging out of their immediate situations and perceived sets of problems, yet guided and to some degree framed by the interventions of external activists, professionals, and funders.

Many members recognized very soon that they had to meet with municipal officials, male community leaders, local churches, political parties, NGOs, and state agencies to obtain their legal status, seek support and funding, request donations, implement their projects, and so on. In many ways, it is through their political skill-building and the interventions of these other institutions that they constructed their strategies and political identities. In this regard, community women's organizations have always had to interact with and negotiate the terms of other social movements and institutions in addition to addressing their own.

Through their interactions with city officials, NGOs, and development organizations, local community women's organizations were linked in new ways to international funding and development strategies, in part through their relationships with feminist NGOs and their new status as recipients of feminist-inspired development projects. What began as poor women's grassroots survival strategies were recognized by many feminists as important political acts, as contributions to the economy and society, as a form of resistance, and as a new kind of "feminism" (Molyneux 1998). Other feminists were cautiously optimistic, noting that many poor women organize out of desperation rather than out of a desire to transform gender relations or other forms of power (Barrig 1996). Silvia Vega, the middle-class feminist activist who worked with Centro Femenino "8 de Marzo," for example, used tactics from her experience in leftist party politics to organize women (Lind 1992). She was a new mother and adopted a notion of feminism that was based on women's traditional gender roles; she also advocated women's entry into formal politics and envisioned the transformation of gender relations in her broader vision of social change. Having been a political candidate herself for the Socialist Party of Ecuador (Partido Socialista del Ecuador [PSE]), she encouraged Chillogallo members to participate actively in politics and public decision making.

Many members did, in fact, attend and participate in meetings and events, including campaign events, research and policy presentations, public speeches, and meetings at the municipality of Quito. Although they presented themselves as mothers, they became actively involved and recognized as citizens in the public-planning process. While this form of citizen participation is not necessarily or automatically integrated into state and municipal planning agendas, it has brought them certain municipal services such as the establishment of a police station in Chillogallo. Politically and symbolically, they gained entry into a sphere that had not previously recognized them and helped transfer a set of principles based on their roles as mothers into that sphere. At the very least, they are engendering the citizen participation process and related notions of citizenship. This aspect of their organizing is proactive; it transforms and puts into question the public/private boundaries of politics, rather than merely reinforcing them, despite their reliance on traditional gender roles. Their "demands for material needs are . . . intricately wrapped up in issues of identity" (Bayard de Volo 2001, 8). As Caroline Moser (1989a) and other scholars have pointed out, women's forms of community activism may be related to their reproductive roles, although they are by no means essentially linked to them. Their strategic essentialism necessarily involves a critique of their roles and identities from the start. This may not be the basis for a revolutionary transformation in gender relations, but it has provided them, and many women activists, with a basis to challenge global forms of power and domination, masculine nationalist ideologies, and political corruption. It is one form of negotiation with broader constructs of femininity as they are shaped by and inherent in globalization and nationalism.

Many members without prior organizing experience claimed in their interviews that they were "not political." This feeds into the misconception, held sometimes by them as much as by outsiders, that they are not contributing to movements for social justice or to feminism itself. One woman explained that "our organization is not political . . . we come here to talk about social issues that we women face" (María, interview, Quito, April 2, 1993). Similar to what occurred within other mothers' movements in which women make the claim that they "are mothers, not politicians" (Bayard de Volo 2001, 16; also see Navarro 1989; Taylor 1997; Power 2002), Chillogallo members distanced themselves from what they perceived as a masculine political domain. Their refusal to identify as "political" indicates their distrust of and alienation from the formal political process and attests to their feeling that they do not belong to that sphere, nor perhaps do they necessarily want to be there. They identified their struggles in terms of their maternal roles, rather than in terms of politics. They felt empowered by this, by this claim of "moral superiority" to male politicians and formal politics, an experience documented in other mothers' movements (see, e.g., Bayard de Volo 2001). They also remained marginalized in national politics and in elite feminist-issue networks as a result of this. They were clients of middle-class organizations and the state, rather than players in the negotiations. They did not view this elite realm as theirs. Their notion of power itself, including how they challenge it and reinforce it, is somewhat contradictory but largely based on their class and racialized experiences and locations.

Their perception of power was something they negotiated, rather than viewed as unidimensional or objectively derived. The external environment, including the broader terrain of discourse and representation, contributed to their conception of power and their perceived political successes or failures. Feminists, in particular, have influenced their gendered conception of power; several other actors and a number of institutions and discourses have mediated their internal process of identifying their identities, roles, notions of power, and relative form of empowerment or disempowerment. In this respect, gender identity politics in community women's organizations are best understood in the context of struggles over material and interpretive power, in which women activists produce and interpret their identities internally, in the process of organizing and through their negotiations with external actors. As Lorraine Bayard de Volo (2001) notes in her research on mothers movements in Nicaragua, "Gendered discourse, like all discourse, contains gaps and contradictions that present conflict and opportunities for change. Movements and individuals alike contradict themselves and manipulate their self-representations" (16). Indeed, there is much at stake in the outcome of women's community-based struggles for survival, not merely for the members themselves but also for development institutions and

NGO activists who themselves struggle for power in the context of global economic restructuring and national politics. In relation to this, it is unclear if their
increased political visibility is helping them economically; nor is it clear whether
their disadvantaged locations in the public and private spheres are being addressed. Their performance of motherhood may help them negotiate issues related to community development and poverty, but it also plays into state and
international development policy frameworks that assume their maternal volun-
teerism.

The Paradoxes of Struggle and Survival

The paradoxes of women's survival and struggle occur within the culturally constructed boundaries of the "public" and "private," sometimes challenging or
transgressing these boundaries, other times reinforcing them. They operate on
various levels, including institutional, policy, cultural, political, economic, and
identity production. These paradoxes involve an engagement with ideas and
concepts about gender, survival, and political identity that occur within and
across national borders, in various imagined communities (Anderson 1983) and
publics (Fraser 1997), among these community, national, and feminist publics.

On one side of the paradoxes, organized women have gained political visibility since their inception in the early 1980s. Many observers have vested great
hope in the transformative potential of these women's organizing efforts, as
Sonia Alvarez alludes to in this chapter's opening quote. In Ecuador, many
have worked in solidarity with and/or helped strengthen community women's
organizations, through leadership and training, funding, and political support.
In this regard, political parties, feminists and women's NGOs, international development and philanthropic institutions, state agencies, and other entities of
social movements such as the labor and indigenous movement have played important roles in shaping and supporting women's community activism, at specific moments in time. Feminist scholars have heralded poor sectors of women
for organizing themselves in the midst of great adversity; in addition, international and state development policies have recognized women's contributions
to community development and social welfare distribution.

Indeed, many women have benefited personally from their participation in
community organizations. They have learned new skills, such as organic gardening, arts and crafts, conflict resolution, local planning, and how to establish a
small business. A few of them have received small salaries for their roles as

organizers and leaders; while insignificant for sustaining their households, they are a form of income nonetheless. Some speak more comfortably about family issues that they had previously viewed as private and or shameful. Some felt empowered about speaking out loud, in front of a group; others felt empowered by sharing with other women a personal experience or past form of victimization (incest, sexual abuse by a local priest, domestic violence from a partner or in-law). These are forms of empowerment that cannot be taken away from them; nor can their new understandings of their gender roles and political and economic participation be removed.

Similarly, as a group, the organization has gained political power and visibility through members' participation in protests, marches, and collaborations with their community, NGOs, and local politicians. Now the women are part of a much broader network of women's and feminist groups in civil society. Without their personal empowerment or their new consciousness derived from their shared identity, they could not effectively protest against the government's lack of support for poor women at a local march or a mobilization against a foreign bank. Without them, they could not make links between their daily lives, their status as members of specific groups or classes, and global economic restructuring. In these ways, Ecuadorian women's community organizations significantly transform the lives of their members, in addition to influencing the nation's societal and cultural norms.

Yet despite their local success—and herein lies another paradox—their political participation plays into the client-based neoliberal model of social welfare distribution. To begin with, Chillogallo women experienced economic instability and downward mobility from the early 1980s to the late 1990s; none reported upward mobility during this period (Lind 1990). Although their organization continues (unlike several others), they have been affected by the broader reforms. Their own survival strategies have converged well with one of the goals of neoliberal economic and social development policies: to redistribute the responsibility and management of social welfare to private sectors. Although, or perhaps because, the private domain of women's work is largely invisible in neoliberal development frameworks (Elson 1995, 1998), it is these women who bear the biggest brunt of this form of restructuring. The broader restructuring of the economy also entails a restructuring of everyday life; to the extent that their political mobilization converges with neoliberal policies that expect families, and especially mothers, to absorb the crisis, their struggles for survival have been "privatized" as well (Benería 1992b).

The women's political identities reflect and give meaning to these paradoxes.

Neoliberal restructuring has exacerbated the paradox of their struggle, since women have been galvanized (or forced, as the case may be) to act because their perceived identities and roles as mothers have been threatened by economic scarcity, foreign debt, and globalization. They struggle to address material needs such as food distribution, yet they have been increasingly positioned to absorb the largely invisible transfer of welfare responsibilities, in essence, to serve as mothers of the crisis. Thus they struggle to be included while they are simultaneously excluded; they have gained much political visibility, yet primarily in their roles as mothers of the crisis, as the very women who have helped many families endure the economic hardship. However, while as individuals and as members of a group, many of them are critical of the gender division of labor in society, and of gender biases in neoliberal development policies, as participants in a movement they face political uncertainty as they address further adjustment measures and the broader, neoliberal-inspired reinforcement of their traditional gender roles. Thus simply increasing their roles in the development process or in the market does not necessarily translate into their "empowerment." It is true, though, that women's participation at the community level can conceivably have a stronger impact on democratization processes and citizen practices, particularly those associated with Ecuador's decentralization process (Arboleda 1994), since the local level is potentially "more permeable" and "more vulnerable to citizen scrutiny and intervention" (Alvarez 1996, 141). Women's struggles for survival, then, are best viewed as paradoxical and as economic- or material-based, as well as cultural-political, struggles over the meanings ascribed to their identities, citizen status, and "roles in development."

Conclusion

By 1990, groups such as Centro Femenino "8 de Marzo" had caught the attention of global feminists. The politicization of groups of urban poor women such as this one contributed to high levels of debate, policy redefinition, and action surrounding "women's roles in development." Likewise, Chillogallo women's relationships with feminists and development professionals, along with global and regional feminist discourses, shaped group members' own political identities and strategies. It was also clear by 1990 that their struggle was becoming institutionalized and depoliticized by development planners. The 1997 political crisis in Ecuador created a new set of political and economic circumstances that led Chillogallo women to continue their protests against the state and foreign

banks and institutions. While community-based women's organizations negotiated the terms of neoliberal social and economic policies in the local sphere,
other groups of (primarily middle-class) women negotiated and helped implement these very policies at the state level, in NGOs, and internationally. Whereas
elite feminist issue networks became stronger during this period (a topic I address in Chapter 5), poorer women's groups remained relatively marginalized,
despite their increased participation in national networks. In many ways, the
1997 political crisis revealed, through the organizing of four professional strands
of the Ecuadorian feminist movement, how this struggle continued. Because of
these structural issues and paradoxes, it is difficult to say with certainty that
women's community mobilization entirely benefits them or is a disservice. How
they express their gender identities and perform specific constructions of femininity converge with the broader processes at play in the political terrain. Institutions such as the state and NGOs have a stake in directing their struggles and
their constructed political identities, although their individual identifications
with society also guide their own feelings about their identities. Clearly, their
activism has been noticed in national and international political arenas, in addition to in their own communities. The question remains, however, of to what
extent their local struggles have contributed to broader social change and to
changes in their own lives.

[5]

Remaking the Nation:
Feminist Politics, Populist Nationalism,
and the 1998 Constitutional Reforms

The 1997 political crisis reveals some of the gendered contradictions of neoliberal development, particularly as they play out in the context of nationalist politics. In August 1996, President Abdalá Bucaram entered office on a populist platform. Bucaram had secured support for his election by promising to implement less severe economic policies and alleviate poverty, by identifying with the masses through, among other things, his musical talent (he produced his own CD while in office and performed publicly), and by handing out money to impoverished supporters as he toured the country. He appointed family members or people with close family ties to key political positions and was therefore criticized for nepotism,[1] yet he also appointed the first female vice president, Rosalía Arteaga, and the first self-defined feminist labor minister, Guadalupe León. Once in office, Bucaram utilized a range of populist strategies to maintain his political support, some of which were laden with gendered contradictions. One controversial and well-documented event was Bucaram's formal support of Ecuadorian-born Lorena Bobbitt, a woman widely addressed in the media as a domestic-violence victim arrested for having severed the penis of her husband, John Wayne Bobbitt.[2] Following her publicized trial in the United States, Bucaram invited Bobbitt to the Ecuadorian National Congress and honored her as a national hero for having "cut off neocolonial relations." During the same

1. President Bucaram appointed his brother Adolfo as social welfare minister. Another brother, Santiago, held a seat in Congress. His brother-in-law, Pablo Concha, was finance minister. And his sister, Elsa, a well-known populist and former mayor of Guayaquil, continued to play an informal yet strong role in political decision-making during this period.

2. Bobbitt was tried and acquitted for her crime in 1993. Her acquittal was based on her testimony that she acted in self-defense. In Ecuador, President Bucaram, along with several sectors of society, men and women alike, supported her on the basis that she was a victim of her (white male) husband and a victim of the U.S. welfare system. Thus in Ecuador she was construed as embodying the underdeveloped nation vis-à-vis the imperialist United States. The fact that her husband was named John Wayne, like the Hollywood actor who portrayed cowboys in the U.S. West, only intensified Ecuadorians' interpretations of Lorena Bobbitt as "colonized" or victimized by white, masculine, Western power.

period, he proposed legislation that called for castration for certain convicted rapists and child molesters. Bucaram made this proposal with little if any prior consultation with feminist state policy makers and activists, despite the long history of feminist organizing and institution-building in Ecuador by that time. These populist antics, addressed by scholars such as Carlos de la Torre (2000), worsened relations between Bucaram and elements of civil society, including business and political elites, nonprofit and other private organizations, and the very sectors that had supported his candidacy in the first place: the urban and rural poor.

During this same period, Bucaram and other male appointees in his administration were charged with misogyny and, in at least one widely reported case, outright physical abuse of female state employees.[3] In addition, Bucaram did not follow through on his promise of milder adjustment measures; rather, his administration implemented a stricter set of adjustment measures than those of the previous administration of President Sixto Durán-Ballén. As a result, Bucaram lost his primary base of support—urban and rural poor sectors—and ultimately, in February 1997, he was forced to resign, following an unprecedented, spontaneous mobilization of more than two million Ecuadorians and a congressional vote to remove Bucaram for "mental incapacity."[4]

Bucaram's term in office was short-lived yet significant. His populist strategies and the political crisis that ensued during his time in office provoked a series of important national debates about redrafting the constitution and political system. These debates culminated in the drafting of the new 1998 constitution and in significant reforms in political parties and campaigns, including the introduction of a quota system for female candidates, and in several other gender-based legislative actions. What was at stake in these discussions was nothing less than the nation itself; what was accomplished through this process was nothing less than remaking the nation through a series of negotiations, disagreements, and compromises among state and civil-society actors. Significantly, the political crisis—Bucaram's unmaking of the nation—led in some ways to further democratization of civil society, at least as inscribed in law and policy, if not in practice. During the drafting of the constitution, indigenous, women's, and other social

3. This concerned Minister Alfredo Adum's derogatory statements about women and one well-publicized incident in which he allegedly slapped one of his female employees in a public space (see Vega 1997).

4. On February 6, 1997, Congress voted 44–34 to remove Bucaram after a nationwide strike in which two million people marched through the streets of cities, towns, and villages in Ecuador. Many factors led up to this national crisis. For a comprehensive discussion of the events surrounding Bucaram's ousting, see Báez et al. 1997.

movements were represented in the discussions alongside politicians and party representatives. While their perspectives were not entirely incorporated into the final documents, they nonetheless were influential. And while these groups continue to be marginalized political actors, they have developed important issue networks, and their presence can no longer be ignored.[5]

Significantly, women's organizations worked actively for institutional change within this context. Women's NGOs along with women working within the state, in rural and community-based organizations and in political parties all participated in the national strike leading up to Bucaram's removal from office. At least four strands of women's activism were influential during this period: feminists working within the state, in CONAMU; CPME, a network dedicated to engendering all state and political institutions; the FNPME; and the so-called autonomous feminists. The Permanent Specialized Committee for Women, Children, and the Family in the National Congress also worked directly in this process and coalesced with the NGO-based movement. As I illustrate in this chapter, these strands of feminist action, which together formed a feminist-issues network, serve to illustrate some of the gendered contradictions of neoliberal reform in the context of Bucaram populism and its aftermath. I demonstrate how social actors, while operating from locations as divergent as the Office of the President, CONAMU, NGOs and community-based grassroots organizations, have contributed to remaking the Ecuadorian nation through new legislation, public political discourse, and direct protest. Their strategies operate in the context of transnational discourses about gender, nation-building, and development in Ecuador. They strategically invoke essentialist notions of gender and national identity (among others) in their political interventions in the public arena in order to challenge the state and remake the nation. To the extent that their efforts converge with the neoliberal state development framework, they contribute to its institutionalization.

The Bucaram Administration, 1996–1997

President Abdalá Bucaram announced his economic policy strategy relatively late, in December 1996, four months after entering office. By this time, Ecua-

5. This was most evident in the January 2000 takeover of the Ecuadorian National Congress by the indigenous movement, in which tens of thousands of indigenous people marched to the capital city of Quito and gained entry into the National Congress, where the leader of the Confederation of Indigenous Nationalities of Ecuador, Antonio Vargas, declared it the "People's Parliament." Other protests and strikes occurred simultaneously, in Quito and throughout the country. Although a faction of the military supported the protestors, a larger faction did not, and President Jamil

dor's national foreign debt had reached more than U.S.$12 billion and the government's budget deficit reached more than U.S.$1 billion (World Bank 1999). The Bucaram administration further institutionalized neoliberal policies, at least in intent (as his power lasted little more than two months longer). While President Bucaram, along with Adolfo, his brother and the then social welfare minister, handed out money to impoverished supporters throughout the country, he simultaneously asked citizens to contribute to paying back the U.S.$12 million national debt by "sacrificing" for the nation, in part by "pulling themselves up by their own private bootstraps" (Alvarez et al. 1998a, 1). While this logic is not unique (Phillips 1998), Bucaram's proposal was seen as deceitful, since just months earlier he had promised a lighter adjustment. His proposals during this period caused the prices of electricity, fuel, and telephone service to increase by as much as 300 percent. High prices fueled protest by consumers as well as labor unions of many kinds; among the protesters were taxi drivers, street vendors, truck drivers, and elements of small and large businesses. Bucaram's populist strategies may have pushed some sectors into further isolation, but they propelled others into immediate action—a common contradictory effect of neoliberal reform on various social sectors (Benería 1992b; Lind 1997). As a result of his policies, coupled with charges of corruption and a general distrust for his government, Bucaram faced opposition by people of all social classes and geographic origins.

Bucaram's ousting was significant in many ways. To begin with, the massive protest that led to his ultimate departure from office was unprecedented in contemporary Ecuadorian history. A wide range of interests, reflecting diverse political positions and identities, were represented in the protest. Working-class, upper-class, rural, urban, political, and nonpolitical individuals alike joined the massive protest. Upper-class women were a visible sector of the demonstrators, which was significant because they are often viewed as apolitical and as the last to enter the streets to protest. As one observer explained their presence to a journalist, "[W]hen high-society ladies join demonstrations, governments fall" (Ortiz, quoted in de la Torre 2000, 101).

One result of the protest was that previously disconnected political movements began to develop networks. New identity-based social movements (such as Afro-Ecuadorian and women's movements) worked more closely with the already strong indigenous movement and more traditional labor movements in

Mahuad deployed approximately thirty thousand troops to repress the protests. In the end, the dominant faction of the military won, and on January 21, Vice President Gustavo Noboa was declared president.

demanding political and economic change. As during the redemocratization process in the late 1970s and early 1980s, political sectors were involved in a mutual appropriation of spaces; they shared resources, unlike before, and, to some extent, a common vision about the current political situation. *Neoliberalism* provided the political rubric under which seemingly diverse political movements and actors converged to address the political and economic crisis. The broad-based challenge to neoliberal reform reflected dissatisfaction with the current economic model as well as with Bucaram's populist antics and the general lack of democratic process.

Neoliberal Restructuring and Gender Politics: Four Feminist Strands

Few, if any, studies of the Bucaram protest provide in-depth analyses of political participation other than that of labor, CONAIE, and the broader indigenous movement.[6] Yet women played important political roles during this period, in the February protest itself and in the subsequent period. While there is overlap among feminists working in each of the four strands, feminists themselves have distinguished them as separate, sometimes polemical positions during the process of organizing in 1997 and following the Bucaram administration. Interestingly, they also reflect growing disagreement among feminist policy-makers and activists regarding feminist action within the neoliberal state and within the development arena. Each strand has responded to the heightened political and economic crisis by developing an explicit strategy to address state, constitutional, and economic reform.

Feminists from all four strands criticized the contradictory practices of the Bucaram administration, the political transition, and the interim government of Fabián Alarcón (April 1997–August 1998). In a statement presented in Quito on February 27, 1997, after the national mobilization, CPME listed the following reasons for their dissatisfaction with that administration: (1) the designation of an unqualified director of DINAMU; (2) the intent to modify laws on presidential succession (so that Vice President Arteaga would not become president); (3) President Bucaram's appropriation of legal-reform proposals submitted by feminist organizations, including CPME; (4) the invitation of Lorena Bobbitt to appear before the National Congress, and Bucaram's decoration of Bobbitt as a national hero; (5) subsequent reform of rape legislation, in which Bucaram pro-

6. See, for example, Báez et al. 1997 and Muñoz Jaramillo 1998. Important exceptions include articles by Rocío Rosero (1997) and María Arboleda (1998).

posed chemical castration for rapists (again, without consulting feminist lawyers and policy makers on their proposals for violence-against-women legislation); (6) Minister Alfredo Adum's declaration that he wanted to be a "caveman and eat women alive" (hombre de cromagñón para comerse vivas a las mujeres) and his aggressive behavior toward women at state-owned Petroecuador, which included slapping a well-known female political figure in a public meeting (Vega 1997).

Most, if not all, feminist professionals and local women's organizations protested Bucaram's simultaneous rejection and appropriation of feminist interests. By appointing the feminist Guadalupe León as labor minister, Bucaram attempted to gain feminist support (similar to his attempt to gain support from other social movements), yet he did so to achieve his own nationalist agenda. León's appointment, which lasted until her resignation in late 1996, led to some of the conflicts between the three strands of feminist action. While León's appointment was significant, as she was the first openly feminist minister in Ecuador's history, some feminists viewed her acceptance of the position as her selling out to Bucaram populism.

Following Bucaram's ousting, as national committees were formed to redraft the constitution, there was increasing national debate about the role of social movements in formal party politics. In this context, feminists addressed corruption and misogyny within the Bucaram administration as a way to advance their own goals of engendering and democratizing political participation, formal democracy, and national development. In this way, gender served to galvanize feminists, along with other social sectors, to act and to frame their own struggles against the neoliberal state. Many of them have chosen to challenge the state from within it; others, from outside it. And, as in other countries undergoing neoliberal reform, while they claim to be against neoliberalism, their discourse does not always coincide with their practice and vice versa.[7] In particular, feminists who struggle from within the state may be critical of neoliberal reform yet

7. Here I am not implying that discourse and practice are entirely separate processes. Rather, I am arguing that an organization's or movement's "discourse" (the realm of language and representations within which an organization is defined by its members; the organization's self-representation vis-à-vis the broader society, including its vision of political and economic strategies) can be quite different from its "practice" (the deployment of political and economic strategies). In this sense, discourse and practice are interconnected and overlapping, yet they can also be distinct and contradictory. Furthermore, how members of an organization publicly define the group itself and how they interpret a context or event (e.g., "neoliberal development," "political crisis," and so on) are more often than not different from how they actually intervene in those contexts and develop strategies.

contribute to the overall project of neoliberal state formation. In this sense, they are working simultaneously within and against the state. Yet the question that continues to divide many people is, To what extent can feminists work creatively and critically from within the neoliberal state?

Within/Against the State: CONAMU

CONAMU is one example of feminists working within/against/for the neoliberal state. In many ways, CONAMU's history is similar to that of other state women's agencies in Latin America (Placencia and Caro, 1998; Alvarez, 1998b; Valenzuela, 1998). Historically, some CONAMU directors have been self-defined feminist leaders from the NGO sector, but most have been from traditional, nonfeminist political sectors. Since this state agency became active in 1980, a series of proposals have been put forth by feminist consultants on its behalf to the government-appointed team responsible for designing Ecuador's national development plans. Throughout the 1980s, these proposals largely reflected the liberal WID approach to "integrating women into development (Rathgeber 1990; Placencia and Caro 1998). The impetus for CONAMU came primarily from international sources, such as the United Nations and solidarity organizations, as well as from local women's organizations. Although the agency was responding to its constituents, namely the women's movement, it was also subject to funding rules and other forms of discipline that were set by international donors, including European governments, UN agencies (especially UNIFEM and UNICEF), and foundations. The state, in turn, accepted feminist demands partly because they knew they could receive additional funding for projects with a gender component and partly as a political concession to female voters.

It is interesting to note than at an institutional level, since the state women's agency acquired a new status within the state when it moved from the Ministry of Social Welfare to the Office of the President (hence its name change from DINAMU to CONAMU), it has gained rather than lost institutional power in the neoliberal context. This is similar to trends in other Latin American countries, where state women's agencies have gained institutional status despite the general move toward privatizing state-led social welfare programs (Barrig 1998; Alvarez 1998a). In the 1998–2000 period, CONAMU employed approximately thirty-four employees (Rocío Rosero, interview, Quito, April 21, 1998). The primary objective of CONAMU is "to serve as the interlocutor of gender and development projects on a national level" (Martha Ordoñez, interview, Quito, April 25, 1998). Its main tasks are to design policy frameworks and to delegate project management and implementation to local women's organizations, local municipalities, and others who bid on projects. Funding for projects is received from the IADB, UNICEF, UNIFEM, and other international organizations and is complemented by a minimal amount of state funding. The primary emphasis is on project design, rather than service delivery. As with other entities engaged in hegemonic state practices, its role as interlocutor of gender and development policy serves to normalize a certain set of ideas about women's roles in development, while rendering others invisible or less important. Some groups of women are marked as needing aid; others are not. Some activities are considered useful or productive; others are not. This reflects the more general desire implicit in the development field to name the problem or target group: through this process of naming, some groups become visible while others remain hidden (Escobar 1995). As Judith Butler has stated, "It is important to remember that subjects are constituted through exclusions, that is, through the creation of a domain of deauthorized subjects, presubjects, figures of abjection, populations erased from view" (Butler, quoted in de la Torre 2000, 87). Development plans tend to "silence and exclude large portions of the population," as Carlos de la Torre points out (2000, 87).

While CONAMU has power in defining who gets funding and why, it is also restricted by the conditions of development funders. It designs gender and development state policies and therefore contributes to defining the discursive and institutional boundaries within which knowledge is produced about WID, yet it must frame its agenda within a context that is acceptable to international funding institutions. In this sense, CONAMU itself must operate within the discursive and institutional boundaries of development.

Engendering the State: CPME

CPME was established in 1996 to address state reform and, most directly, to address the growing political crisis surrounding the Bucaram administration. CPME is composed of feminists from the NGO sector, political parties, and the popular women's movement, most with experience in the state or private sector or both; some of the women with such experience have participated in feminist organizations. A primary goal of CPME is to engender the state and political system. At the state level, this involves engendering all state ministries—in terms of personnel, policy frameworks, and project implementation. While CONAMU has worked to add a chapter on gender and development to each government's National Development Plan, CPME argues that this is not enough; rather, every section of each plan should contain a gender dimension, rather than there being only one section in which gender issues are discussed exclusively. From CPME's perspective, CONAMU's efforts thus far have remained largely ghettoized within the larger state; CPME seeks to overcome this ghettoization by making gender an important aspect of the entire state.

To achieve this goal, CPME has set up vertical relations among CPME-appointed expert committees and ministries, with the aim of providing expertise on gender issues to policy makers within each ministry. For example, the CPME committee on women and housing has set up a relation with the Ministry of Housing, with the hope of adding a gender component to all housing policy produced in the ministry. Likewise, committees have been set up with the Ministries of Social Welfare, Labor, Finance, and Education, as well as with other state agencies such as CONADE.

To engender the political system, two goals of CPME have been (1) to establish a female quota system in the political process, and (2) to acquire political party status for the women's movement. First, CPME spearheaded the initiative to pass legislation mandating a minimal quota of female political candidates in national, provincial, and municipal campaigns, in which initially 20 percent of all political candidates be required to be female, with the expectation that this figure would be raised incrementally to 50 percent (Vega 1998). CPME spent years on this issue and was joined by FNPME and some CONAMU employees, leading to the passage of this legislation in 2000 (Herrera 2000). To the extent that the quota system introduces more female candidates to the party system, the "formal" political arena has become engendered; this is so despite the fact that this system does not necessarily ensure feminist candidates (that is, female candidates with a "feminist" consciousness) nor does it necessarily translate into any form of public, educational awareness about gender discrimination or difference. What it does signify, though, is the growing presence of feminist *demands* in the public, political sphere, a sphere characterized by masculine interpretations of political power and citizen demands.

Second, CPME fought for party status for the women's movement, largely following the political strategy of Ecuador's indigenous movement. In the 1990s, social movement leaders fought for certain privileges previously held only by political parties, including the right to launch their own political candidates. Legislation based on this approach was passed in 2000 and allows social movements that meet a particular set of legal requirements to have a certain amount of candidates for each election for local, provincial, and national seats in the Congress and Senate (Viviendo la Democracia 2002). The largely CONAIE-led indigenous movement formed the Movement of Plurinational Unity: Pachakutik New Country (Movimiento de Unidad Plurinacional Pachakutik Nuevo País [MUPP-NP]), commonly referred to as Movimiento Pachakutik, based on the movement vision to establish an "indigenous party."[8] In contrast, rather than create a "feminist party," the women's movement fought to gain a platform as a movement, something that was more loosely defined as an organized network rather than in terms of party membership (Vega 1997). With no party name, the women's movement has attempted to formalize certain aspects of the political process; namely, electing women to political positions, while opting out of creating an actual party similar to MUPP-NP. To date, the women's movement and the indigenous movement are the only two movements that have acquired this status, and Ecuador is one of the few countries worldwide where the women's movement has met the requirements for party status.

Importantly, these two CPME strategies preceded the women's movement's historically unprecedented participation in the meeting of the 1998 National Assembly in which the constitution was redrafted. Had it not been for the new party legislation, feminists and indigenous activists would not have acquired formal seats in the National Assembly. CPME's strategy, to engender the political and state system at large, was successful in part because of these conjunctural conditions following the chaotic political crisis. More directly, CPME was motivated by some members' frustration with other feminist strategies, especially that of CONAMU. CPME perceived CONAMU as ineffective and powerless vis-à-vis the broader state. At the same time, CPME perceived CONAMU as distant from the interests of the civil-society-based women's movement and at times as controlling their interests. Indeed, it is this perceived contradiction, that CONAMU simultaneously has too much power (vis-à-vis the women's movement) and not enough power (vis-à-vis the state), that has contributed to disagreement among feminists regarding how to proceed with feminist action within the state, alongside neoliberal state reform. Of course, this type of disagreement also stems from personal divisions and depends to some degree on who builds alliances with whom. In this sense, political alliances are constructed, maintained, dismantled, or transformed over time based on *not* solely ideological alliances but on per-

8. MUPP-NP was originally composed of three indigenous federations: CONAIE, the Confederation of People of the Quichua Nationality of Ecuador (Confederación de Pueblos de la Nacionalidad Kichwa del Ecuador [ECUARUNARI]), and the National Confederation of Affiliates of Peasant Social Security (Confederación Nacional de Afiliados al Seguro Social Campesino [CONFEUNASC]).

sonal alliances as well. Just as clientelism and coalition-building were evident in the Bucaram administration at large, divergent perspectives on feminist action reflect ideological differences as well as personal disagreements.

The CPME strategy to engender the entire state also reflects growing discontent among some Latin American feminists about the effectiveness of state women's agencies in promoting gender-sensitive policies, laws, and practices. Women's interests within the state are often compartmentalized in one agency. Many states have established agencies that specifically address women's issues, such as in Chile, Mexico, Argentina, and Peru (Valdés 1994; Placencia and Caro 1998). Some have situated gender issues alongside those of non-gender-based groups, as in the case of Bolivia, where until recently gender issues were addressed under the same institutional roof as indigenous and elderly issues (in the Vice-Ministry of Gender, Ethnic, and Generational Affairs); now gender issues are addressed alongside family issues (in the Vice-Ministry of Gender and Family Affairs; a Vice-Ministry of Ethnic Affairs was also created [see Paulsen and Calla 2000]).[9] In effect, CPME was attempting to overcome this compartmentalization of gender issues by adding a gender component to a wide range of state agencies and offices.

In some ways, CPME's political approach represents the most conventional political strategy among the four strands, in that it promotes the integration of the women's movement into the formal, traditional political process. This is the basis for criticism of CPME by other feminist strands. Yet, clearly, they have contributed to enormous positive changes in the political structure of the country and to innovative new practices. Currently the group is recognized by the Ministry of Government as the leader of the women's movement (which grants them party authority), although at times they also act as a voice for the NGO-based and community-based women's movement. Thus they must perform a political balancing act and have been criticized by other strands for "confusing

9. This institutional shift was based on the assumption that gender and ethnic issues are separate, something that many policy makers and scholars have argued against because it positions women (in the case of gender) and indigenous people (in the case of ethnicity) as the "targets" of development policies. This does not allow, for example, an analysis of middle-class mestizo men or other groups with privilege in society (see Paulsen and Calla 2000). In placing gender alongside family issues, the state effectively conflated "women" with "the family," despite the fact that feminist policy-makers have long argued for a separate analysis of women's lives (see Montaño 1996). It is best seen as a product of the ideological battles taking place in many Latin American countries (and elsewhere) about "gender" versus "family values" (Franco 1996): in this case, the state effectively undermined feminist interpretations of gender by collapsing gender issues with family issues and framing them all as "family related."

their political roles" (Rocío Rosero, interview, Quito, August 3, 2000) and for dominating the women's movement.

A Civil-Society-Based Coalition with a Place in the State: FNPME

FNPME was established in 1994, during the regional preparatory meetings for the 1995 UN conference in Beijing, China. FNPME represents organizations from a wide range of political sectors and includes women of middle-class, professional and NGO sectors, among others. The group was founded by Guadalupe León, then Director of the Center of Studies and Research About Abused Women in Ecuador (Centro de Estudios y Investigación Sobre Mujeres Maltratados del Ecuador [CEIMME]). FNPME originally relied on institutional support from CEIMME, although the former was designed as an umbrella organization of women's NGOs and local organizations committed to incorporating women into community-based and other development initiatives as well as into informal political networks. In general, FNPME does not advocate women's participation in the formal political process. Rather, it operates more from within a development framework than from within a traditional political framework, and it advocates the incorporation of women into public decision-making and planning.

During the Bucaram period, FNPME advocated a civil-society approach to politics, one in which civil-society institutions, rather than the state or political parties, would be engendered. This engendering would occur both through women's actual participation in community-based and national initiatives as well as through the promotion of an awareness of the gender dimensions of organizational structures, policies, project design, implementation, and so on in local organizations. Interestingly enough, its original advocate, Guadalupe León, was also the labor minister during a short period of Bucaram's administration in 1996. Thus while FNPME focused on strengthening civil-society institutions, its leader took a place in the state.

Not only did León take a place in the state; she took one in Bucaram's government, during a period of heightened anger and frustration among feminists surrounding Bucaram's policies, which were laden with gendered contradictions. Perhaps the most fundamental issue for other feminist strands was that León chose to work with an unpredictable government that was known for its misogynist acts and gendered political antics, including the honoring of Lorena Bobbitt as a national hero, which had already alienated several political sectors. Moreover, León's appointment further fragmented feminist politics in the state:

between CONAMU, CPME, and León's position as labor minister, feminist interests were dispersed throughout the state. However, rather than creating a
stronger feminist network within the state, this led to further divisions between
feminists, thus contributing to the separate strands of feminism that I address in
this chapter.

Feminists Remake the Nation: The Autonomous Feminists

Frustrated with the limitations of working within the state or under the guidelines of international development organizations; disillusioned with partisan and
other ideological and personal divisions between CONAMU, FNPME, and CPME
feminists; and desiring a new form of politics, a small number of feminists organized an informal group to discuss and reflect on the political crisis stemming
from the Bucaram administration.[10] Self-defined as autonomous feminists, they
maintain a strong critique of the bureaucratized structures within which they
must often work if they wish to earn an income or receive institutional funding.
Similar to other groups of autonomous feminists that have emerged in the region during the 1990s, this group is composed of feminists who have worked in
NGOs or in the state and are now disillusioned with what they perceive as an
overburdened, ideologically and financially limited gender technocracy. The
group is small and grassroots in nature, yet it has made its presence known
through public, performative acts of protest in Quito.

One symbolic protest that received national attention occurred on International Women's Day, March 8, in 1998.[11] The autonomous feminists dressed up
as Manuela Sáenz, liberator Simón Bolívar's lover and a recently revived heroine in Ecuadorian postcolonial history, and rode on horses to the Plaza de Independencia in the central historic district of Quito. While this protest was
relatively small, the symbolic move to reappropriate Sáenz's image was significant on more than one level. Known as "the liberator of the liberator" (*la liber-
tadora del libertador*) for having once saved Bolívar from being captured by

10. It is important to emphasize that several of this group's members also participate in another
strand of feminism. For example, some members of the Foro also participated in the autonomous
feminist group. In practice, these groups are not entirely separable, although in terms of their political ideology and visibility they represent a separate strand of feminist action. In the present context,
this strand has become even more distinguishable from other strands and is led most visibly by the
group Feministas por la Autonomia.

11. For my analysis of this performative protest I rely on interpretations of the event by protest
participants, conversations with observers, and media coverage.

the Spaniards, Sáenz has recently been celebrated in Ecuadorian literature and popular culture as a heroine in her own right—and not just as an appendage to Bolívar. She has been revived in the imaginations of many Ecuadorians at a time of heightened public debate, and sometimes outright conflict, over national identity. The group of autonomous feminists who replicated Sáenz's image in public did so to reappropriate her as a modern national hero. In this sense, autonomous feminists helped to remake the nation by tapping into the collective memory of Ecuadorians—into memories of resistance from Spanish conquest and rule—and by engendering that collective memory.

This protest is also significant because feminists invoked a collective, historical notion of national identity, yet also put into question the boundaries within which nation-building and development have occurred within Ecuador. As they performed the nationalist image of Manuela Sáenz, they did so to reclaim the very project of nation-building with which Sáenz is associated. In this sense, they drew from her historical representation to engender, and challenge, the modern practice of nation-building. They questioned, for example, political corruption and the nation's debt burden and advocated economic redistribution and democratization of the political system. Inherent in their march was the idea that women are affected in gender-specific ways by the current economic and political reforms. Their public portrayal of Sáenz, a historically "invisible" heroine of the colonial independence movement, thus became a modern icon of feminists' remaking the nation in the context of neoliberalism. They are perhaps the most explicit example of how feminists self-consciously critique the context they work within through an awareness of how their own gender identities become sites of power and struggle. They are also an example of recent feminist movements that have learned from second-wave feminism and are critical of feminist movements' reliance on the international development arena, including Western development discourse and institutional practices.

Dilemmas of Engendering the Neoliberal State

The four strands of feminism I address in this chapter have simultaneously struggled for access to institutional spaces such as the state, while also questioning the premises within which the state and other patriarchal institutions or practices (the party system, the constitution, national development plans) are constructed. In the process, they represent the interests and identities of some sectors of women—but not all women. In the neoliberal context, economic and social disparities between, for example, state feminists and women who are recipients of state policies have become even more apparent. While in theory feminism as a political project challenges the exclusion of women in historical processes of modernization (Olea 1995), it cannot successfully benefit all women. In practice, some women are included more than others. Much of this is caused by racial, sexual, and class biases that permeate the feminist movement and all of society. It is partly for this reason that some feminists have argued that modernization will always be an "incomplete project" for women (see Vargas 1992).

   In Ecuador, these historical contradictions were accentuated during the Bucaram administration, as feminists actively discussed whether to participate in the state—and if so, in what capacity and for whom. Any clear ideological agenda was absent in Bucaram's government; some feminists justified working within the state, while others were opposed to it. Perhaps what was most apparent about the state during this period was its fragmentation. The Bucaram administration lacked a clear ideological agenda. Furthermore, a wide range of opposing political interests were represented in state agencies during that administration, more so than during other periods, creating major conflicts between, for example, feminist and religious-fundamentalist ministers. During the Bucaram administration, the state did not appear cohesive, but rather fragmented and weak, despite Bucaram's popular nationalist discourse of unity. Some CONAMU employees were deeply opposed to Bucaram's policies and leadership style, creating enormous conflict and a general lack of efficiency in governance. CONAMU employees were also faced with opposition by women's community organizations and NGOs, a result of Bucaram's politics but also of the broader restructuring process. One factor that contributed to this conflict was the differential class effects on women of different social classes and societal locations, including between policy makers and policy recipients (Schild 1998).

   CONAMU's symbolic and institutional location serves as an example. CONAMU employees earn state salaries. While their livelihood and institutional political strategy is derived from working within the state, CONAMU employees disagree on how neoliberal policies affect CONAMU's institutional structure and the so-called recipients of CONAMU's policies and programs: sectors of "poor women." One example of this concerns CONAMU's institutional shift from direct service provider to facilitator of gender and development policy—the privatization of CONAMU's project implementation, a process that may potentially exacerbate the work lives of local women's organizations and communities (Lind 1997). In this sense, and in the sense that CONAMU plays a powerful role in defining the symbolic and institutional boundaries within which "poor women" are constructed as recipients of development and as clients of the state, CONAMU's goals are an extension of or converge with the broader project of neoliberal state formation. CONAMU's practices therefore contribute to what Verónica Schild (1998) has called the "new gendered market citizens," as women as constituents are increasingly defined in terms of the market. As CONAMU defines its recipients ("poor women") in terms of their work and their market value, they are using a market-oriented conception of citizenship. Thus, CONAMU practices help to institutionalize women as market citizens. This resonates with observations about state women's agencies in Peru (Barrig 1998), in Chile (Schild 1998; Valenzuela 1998), and in comparative studies (Alvarez 1998a).

Yet despite this convergence, CONAMU as an institution has played an important historical and political role in engendering state development policies, in addressing the gender dimensions of neoliberal reform (and more broadly speaking, making visible women's roles in the economy and in politics),[12] and in negotiating the highly contested boundaries of the public and private in the context of neoliberalism. CONAMU's institutional activism, and divergent scholarly views on state women's agencies' complicity with or contradictory relationships with neoliberal states (Schild 2000a, 2000b), reveals some of the contradictions of feminist politics in the context of neoliberalism. CONAMU is caught in a paradox of feminist action within neoliberal contexts: relying on an increasingly "undependable" state (Alvarez 1996), yet doing so from within a state agency with more institutional power than ever, with funding to employ thirty-four people, and with significant knowledge to address the gender dimensions of neoliberal reform. CONAMU's decisions about how gender and development issues are framed in state documents contribute to shaping, sometimes in powerful ways, the institutional environment within which policy making, project design, and political decisions about women's roles in economic development take place. In this sense, CONAMU as a state institution is an important site of interpretive power (vis-à-vis the women's movement and civil society) despite its limited power within the male-dominated state. It has also been an important site of resistance to state hegemony.

In the neoliberal context, it remains to be seen what CONAMU's contradictory role will signify for feminist politics and for CONAMU's self-defined recipients,

---

12. One recent example includes CONAMU's project on gender and property rights. CONAMU is the first in Ecuador to employ such a study of the relationship between gender, land, and property rights since the accelerated process of trade liberalization and agricultural restructuring, beginning with the Durán-Ballén administration in 1992 (see Deere and León de Leal 2001a, 2001b).

poor women. Ecuadorian community-based women's organizations have received minimal support through state and international development aid since the initial period of structural adjustment in the early 1980s. Decentralization measures, too, have contributed to institutionalizing this process by which women and their labor are incorporated into the new political structures (Arboleda 1994). While this process has had positive effects on specific sectors of women who gain political visibility or economic independence, it nonetheless institutionalizes women's struggles for survival to the extent that their informal political and economic participation remains unacknowledged and to the extent that they are targeted as volunteers in neoliberal development projects.

Like CONAMU employees, feminists from CPME, FNPME, and the autonomous strand also engage actively in these debates on development and neoliberal reform. CPME served as an observer of the 1998 elections, documenting female candidates' campaigns as well as citizens' gender-based attitudes toward voting for or against these candidates (Vega 1998). The group publishes a newsletter, La otra mitad (The Other Half), which focuses on gender-based reform in the state and political system. Each newsletter treats a different theme or state agency; housing, rural development, employment, political participation and citizenship are some of the topics. CPME continues to work toward engendering the entire state, rather than only one state agency (such as CONAMU). This raises concerns for feminist action, as engendering the entire state does not automatically translate into a feminist state, although it might help to place gender issues on various ministerial agendas. The extent to which such a strategy is sustainable is another question altogether; much will depend on the current and future government's willingness to cooperate with CPME by integrating gender into ministry frameworks and projects. Furthermore, some have argued that CPME lost its political effectiveness once it started working within established male-dominated institutions. For example, CPME's proposal to back female politicians may be increasing the amount of female political candidates, but it remains unclear whether this will result in electoral wins for these candidates. A preliminary study of Bolivia's female quota system found that the actual number of women holding formal political positions decreased, rather than increased, following the first three years after the female-quota legislation was passed (Zabala, interview, Cochabamba, Bolivia, April 15, 1999). A second issue concerns whether the quota system will result in any shift of gender consciousness or political perspective among female or male politicians; at the very least, this needs to be further examined. Thus engendering the state may lead to further awareness of gender issues but does not necessarily imply a change in values, assumptions, or ideologies of gender as they are implicit in state institutions and society at large.

Since 1998, FNPME has acquired official status (*personería jurídica*) as an independent organization, works in at least fourteen provinces, and has its own projects that focus on strengthening the capacity of local women's organizations. It continues to work within civil society more than from within the state to affect change, although FNPME members and consultants have played key roles in national debates and sent members to the National Assembly in 1998. In 2000, FNPME leaders published a book on feminist involvement in redrafting the 1998 constitution (Rosero, Vega, and Reyes Ávila 2000). The autonomous strand, a small and informal yet symbolically important strand, questions institutional complicity with the state and international development apparatus. It has been represented most visibly by the network Feministas por la Autonomia. Feministas por la Autonomia constituted one of the most critical spaces for feminist reflection in the early 2000s, and has focused to a large degree on sexual rights, including the right to abortion, lesbian rights, and the promotion of anti-incest and pornography laws. Feministas por la Autonomia takes an antistate position and chooses to focus on its own activities "rather than be co-opted by other political sectors" (Rocía Rosero, interview, August 3, 2000).

In general, autonomous feminist groups operate to disrupt institutionalized feminist practices and to question feminists' own roles in (re-)producing hierarchies and inequalities. In this way, they make explicit the contradictions of feminist actions to remake development and the nation. It is perhaps because of their direct challenge to feminism that, until recently, other feminists have not taken them seriously. Another reason for this may the fact that some groups (for example, Mujeres Creando, in Bolivia) use agitation and direct confrontation as a political strategy, thus forcing many feminists to take a position either for or against them. Yet it is also because they are challenging the comforts that some feminists have attained over the years—comforts derived from their own class positions or complicity with state and international development interests. This skepticism of autonomous feminism is changing, however, and it must be acknowledged that feminists from all strands have become disillusioned to varying degrees by the bureaucratization and NGOization of feminist struggles (see Alvarez 1998b). In addition, many autonomous feminists themselves often still work within the very context that they critique—the so-called gender technocracy—some out of necessity, some out of choice. Thus even for them, it has been difficult to maintain institutional autonomy alongside their ideological autonomy from the international development apparatus.

Conclusion: Neoliberal Failures, Feminist Successes

A number of professionals and activists from all four strands have participated in transnational networks, international conferences, or both. Some have participated in or organized graduate courses in which debates on women's movements, gender, and neoliberal state policy have been explicitly discussed.[13] Through this process, new cultural framings of development may appear; framings that question the role of feminism within the state. Yet the extent to which feminist interpretations of development are put into practice is another question altogether.

One positive result of the otherwise difficult 1997 political crisis was that feminists from various locations struggled for change in new ways. The success of their actions are already evident: in the new constitution, which includes a stronger gender focus than ever before; in the structure of political party candidacies and elections, which now calls for a minimal participation of female candidates; in the new social movement–based political party structure; and in numerous publications, meetings, and public events that address the topic of gender and state reform. Yet in 1998, amid these sweeping changes, many of which were considered successes by women's movement activists, it remained a period of political uncertainty and economic hardship. It was questionable, for example, whether CPME's agenda would translate into sustainable institutional state practices, particularly with the financial crisis on the horizon.

President Jamil Mahuad (1998–2000) introduced a series of measures in March 1999 to deal with the growing budget deficit (then at U.S.$1.2 billion), rising inflation rates, and a U.S.$16-billion foreign debt. His measures, which included drastic price hikes, increases in the sales tax, and a partial freeze on the withdrawal of funds deposited in private and institutional checking and savings accounts, led to the closure of major banks and to widespread protest and economic paralysis (North 1999, 6). This culminated in the ousting in January 2000 of President Mahuad, following the indigenous takeover of the National Con-

---

13. FLACSO, for example, has offered a graduate program in gender and development studies. The first time this program was offered was in 1997–98, when FLACSO won a bid from CONAMU to manage the program. Originally, CONAMU received funding from the Inter-American Development Bank to establish a master's program in gender and development studies, with the goal of providing training in gender and development to public-sector employees (national and municipal government employees) and to some nonprofit sector employees. This is an interesting example of the ways in which feminist political practice converges with the objectives of the broader development field, yet also provides an institutional space within which feminists can formulate and provide constructive criticism on development itself.

gress and an unsuccessful military coup on January 21, as well as national protests by many social sectors. Given the continuing economic and political
paralysis in the country, in part caused by the effects of dollarization of the
economy, it remained to be seen what would occur within the state itself and in
civil society.[14]

The four feminist strands that were consolidated in the late 1990s reflected
the fragmented nature of feminist politics in Ecuador and throughout the region. Separate strands and struggles characterized feminist politics more than
did a unified notion of a social movement; nonetheless, the strands worked together on key issues such as the social movement party legislation and the new
constitution. Although the conventional notion of a unified women's movement
seems to be a remnant of the past, when, for example, women mobilized against
military authoritarian states (Alvarez 1990), some unity arose in the post-
Bucaram era surrounding political democracy and participation. The arguments
and perspectives of the four strands reflect historically divergent views on successful feminist strategies, yet they also reflect feminists' growing concerns and
discontent over heightened economic disparities between women activists
themselves. The fragmented nature of 1990s Ecuadorian feminist politics was
characterized by competition and access to the market (access to funding, to
institutional power, to international funders) rather than by cross-class solidarity,
a strong, earlier ideology of feminism in the 1960s and 1970s. The new economic
conditions placed strains on and fundamentally called into question earlier feminist notions of "doing politics," such that feminists were willing to explore a
variety of strategies to achieve political success—not the least of which was the
emerging critique of "institutionalized feminism" by autonomous feminists.

To some degree, autonomous feminism represents a break with earlier forms
of feminist politics, forms of politics that feminists themselves have had to recon-
sider in order to address the increasingly globalized nature of economic and
political change. As Ecuadorian and other Latin American feminists have acknowledged for years, women's movements necessarily have constructed strategies that address a transnational rather than merely a national arena (see Alvarez
1998b). Indeed, the history of women's organizing in Latin America has been
transnational in the sense that feminists have received international support and
funding and have been in constant communication with feminists from other
countries in order to construct their own local (community, national) struggles.

14. President Noboa carried out former president Mahuad's plan to dollarize the Ecuadorian
economy. This currency transition took effect on September 11, 2000. More on dollarization in
Chapter 6.

The "traveling" nature of feminist discourse and practice in Ecuador influenced Ecuadorian feminist strands, as they translated global ideas into the local, national political context (Kaplan 1996; Thayer 2000).

Clearly, all four strands have contributed in important ways to transforming national politics during the Bucaram period. As a visible force in anti-Bucaram protests and in the drafting of the new constitution, feminist activists and policymakers undoubtedly played crucial roles in transforming the political process. Despite the failure of the neoliberal project and politics of the Bucaram administration, feminists were successful in their organizing strategies at the national level, a reality that continued into the next century amid further financial and political crises.

[6]

Making Dollars, Making Feminist Sense of Neoliberalism: Negotiations, Paradoxes, Futures

In this book I have aimed to address a set of gendered paradoxes concerning Ecuador's trajectory of "development" and state restructuring preceding and during the neoliberal period of the 1980s and 1990s. These paradoxes are derived from several factors: ideologies of womanhood and imaginings of Ecuador as a nation; the negotiated relationships between sectors of women and the state, an institution that has changed over time; the historical construction of the social welfare system; post–World War II relationships between global development agencies and the Ecuadorian state; the institutionalization and privatization of women's struggles for survival; and the roles played by the many actors involved in feminist-issue networks who have had a stake in women's grassroots struggles. These paradoxes are embodied in women's political identities and strategies; they also significantly shape and transform broad processes such as democratization and constitutional reform. They affect women's lives, as I have shown, and have important consequences for a rethinking of politics, the economy, the state, and citizenship. Finally, they illustrate the global tensions that exist between (1) women's integration into Latin American modernities and their ongoing social exclusion, and (2) the goals of international development, construed largely through a Eurocentric lens, and the realities of Third World societies.

By way of conclusion, in this chapter I discuss the context of neoliberal state restructuring during the 1998–2004 period, including the cultural and economic effects of dollarization on women's lives and gender identity politics, and the possible outcomes of the Lucio Gutiérrez administration's (2003–present) populist agenda for national gender and ethnic politics. This is followed by my more general conclusions about rethinking gender and neoliberalism in Latin America in the context of struggles for citizenship, sovereignty, and national identity.

The Ecuadorian Financial and Political Crises, 1998–2002

In January 2000, President Jamil Mahuad (now a professor at Harvard) was overthrown, following a series of national protests that ultimately led to his forced resignation. Based on Ecuador's constitutional law, then vice president Gustavo

Noboa became the next president of the country. In November 2002, Lucio Gutiérrez, the young populist military leader who joined with the indigenous movement to oppose the Mahuad administration in January 2000, was elected as Ecuador's next president. Considered both centrist and leftist by Ecuadorians, he refuses to label himself in terms of conventional political ideologies.[1] His political victory was largely a result of the indigenous movement and military alliance created earlier and CONAIE's support for him during the 2002 presidential elections (Van Cott 2002). The obvious irony of his election is the fact that while many Ecuadorians have been skeptical of military power since the transition from military rule to democracy in 1979, (that is, skeptical of the military governments that first accumulated debt, in addition to suspending democratic freedoms and protections), they have now elected a military leader to be their president. As political analysts have pointed out, this type of neoliberal populist leadership would not have been possible twenty years ago, when the country and region first underwent redemocratization; it has only been with the introduction of neoliberal governments, in which some types of political protections have been suspended in the name of restructuring the country's economy, combined with an increase in populist governance, that a military leader would win a democratic election (Van Cott 2002; Burt and Mauceri 2004).[2] This coalition has not been supported by the U.S. government, which has worked to destabilize the indigenous movement in recent years (Whitten 2003a).

The Gutiérrez administration was faced with many political opportunities resulting from the legislative reforms but also a complex economic situation. Dollarization had begun in September 2000 and had exacerbated some of the country's economic problems in the short term.[3] This policy, which is being con-

1. During his inaugural ceremony on January 15, 2003, Gutiérrez publicly stated, "If sharing and acting in solidarity, if combating corruption, social injustice and impunity is leftist, then I am a leftist! If generating wealth and stimulating production is right wing, then I am right wing!" (Si compartir y ser solidario, si combatir la corrupción, la injusticia social y la impunidad es ser de izquierda, pues soy de izquierda! Si generar riqueza e impulsar la producción es ser de derecha, pues soy de derecha! [Cornejo Menacho 2003]).

2. Peru offers a well-known example of this type of neoliberal politics: President Fujimori (1990–2000) deployed a "self-coup" following his election in 1990 (Burt and Mauceri 2004). Venezuela is another well-known case, where military leader Hugo Chavez was democratically elected in 1998. Perhaps even more ironic is the case of former Bolivian dictator Hugo Banzer (1971–78), a close friend of Klaus Barbie and other Nazi refugees in Bolivia, who returned to politics and was democratically elected to the presidency in 1997. In 2000, following a serious bout of cancer that led to his death the following year, he was replaced by Vice President Jorge Quiroga.

3. President Mahuad first introduced this legislation in late 1999, and it was partly for this reason that he was forced to resign in January 2000. As a result, the dollarization legislation took effect under the subsequent leadership of Gustavo Noboa (January 2000–August 2002).

sidered for adoption in several countries undergoing SAPs (World Bank 2003e), was meant to stabilize Ecuador's failing economy. Changing the currency did not happen overnight; for several months (and even now) people have exchanged sucres in the streets while exchanging dollars in most formal businesses. Throughout the country, there is a scarcity of U.S. coins, including pennies, nickels, dimes, and quarters. International charities have promoted "penny drives," whereby volunteers collect U.S. coins and bring them to distribute through their institutional channels in Ecuador. Because of this shortage, the Central Bank of Ecuador has begun to produce its own version of U.S. coins. However, Ecuadorian quarters are perceived as less valuable than U.S. quarters, despite the fact that they are supposed to hold the same value. Even the value of change, in this case, reflects perceived inequalities between Ecuador and the United States. During the 1990s, many new high-rise buildings have been built, often inspired by postmodern architecture. Hotels abound; large, modern buses fill the streets; a new electric train service has been established; there are more cars on the roads; new foreign-owned franchises have arrived, including several new fast-food restaurants, movie complexes, and shops in malls. It appears that Quito's wealthy are doing quite well. Many of them support Ecuador's dollarization, since most have accounts in dollars both within and outside the country and no longer have to worry about an unstable exchange rate for sucres. "It's much better," an upper-class woman told me during my trip to Quito in summer 2001.

In contrast, dollarization has not benefited many poor and middle-class Ecuadorians. Although this process was meant to control inflation, instead it has increased. While the dollar was meant to stabilize the economy, given that the sucre had devalued tremendously in the past decade and especially since 1997, it has not stabilized the economic lives of the poor and middle class. Rather, what we see is even more dire circumstances for people who lost their savings during the banking crisis, higher rates of unemployment and underemployment, and extremely devalued social security benefits and payments. The Mahuad administration made the initial decision to dollarize without consulting international lending institutions or fully assessing the economic risks involved; as a result, an additional factor was that the international financial community was wary of the Ecuadorian legislation, although ultimately the IMF, World Bank, and IADB all supported the government's decision. Mahuad's announcement of the dollarization legislation in late 1999 followed a period of severe instability in Ecuador's financial sector, leading to the closure of more than twenty leading national banks. Several banks are still undergoing legal processes to determine how each of their cases will be handled.[4] Originally, many people's accounts were frozen and, following their bank's legal case, they were not returned any of their savings.[5] Other people have received a percentage of their savings. Yet others were fortunate enough to be able to withdraw all their money. Now their savings accounts are under their beds or in foreign banks; those who can afford it might invest in a commodity such as a home or a new car, rather than in a savings account.

For example, a middle-class feminist from Quito once explained to me that "she is glad she invested most of her savings in her home" in 1999, since otherwise she would have lost that money. One of the origins of the crisis lies in the fact that the Ecuadorian banking system was largely unregulated: many banks, for example, offered up to 20 percent annual percentage rates on savings accounts, making these accounts a significant form of investment. In addition, several banks used their clients' savings to invest outside the country, particularly in countries where their financial transactions could not be tracked.[6]

Another consequence of this crisis is that banks that traditionally have paid out social security checks are now only paying them out on a limited basis, if at all. Banks cannot afford to make full payments when their own savings have been devalued and they are headed toward bankruptcy.[7] The Central Bank of Ecuador does not have large savings either. In 2001, outside those banks on payday, one saw lines of women and men waiting to receive their payments; payments that probably would not cover their monthly expenses. In August 2001,

4. The results of each case determines whether a particular bank (or the Central Bank of Ecuador) can pay back bank clients, and how much (that is, what percentage of their accounts), if anything, will be returned to them.

5. This is true both for accounts in sucres and for those in dollars. Many banks offer both types of accounts. It is important to note, however, that bank accounts in sucres were among the first to be frozen. Some banks allowed their customers with accounts in dollars to continue using them as usual. Banks changed their policies over time, depending on their precarious financial and legal situations. By that time, people with accounts in dollars (typically wealthier people) were able to remove their money and, if they wished, transfer it to foreign banks. Thus people with accounts in sucres, particularly those who did not have access to or knowledge about foreign banks and the broader financial market, were the most likely to lose from the bank closures.

6. For example, some banks hid their investments in Caribbean countries with offshore financial industries, where privacy laws are such that there is little regulation and control over money laundering.

7. As banks exchanged their sucres for U.S. dollars, they typically lost money in the transaction as a result of the exchange rate (at the time, it reached up to S/30,000 per U.S. dollar). Although in theory dollarization may contribute to stabilizing the economy, in Ecuador it also led to further inflation, since it hiked up consumer costs. This resulted from multiple factors, including the fact that the value of the U.S. dollar was strong and the Ecuadorian business sector often opted to hike up prices to match the strength of the dollar. The scarcity of change added to this situation as well.

a young middle-class woman in her late twenties described her own family's economic situation:

> My parents are both retired teachers. My father worked at the public university until his retirement. My mother was a high school teacher. They both counted on their monthly social security checks to survive. Before the crisis, they lived quite well. They owned their own home, they had a car, and they didn't need any more money to be happy. But since the crisis they are no longer receiving their full social security checks. Now they receive only sixty dollars a month, rather than over three hundred dollars. They cannot survive on that money alone. My siblings and I have to help them now. There is no other alternative.

This woman was formerly an American Field Service (AFS) exchange student in the United States. She spoke English quite well. She continued, "I want to return to the United States but now I can't, I have to stay here and take care of my parents." A feminist policy-maker who represented the women's movement in the 1998 National Assembly commented on how she and her adult siblings now support their mother. "We all give her money every month; there is no other way to handle this." Having invested her savings in a new home, the daughter now has very little left to save, given her house payments; monthly expenses for herself, her partner, and two children; and supporting her mother.

Many people have also been affected by rising unemployment and underemployment rates. In addition to women and men waiting in lines for their social security checks outside Quito banks, one can also see lines of younger women, many of them laid-off bank tellers still wearing their bank uniforms, waiting in lines to apply for new jobs or hoping for severance payments that rarely come. Their experiences are exacerbated by the fact that there is less and less public and private aid available to them, including state aid, bank loans, and affordable mortgage rates on new homes.

Dollarization is just one outcome of the Ecuadorian neoliberal restructuring process. It is partly a consequence of the failure of the Ecuadorian financial market to survive under a changing development model. Initially, dollarization affected people of all classes to the extent that their accounts were frozen or entirely lost following the bank failures. The gender dimensions of this situation remain largely invisible to most people, despite the fact that, like SAPs, dollarization disproportionately affect women in the private realm of family and community. Reduced social security benefits (for the small percentage of Ecuadorians who receive them) translates into more care-based work for seniors, a role held traditionally by female family members (Folbre and Bittman 2004). Inflation and unemployment, particularly in economic sectors gendered as "female," such as bank telling, directly affect job opportunities among middle-class women. Because U.S. coins and dollars have a higher value than sucres and the comparative currency value is often unclear, daily economic transactions have become more costly. For example, whereas a kilo of potatoes may have cost S/ 4,000 (U.S. 18 cents in 2001 dollars) prior to dollarization, they may now cost U.S. 25 cents, since the U.S. quarter is often the only change people have. The cost of daily items such as food and transportation (such as buses and taxis) tend to be converted up to the nearest dime or quarter, rather than down. In addition, because there has been a lack of U.S. coins in circulation, when an item costs, for example, U.S. 20 cents, one might have to pay a quarter to buy it, with no change returned. These unintended price increases have important conse- quences for poor women, who are primarily responsible for shopping on a daily basis, managing the household budget and caring for children. Here, too, we see that the public/private restructuring of the economy falls indirectly into the hands of poor women. Similarly, the welfare network that is supposed to have been created throughout civil society, as a result of shifting state welfare respon- sibilities to NGOs and other private organizations, may be partly addressed by civic organizations but continues to be mothered by poor women.

The implications of dollarization, as one result of the economic restructuring process, go far beyond the economic, as culture, politics, and power are also put into question. The trend to dollarize, coupled with hemispheric trade and other initiatives to foster market competition in the Americas, exemplifies the ways in which this new emphasis on the global market contributes to heightened gender inequalities that permeate social welfare distribution.

Antineoliberal Coalitions: The Women's Movement and the Indigenous Movement

Although Ecuadorian social movements could not block the dollarization legis- lation from passing, many women have, in fact, been actively involved in shap- ing the political process to the extent possible. The indigenous movement, too, opposed dollarization and pointed out the ethnic and class disparities that arose from the neoliberal development model and the introduction of Western market values. Significantly, since the late 1980s when NGOization first began, the prior political organizing of these two movements had paid off. Women's NGOs such as CPME continued to play a key role in the campaigns, and FNPME plays a pivotal role in shaping the civil-society-based community of social welfare providers.

One conceivable success of antineoliberal protest in Ecuador concerns the fact that both indigenous and feminist interests are present in the current administration. After taking office in January 2003, President Gutiérrez appointed two CONAIE leaders to ministerial positions. Nina Pacari, lawyer, feminist, and CONAIE leader, was appointed minister of foreign relations. Luis Macas, former president of CONAIE, was appointed minister of agriculture and livestock. His appointments of indigenous leaders has been seen by his supporters as a victory, to the extent that he has acknowledged Ecuador's 1998 constitutional declaration of the "pluricultural and multiethnic state" (Van Cott 2002, 47). Feminists applauded Pacari's appointment on the basis that she represented, for the first time in history, both feminist and indigenous interests in the Ecuadorian state. Importantly, her position is a symbolic victory for the many indigenous and feminist activists who have sought to build coalitions and address the concerns and interests of indigenous women, in both the male-based indigenous movement and the urban-based women's movement. This has not been an easy alliance, given the different agendas, interests, and perspectives of these two social movements.[8]

It has yet to be seen if feminist and indigenous interests will actually translate into a feminist or multiethnic state. Given the tendency of neoliberal populist governments to combine a socially-aware political agenda with traditional SAPs and to appeal to marginalized sectors while pursuing neoliberal reform, a substantive change in the state's approach to gender issues and indigenous concerns is unlikely. In many ways, what we are witnessing is a reordering of gender and ethnic difference rather than an equalization of power, a process that is integral

8. Here I am referring to the distinct historical trajectories of each social movement, and to the distinct sets of interests that indigenous political sectors have developed versus those of feminist sectors. The ethnicity-based claims of peasant and indigenous struggles have derived from legal notions of community- or group-based rights, with little or no consideration of gender differences between men and women within a given community. The gender-based claims of women's movements, by contrast, have emphasized the individual rights of women as a means through which women may acquire their rights within the realm of family law and policies, often defined through a Eurocentric lens (Shachar 2003). While feminists emphasize individual self-transformation in their vision of societal change, indigenous activists focus on communal rights to ownership and political leadership. Indigenous women have had to negotiate both these political discourses in order to create their own vision that incorporates elements from both movements, a process that has only recently begun at a more organized level.

to, not separate from, contemporary globalization and neoliberalism (García Canclini 2001).[9]

Yet alongside this reordering of difference, we have witnessed some important forms of social change. Since 1998, what has been interesting about Ecuador's women's movement and indigenous movement is the extent to which they have successfully coalesced to oppose the neoliberal development model. In this sense, Ecuadorian social movement responses to neoliberalism is not unlike those of other countries in the region where gender rights and multiculturalism are being promoted, perhaps ironically, alongside and sometimes as an integral part of the state's development agenda (Stephenson 2001; Paulsen and Calla 2000; Radcliffe, Laurie, and Andolina 2004; Sieder 2002). Although, clearly, Ecuador's neoliberal development approach has varied depending on the administration in power and has been more successful at some times than at others, the women's movement and indigenous movement have been incorporated into the state planning process in unprecedented ways, an observation made by other researchers of neoliberalism and the restructuring of state–civil society relations (Segarra 1994; Salinas Mulder et al. 1994). Regardless of one's perspective on neoliberalism, this has led to increased political opportunities for women and other groups.

It is also true that in Ecuador, neoliberal policies have been highly negotiated and publicly debated, more than in other countries, such as Bolivia or Peru. By creating umbrella networks of NGOs; strengthening institutional links between state agencies, NGOs, and community associations; and formalizing the representative status of the women's movement and indigenous movement in the national electoral process, well-established and prepared social movements and civic organizations have had the opportunity to participate in the dialogues. Yet the relative success of this series of negotiated encounters with neoliberal development depends largely on the lens through which one measures the outcomes: for feminist policy-makers the outcome may be more positive to the extent that some of them directly participated in the public decision-making process, including the redrafting of the constitution; for poor women, who do not have interpretive power in Ecuador's changing civil society, the outcome may not be as positive. And despite the increased political opportunities for women, the economic situation has not improved.

Several questions about women's movements, state modernization, and neo-

9. As cultural critic Nestor García Canclini (2001) notes, "[R]ather than homogenize the world, globalization reorders differences and inequalities without eliminating them. Hence, the rise of multicultural societies should be seen in connection with globalizing movements" (3).

liberal development remain. For example, what additional obstacles do sectors of urban poor women face as the neoliberal development model is further institutionalized? What are the long-term implications of these structural changes for the Ecuadorian women's movement? How have neoliberal policies shifted power relations between poor and middle- to upper-class women, including within the women's movement? What is the future of feminism in this context? How will this transform, it at all, the relationship between women and the state? Important differences exist between classes and political sectors of women, both within Ecuador and between nations; not the least of these is class difference. These differences shape women's divergent views on state modernization and global development, including how they prioritize their needs and create political strategies, and present a political paradox to contemporary feminists.

Engendering Neoliberalism

In this book I have addressed two primary ways in which the living conditions of sectors of urban poor women in Ecuador have deteriorated since the inception of SAPs in 1980: through the intensification of women's work and through the institutionalization of their struggles for survival. Importantly, we have seen how women have served as buffers of the economic crisis through their provision of voluntary labor in the economy and for the state. These findings resonate with those of regional and international studies on gender and neoliberal reform in Latin America (e.g., Moser 1989b; Benería and Feldman 1992; Bakker 1994), the Caribbean (Safa 1995), Africa (Emeagwali 1995; Mikell 1997), South Asia (Kabeer 1991), North America (Bakker 1996) and Eastern Europe and the former Soviet Union (Aslanbeigui, Pressman, and Summerfield 1994).

Women's household and community labor has intensified as a result of the restructuring of the state and economy, most specifically through macroeconomic and social welfare policies that shift traditional state responsibilities to the private sector. This is a recent chapter in the much longer history of the making of so-called modern states in postcolonial nations. Through gender biases in the policy frameworks themselves, coupled with biases in their implementation, the restructuring of the economy has shifted responsibilities to the realm of women's work. The United Nations and other development organizations have attempted to "integrate women into development," but their efforts have had contradictory results. It is significant that the amount of time and energy women spend on work each day has increased, rather than decreased, since the inception of the development field in Ecuador (World Bank 2001). Neoliberal policies that include privatization measures exacerbate this tendency by further shifting responsibilities to the family, household, and community, thus leading to this intensification of women's work and to their need or desire to organize collectively.

In relation to this, poor women and community-based women's organizations have become the ideal recipients for neoliberal development projects that rely on volunteer labor. Despite the best intentions of WID planners and feminists to empower poor women, women's incorporation into volunteer-based development projects tends to reinforce their marginalized class status and institutionalize their struggles for survival rather than empower them in meaningful ways. This is true, at least, for the case of most Ecuadorian women's organizations. Those that continue to survive tend to be the best supported financially and institutionally, by a combination of NGOs and foreign philanthropic institutions. Only one women's organization in this study, for example, has grown in size or institutional capacity since its inception. Others continue to exist but with few or no resources. These economic consequences of neoliberal policy frameworks, including WID policies, stem largely from the ways in which the public and private are understood in development frameworks and from the assumption that members of poor women's organizations *should* be trained to participate in community initiatives such as day-care centers, soup kitchens, and communal stores.

Contradictions that Endure: Women's Movements and Neoliberal State Restructuring

Paradoxes abound about the goals of development (those to eliminate global poverty) and the actual gendered consequences of concrete development practices such as those associated with neoliberal restructuring. How NGO professionals and state policy makers should (or should not) intervene in women's community organizations continues to be a key area of concern for feminists. Rather than improving the living situation of many women, the economic crisis and neoliberal policies have exacerbated women's so-called burden, one that was gendered and unequal from the start (Benería and Feldman 1992). The implications of this are contradictory. It is true that women have gained important forms of visibility through the political reforms of the past two decades, including through new affirmative-action and antidiscrimination laws; the introduction of the female-quota system; decentralization laws; the representation of social movements in party elections; and funding for research on women at CONAMU, women's NGOs, and universities and research institutes such as FLACSO. And perhaps ironically, despite the broader process of state retrenchment and restructuring, the Ecuadorian state women's agency has gained higher institutional status then before, a trend we see throughout Latin America.

Yet it is important to highlight which women have gained and which have lost. Some women have lost more than they have gained, despite development discourse that claims that civil society is being strengthened or that poor women are benefiting from development. While differences have always existed between Ecuadorian women's organizations (as they have elsewhere), their perceived fragmentation has been exacerbated by neoliberal reforms. Community-based women's organizations, for example, have been targeted, more than during earlier decades, as the new service deliverers in increasingly privatized economies. While the redistribution of social welfare has led, in some cases, to increases in grants and funding for community-based women's organizations, these organizations nevertheless are expected to take over service delivery and distribution where the state no longer provides it, much as is seen in U.S. policy from the 1980s to the present, in Britain's Thatcherism, and in IMF and World Bank adjustment policies worldwide. In essence, women's organizations provide an important economic foundation for communities, cities, and nations around the world.

This is certainly the case in Ecuador, where historically poor women in urban areas were incorporated into government schemes such as communal stores and day-care centers, albeit somewhat unsuccessfully. The new NGO-based welfare network has more effectively facilitated the redistribution of social welfare among community groups, including women's and neighborhood associations. In addition, women continue to individually support the economy through their informal (paid and unpaid) labor. Similarly, in Peru and Bolivia, women have been systematically targeted to participate in Glass-of-Milk programs (Peru), food-for-work programs (Bolivia [see Ochsendorf 1998]), and communal kitchens (Peru and Bolivia [see Sara-Lafosse 1984; Delpino 1991; Salinas Mulder et al. 1994; Barrig 1996]), both by the state and by NGOs. All these programs, whether sponsored by governments, international development organizations, or NGOs, rely on the assumption that women have endless amounts of time to participate, do not require high (if any) salaries, and do not mind extending their traditional reproductive roles to the realm of community management. This institutional reliance on community-based women's organizations has perhaps financially benefited some members, yet poor women no longer can rely on the state, or even NGOs, for support. In many cases, the funding they receive is not enough to allow them to gain self-sufficiency in their struggles or in their daily survival. In this sense, the privatization of social welfare has not been justly redistributed to women's organizations or to the communities they serve and represent.

A related factor concerns the range of visions and political strategies that women in Quito have used to oppose neoliberalism. While it is true that many poor women throughout the world's cities may have a shared identity based on their socioeconomic locations in processes of development and globalization, a point I addressed in Chapter 4, this study highlights the fact that Ecuadorian women's organizations do not always share a common vision of development, in part because of their distinct political interests and visions. Neoliberal development policies have reordered classes of women and exacerbated class inequalities in two important ways. First, they have contributed to the widening gap between rich and poor in the country, an issue that affects all marginalized groups. Second, the new public-private arrangements have led to an increased division between women who design and implement neoliberal policies (that is, state and NGO feminists) and those who are targeted as clients of state- and NGO-based development projects—namely, poor women. As a result, some women activists (including, for example, community-based activists and autonomous feminists) criticize CONAMU professionals for supporting the state's neoliberal agenda. Critics view CONAMU professionals as working in the interests of neoliberal and First World elites, rather than in the interests of poor women.

Certainly the issue of class differences between and within Latin American women's movements is not a new issue (Saporta Sternbach et al. 1992; Vargas 1992). Professionally trained and formally educated, typically middle-class women activists tend to find jobs in the NGO sector, UN agencies, foreign government agencies (for example, Canadian, Dutch, Swedish, and U.S. agencies) and/or state agencies. They also tend to be the movement representatives that are funded to attend international and regional meetings, including UN conferences (such as the UN women's conference in Beijing, UNFPA meetings in Cairo) and the regional preparatory meetings for those conferences. Working-class, poor, and rural women have less access to political power and employment, and therefore often participate in more informal, community-based organizations and networks. There are some exceptions to this, of course, as many poor women have also attended international conferences, although the divide between those who create and implement WID policies and those who are the recipients of these policies is great. This division leads to extremely divergent views on feminism and politics in general.[10]

An irony is that despite these class differences, neoliberal policies have also galvanized women into participating in broader unified fronts at unprecedented levels. Ecuadorian women's organizations, although they constitute diverse strands of action, have all worked toward strengthening democracy and citizen practices—and in reshaping biased economic policies. Their activism constitutes a web of institutions, meaning, and mobilization, a web that is influenced by local, national, and global discourses of feminism and neoliberalism, among others. The women are part of larger social movement networks and sometimes walk together in marches or attend the same meetings, yet they also operate in distinct spaces in Ecuadorian society. It is these distinct spaces, in household, community, civil society, state, and nation, that I have addressed in this book as a way to understand the coalescing of women activists in a struggle against neoliberal development.

Similar processes are occurring in other Latin American countries. Bolivian women's organizations, for example, including the "Bartolina Sisa" National Federation of Peasant Women of Bolivia (Federación Nacional de Mujeres Campesinas de Bolivia "Bartolina Sisa" [FNMCB-BS]) and middle-class, policy-oriented NGOs such as the La Paz–based Women's Network (Coordinadora de la Mujer) and Cochabamba-based Women's Juridical Office (Oficina Jurídica de la Mujer), address a range of issues related to the current neoliberal economic measures and the politics of decentralization. There, too, while there may be a perceived fragmentation of women's organizations in the neoliberal context, in the sense that neoliberal policies arguably exacerbate divisions between women's organizations, women's organizations nonetheless have created coalitions and informal networks and have simultaneously protested as part of larger political unities, against neoliberalism (Lind 2002).

Futures

More than twenty years have gone by since [the inaugural conference
of the United Nations Decade for the Advancement of Women, 1975–

10. Verónica Schild (1998, 2002) finds similar results in her study of the Chilean women's movement. She argues that middle-class Chilean feminists who work in the state women's agency, National Women's Service (Servicio Nacional de la Mujer [SERNAM]), contribute to neoliberal state formation by facilitating and managing WID policies that target poor women. Among other things, this leads to new forms of market-based citizenship among Chilean women and men.

85, in Mexico City]. There have been so many workshops, so many
conferences. Nonetheless, the situation of women has not improved. It
has remained the same. Nothing has changed.

—DOMITILA BARRIOS DE CHUNGARA, interview, Cochabamba,
Bolivia, April 15, 1999

The examples and studies I discuss in this book show clearly that women are
not passive recipients of development but rather proactive, productive (in the
Foucauldian sense) and resisting. Women's everyday, negotiated encounters
with development provide us with important insight into reimagining development, an important task given the historical fact that women's lives have
changed little, if at all, since the inception of the international development
field—a point Bolivian activist Domitila Barrios de Chungara so aptly makes.[11]
There are two general ideas about development that those who herald the "engendering of development" typically assert. First, many scholars of WID, WAD,
and GAD have addressed the need for alternative development practices, such as
those emerging from the original WID subfield established in the early 1970s.
Since the 1970s, women have been incorporated into development projects in a
range of areas, from agrarian reforms to labor policies and antipoverty, small-
business, health, and education initiatives. Neoliberal development projects
have drawn on these earlier modernization frameworks and emphasized private-
sector development while deemphasizing the state's role in the economy. While
many new institutions and practices have arisen as a result of pushing for WID
policy as an alternative development practice, generally speaking these policies
are produced within the discursive realm of development and therefore contribute to reordering gender (and class, ethnic, and national) difference rather than
eliminating gender inequalities. Through labeling population subgroups as "in
need" and as a "problem to be solved" (Mueller 1985; Escobar 1995), "women,"
"peasants," micro-entrepreneurs," or more recently, "men" (Cleaver 2002) and
"cultural laborers" (Radcliffe, Laurie, and Andolina 2004), are added to development and even given their own subfield.

Insofar as alternative development practices have helped to channel funding
to women's groups and to engender state and societal institutions, I argue that
they are necessary because they contribute to change within already existing
institutions and practices. Were it not for the activism of CPME, FNPME, CON-

11. Domitila Barrios de Chungara was particularly well known among Western feminists in the
1970s and 1980s, following the publication of the English translation of her autobiography, *Let Me
Speak!* (1978) and her appearances at several United Nations women's conferences (see Lind 2003).

AMU, and the broader civil-society-based women's movement, Ecuadorian women would not have the legal rights and protections that they currently have. Since 1980, international agencies and philanthropic institutions have channeled millions of U.S. dollars to Ecuadorian women's organizations. CONAMU itself is funded largely by UNIFEM and other institutions such as IADB, and the Ecuadorian state typically matches a small portion of the international funding, thus making CONAMU a transnational, rather than merely a national, state agency. UNIFEM and IADB have funded GAD graduate programs in Ecuador, including a master's program that was awarded to FLACSO through a competition administered by CONAMU. Similar academic programs exist throughout the region. If it were not for this funding and emphasis "from above" on these issues, Ecuadorian feminists could not promote their political agendas as effectively. At the very least, it is a transnational process of exchange, whereby local feminist policy-makers negotiate with and place demands on international organizations and the state, while at the same time, international organizations place demands on the Ecuadorian state to address gender issues. In conjunction with this, local feminist actors exchange ideas and resources with participants in other women's movements, regionally and globally, in such a way that the Ecuadorian women's movement has had to address these multiple institutional levels and forms of mediation since the beginning of their movement. Similarly, by drawing from this transnational web of international development and social movement formation, middle-class professionals and activists have intervened in and mediated the struggles of poor women in Ecuador, a phenomena that characterizes most Latin American women's movements.

These types of reforms occur "from below" as well, through, for example, women's grassroots organizing and the construction of national umbrella organizations (such as the Ecuadorian Network of Popular Women) and transnational social movement networks. Cultural representations of women in Ecuadorian development discourse and women's movement political discourse are intimately linked to this global negotiation over cultural and economic meanings of gender, including those meanings derived from women's experiences in Ecuadorian society and those derived from Western development discourse. Although many scholars have rightly criticized development studies of "Third World women" on the basis that they essentialize women's lives and naturalize and privilege the economy over all other aspects of women's identities (Ong 1987; Mohanty 1991; Kondo 1990; Marchand and Parpart 1995), this study directly addresses that debate by rethinking the economy itself. To begin with, this requires a rethinking of the meaning of gender, the market and the public/

private in neoliberal development discourse, along with associated notions of community participation, political participation, and citizenship. Rather than negate or avoid the economy, I argue that feminists would be best served by directly addressing it and developing a concrete agenda for the incorporation of feminist interests into state development planning.

This has already begun to occur at the international level, albeit in reformist ways. For example, the United Nations (spearheaded by UNIFEM) has pushed to engender regional trade initiatives and the WTO. In 2002 in Monterey, Mexico, at the first international conference on financing for development, there was extensive coverage of the gender dimensions of the financing-for-development agenda. UNIFEM's commissioned working paper, "The Gender Dimensions of the Financing for Development Agenda" (Floro 2001), is the foundational document for this discussion. In it, the author addresses the gender dimensions of five key aspects: the mobilization of domestic resources, the mobilization of international resources, international trade, international financial cooperation, and external debt. Dissertations and reports are being completed on the topic of gender and world trade (e.g., Bisnath 2002 and 2004), in addition to many that have already been completed on gender, economic restructuring and foreign debt. In Ecuador, a recent study addresses the fact that very few women in Ecuador's countryside own property, property ownership being a key aspect of women's economic independence, despite the country's past agrarian reforms (Deere and León de Leal 2001a and 2001b).

Yet, clearly, in addition to alternative development practices, including these recent innovative studies, we need alternatives to development, particularly to the global, neoliberal development model. This one is not working for the majority of people in this world, although the fact that it works for the rich—a population where wealth is concentrated now more than ever—has meant that to development continues to operate in the interests of the global financial sector and northern economic interests, despite the fact that this community is extremely small and concentrated. Knowledge production, national development frameworks, and concrete practices are influenced by and embedded in these structures. Women's organizations have achieved much for their members and communities, yet to the extent that they either serve as volunteers for neoliberal development initiatives or as managers of the restructuring process (for example, CONAMU), their agendas converge with the interests of the development elite that supports neoliberal, market-based policies. Women's local change and resistance challenges national and global development structures in important ways. Yet development discourse continues to frame their existence, and many feminists, not only in Latin America but also in the United States and elsewhere, still have to catch up to the global discussions taking place about trade and macroeconomic change and to the states that are being restructured and reconfigured in this process.

Feminists have, however, made interesting strategic interventions in national and global contexts of development. In Ecuador, this is evident in feminist reappropriations of nationalist symbols (such as that of Manuela Sáenz) and also in their historical struggle to name themselves ("women") in the cultural project of modernization and modernity. The more recent emphasis on differences between women is another stage in this cultural-political struggle through which women activists have reappropriated colonialist categories to name themselves and oppose neoliberal development. The struggle for citizenship in the early twentieth century is a historical example of this; feminists' symbolic and material struggles for a new, broader definition of citizenship—women's struggles to "become" full citizens—is a more recent example, one we see occurring in the current context of neoliberal state formation, policy making, and local development practices.

To reimagine gender and neoliberal development, we need to rethink the central focus on "the family" of the micro—all that is linked to the private sphere in modern Western discourse—in order to truly refashion WID discourse and practice and, ultimately, to reconfigure social relations of power. There is ample evidence to show how macroeconomic development frameworks are gendered and affect women and men differently, as I have shown throughout this book, yet until now little has been done to examine how they are culturally and politically negotiated. Introducing an alternative model to neoliberal development, representing women differently, and rethinking development itself requires a much broader shift in thinking about self, society, and modernity, one that entails at the very least a fundamental redrawing of the gendered (and classed, racialized, and heteronormative) boundaries of the public and private in development discourse and practice. Among other things, this requires that we examine women's cultural-political interventions in development as well as our own ethnographic imaginations as researchers. "Scholarship," after all, "is implicated in gender-formations" (Oyěwùmí 1997, xv); formations that are embedded in discourses and practices of development, nation-state building, globalization, and identity production.

People throughout the world are challenging globalization and global neoliberal restructuring, in the North and South. The new McWorld is perceived as inevitable and scary to many, regardless of their socioeconomic status or class-based vision of the world. One video game, now available on the web, allows players to stop at McDonald's in their broader pursuit of capitalist wealth and power. Soon after it was introduced, consumer groups asked players to stage virtual protests of McDonald's while playing the game, by virtually acting sick and not purchasing food there in the course of the game ("Big Mac Is Virtual" 2002). These virtual and real protests reflect people's contradictory identifications with globalization, not merely their acquiescence to Western notions of development, modernity, and globalization, or their absolute rejection of it—indeed, most poor people want access to the benefits of modernization. What they challenge is unequal distribution and the concentration of wealth in their societies.

Constructing an alternative to the neoliberal development model is difficult, despite the best intentions of development scholars, including those who address postdevelopment. Yet envisioning a different kind of society is not, nor is critiquing the economic and cultural arrangements within which we currently live. Deconstructing the philosophical and material foundations of neoliberalism and globalization—two forms of discourse that greatly influence Ecuadorian social movements today—is an important starting point from which to imagine an era beyond global domination and to envision a "feminist future" (Bhavnani, Foran, and Kurian 2003). What continues to be unclear is the extent to which feminism as a political project can be critical and creative while also working from within the institutional arrangements of neoliberal development. As Chilean feminist Raquel Olea so aptly states, "[T]here is a dominant discourse and too often we speak from inside that discourse" (quoted in Alvarez 2000, 53). The challenge remains to find a different language to speak about neoliberal development and globalization without speaking entirely from inside it. Above all, this envisioned future includes a push for effective antipoverty policies and the defense of all people's rights to live without poverty.

A P P E N D I X

Chronology of Events

Year	Political and Economic Context	Women's Organizing Efforts
1900–1920s	State liberalization Economic crisis (1925 +) First wave of urbanization High unemployment	Suffragist movement Socialist and nationalist feminisms Pan-American women's congresses Feminist magazines Female suffrage (1929, literate women)
1930–1940s	Velasquista populism Ministry of Social Prevision and Labor (1938) Labor Code (1938) Glorious May Revolution (1944) United Nations (1945 +) Banana exportation	Women's auxiliaries of peasant, indigenous, and labor movements Women in leftist political parties
1950–1960s	Ministry of Labor and Social Welfare (1968) Development aid first channeled Discovery of oil	Women's auxiliaries of peasant and labor organizations formed
1970s	Military rule Oil dollars Heavy state spending Growing deficit Voting rights extended to illiterate people (1976) First election with mass voting participation (1980)	UN women's conference (1975) March of Pots and Pans (1978) Women's participation in antimilitary protest coalitions, human rights, popular education, and labor movements
1980s	Redemocratization Foreign-debt crisis and SAPs Roldós/Hurtado govt. (1980–84) Febres-Cordero govt. (1984–88) Borja government (1988–92)	CEDAW ratified (1981) OFNAMU (1980) CEPAM (1982) AMM established (1986) National Conferences of Feminist Theory (1986 and 1987) First Latin American/Caribbean feminist *encuentro* (1981)

Year	Political and Economic Context	Women's Organizing Efforts
		UN women's conferences (1980, 1985)
		NGOization of women's movement
1990s	Neoliberalism	Violence Against Women Law (1995)
	Indigenous protests and strikes	
	Durán-Ballén govt. (1992–96)	Women's Police Commissaries (1995)
	Bucaram govt. 1996–97	
	Mahuad govt. 1997–2000	CPME (1986)
	New Constitution 1998	CONMEI (1997)
	Financial crisis 1999	Feminists for Autonomy (1997)
		UN Beijing conference (1995)
		Female political quota 20% (1997) CONAMU, Office of the President (1998)
		CONAMU's Equal Opportunity Plan introduced (1998)
		Revised civil/penal codes (1998–99)
2000s	Noboa govt. 2000–2002	Female political quota increased to 30 percent (2000)
	Dollarization (2001)	
	Gutiérrez govt. 2002–present	

BIBLIOGRAPHY

Abad, Angelita, Marena Briones, Tatiana Cordero, Rosa Manzo, and Marta Marchán. 1998. "The Association of Autonomous Women Workers, Ecuador, '22nd June.'" In *Global Sex Workers: Rights, Resistance, and Redefinition*, ed. Kamala Kempadoo and Jo Doezema, 172–77. New York: Routledge.

Abya Yala. N.d. "Alicia Canaviri habla con SAIIC sobre la mujer, los jovenes y la globalización en las comunidades indígenas de Bolivia." *Abya-Yala* 10 (4): 22–24.

Agencia Latinoamericana de Información (ALAI). 2004. "Movimiento de mujeres." http://www.alainet.org/publica/diversidad/movmujer/html (accessed May 8, 2004).

Agreda, E., et al. 1996. *Mujeres cocaleras marchando por una vida sin violencia*. Cochabamba, Bolivia: Comité Coordinador de las Cinco Federaciones del Trópico de Cochabamba.

Alarcón, Norma, Caren Kaplan, and Minoo Moallem. 1999. "Between Woman and Nation." Introduction to *Between Woman and Nation: Nationalisms, Transnational Feminisms, and the State*, ed. Caren Kaplan, Norma Alarcón, and Minoo Moallem, 1–16. Durham: Duke University Press.

Albó, Xavier. 1996. "Making the Leap from Local Mobilization to National Politics." NACLA Report on the Americas 29:15–20.

Alexander, Jacqui, and Chandra Talpade Mohanty, eds. 1997. *Feminist Genealogies, Colonial Legacies, Democratic Futures*. New York: Routledge.

Alvarez, Sonia. 1990. *Engendering Democracy in Brazil: Women's Movements in Transition Politics*. Princeton: Princeton University Press.

———. 1996. "Concluding Reflections: Redrawing the Parameters of Gender Struggle." In *Emergences: Women's Struggles for Livelihood in Latin America*, ed. John Friedmann, Rebecca Abers, and Lilian Autler, 153–84. Los Angeles: University of California, Los Angeles, Latin American Center.

———. 1998a. "Feminismos latinoamericanos: Reflexiones teóricas y perspectivas comparativas." In *Reflexiones teóricas y comparativas sobre los feminismos en Chile y América Latina*, ed. Marcela Ríos, 4–22. Santiago: Facultad Latinoamericana de Ciencias Sociales (FLACSO).

———. 1998b. "Latin American Feminisms 'Go Global': Trends of the 1990s and Challenges for the New Millenium." In *Cultures of Politics/Politics of Cultures: Revisioning Latin American Social Movements*, ed. Sonia Alvarez, Evelina Dagnino, and Arturo Escobar, 293–324. Boulder, Colo.: Westview Press.

———. 2000. "Translating the Global: Effects of Transnational Organizing on Local Feminist Discourses and Practices in Latin America." *Meridians* 1 (1): 29–67.

Alvarez, Sonia, Evelina Dagnino, and Arturo Escobar. 1998a. "The Cultural and the Political in Latin American Social Movements." Introduction to *Cultures of Poli-*

tics/Politics of Cultures: Re-visioning Latin American Social Movements, ed. Sonia Alvarez, Evelina Dagnino, and Arturo Escobar, 1–29. Boulder, Colo.: Westview Press.

———, eds. 1998b. *Cultures of Politics/Politics of Cultures: Re-visioning Latin American Social Movements*, Boulder, Colo.: Westview Press.

Anderson, Benedict. 1983. *Imagined Communities*. London: Verso.

Anderson Velasco, Jeanine. 1985. "The UN Decade for Women in Peru." *Women's Studies International Forum* 8 (2): 107–9.

———. 1990. *Intereses o justicia: ¿Adónde va la discussion sobre la mujer y el desarrollo? Entre mujeres: Un proyecto de cooperación nortesur. Cuadernos de trabajo II*. Lima: Centro de la Mujer Peruana Flora Tristán.

Andrade, Victor Ruben, et al. 1995. *The Weight of Law 1008*. Cochabamba, Bolivia: Andean Information Network.

Andrade, Xavier. 2001. "Machismo and Politics in Ecuador: The Case of Pancho Jaime." *Men and Masculinities* 3 (3): 299–315.

Arboleda, María. 1994. "Mujeres en el poder local en el Ecuador." In *Jaque al Rey: Memorias del taller, participación política de la mujer*, ed. Red de Educación Popular entre Mujeres (REPEM), 41–71. Quito: REPEM/Ciudad.

———. 1998. "Agendas de las mujeres para la Constitución." In *Asamblea: Análisis y propuestas*, ed. Francisco Muñoz Jaramillo, 65–102. Quito: Tramasocial Editorial.

Asad, Talal. 1973. Introduction to *Anthropology and the Colonial Encounter*, ed. Talal Asad, 9–20. Altantic Highlands, N.J.: Humanities Press.

Aslanbeigui, Nahid, Steven Pressman, and Gale Summerfield, eds. 1994. *Women in the Age of Economic Transformation: Gender Impact of Reforms in Post-socialist and Developing Countries*. New York: Routledge.

Ayala Martín, Alexandra. 2004. "El protagonismo de las indígenas: Gran paralización de protesta contó con la decidida participación de las mujeres indígenas," *Nodo 50*, http://www.nodo50.org/mujeresred/ecuador-indigenas.html (accessed May 8, 2004).

———. 2004. "Periodismo feminista y periodistas feministas." http://www.unifemandina.org/unifem/02_03/pandora.htm (accessed May 8, 2004).

Babb, Florence. 2001. *After Revolution: Mapping Gender and Cultural Politics in Neoliberal Nicaragua*. Austin: University of Texas Press.

Baden, Sally, and Anne Marie Goetz. 1998. "Who Needs [Sex] When You Can Have [Gender]? Conflicting Discourses on Gender at Beijing." In *Feminist Visions of Development: Gender Analysis and Policy*, ed. Cecile Jackson and Ruth Pearson, 19–38. New York: Routledge.

Baéz, René et al. 1997. *¿Y ahora que? Una contribución al análisis político-histórico actual*. Quito: Eskeletra Editorial.

Bakker, Isabella, ed. 1994. *The Strategic Silence: Gender and Economic Policy*. London: Zed Press.

———. 1996. *Rethinking Restructuring: Gender and Change in Canada*. Toronto: University of Toronto Press.

Barber, Benjamin. 1995. *Jihad vs. McWorld*. New York: Times Books.

Barrig, Maruja. 1986. *De vecinas a ciudadanas*. Lima: Servicios Urbanos para Mujeres de Bajos Ingresos (SUMBI).

———. 1989. "The Difficult Equilibrium Between Bread and Roses: Women's Organizations and the Transition from Dictatorship to Democracy in Peru." In *The Women's Movement in Latin America: Feminism and the Transition to Democracy*, ed. Jane Jaquette, 114–48. Boston: Unwin Hyman.

———. 1996. "Women, Collective Kitchens, and the Crisis of the State in Peru." In *Emergences: Women's Struggles for Livelihood in Latin America*, ed. John Friedmann, Rebecca Abers, and Lilian Autler, 59–77. Los Angeles: University of California, Los Angeles, Latin American Center.

———. 1998. "Los malestares del feminismo: Una nueva lectura." Paper presented at the thirty-first meeting of the Latin American Studies Association, Miami, Fla.

Barrig, Maruja, Lidia Elías, and Lisbeth Guillén. 1992. *La emergencia social en el Perú*. Lima: Asociación Laboral para el Desarrollo (ADEC-ATC).

Basu, Amrita, ed. 1995. *The Challenge of Local Feminisms: Women's Movements in Global Perspective*. Boulder, Colo.: Westview Press.

Bayard de Volo, Lorraine. 2001. *Mothers of Heroes and Martyrs: Gender Identity Politics in Nicaragua, 1979–1999*. Baltimore: Johns Hopkins University Press.

Becker, Gary. 1981. *A Treatise on the Family*. Cambridge: Harvard University Press.

Becker, Mark. 1999. "Citizens, Indians, and Women: The Politics of Exclusion in Ecuador." Paper presented at the Conference on Latin American History, Washington, D.C. http://www.yachana.org/research/confs/clah99.html (accessed May 8, 2004).

Beckerman, Paul. 2002. "Longer-Term Origins of Ecuador's Pre-dollarization Crisis." In *Crisis and Dollarization in Ecuador*, ed. Paul Beckerman and Andrés Solimano, 17–80. Washington, D.C.: World Bank.

Beckerman, Paul, and Andrés Solimano. 2002. *Crisis and Dollarization in Ecuador*. Washington, D.C.: World Bank.

Benería, Lourdes. 1992a. "Accounting for Women's Work: The Progress of Two Decades." *World Development* 20 (11): 1547–60.

———. 1992b. "The Mexican Debt Crisis: Restructuring the Economy and the Household." In *Unequal Burden: Economic Crises, Persistent Poverty, and Women's Work*, ed. Lourdes Benería and Shelley Feldman, 83–104. Boulder, Colo.: Westview Press.

———. 1995. "Toward a Greater Understanding of Gender and Economics." *World Development* 23 (11): 1839–50.

———. 1996. "Globalization, Gender, and the Davos Man." *Feminist Economics* 5 (3): 61–84.

Benería, Lourdes, and Shelley Feldman, eds. 1992. *Unequal Burden: Economic Crises, Persistent Poverty, and Women's Work*. Boulder, Colo.: Westview Press.

Benería, Lourdes, Maria Floro, Caren Grown, and Martha MacDonald. 2000. "Globalization and Gender." Introduction to *Feminist Economics* 6 (3): vii–xviii.

Benería, Lourdes, and Amy Lind. 1995. "Engendering International Trade: Concepts, Policy, Action." In *A Commitment to the World's Women: Strategies for Beijing and Beyond*, ed. Noeleen Heyzer, 69–86. New York: United Nations Development Fund for Women (UNIFEM).

Benería, Lourdes, and Breny Mendoza. 1995. "Structural Adjustment and Social Emergency Funds: The Cases of Honduras, Mexico, and Nicaragua." Paper prepared for UNRISD's project Economic Restructuring and New Social Policies, Spring.

Berger, Mark T. 1995. *Under Northern Eyes: Latin American Studies and U.S. Hegemony in the Americas, 1989–1990*. Bloomington: Indiana University Press.

Bergeron, Suzanne. 2001. "Political Economy Discourses of Globalization and Gender." *Signs* 26 (4): 983–1006.

Beverley, John, and José Oviedo, eds. 1993. "The Postmodernism Debate in Latin America." Special issue, *boundary 2* 20 (3).

Bhavnani, Kum-Kum, John Foran, and Priya Kurian, eds. 2003. *Feminist Futures: Reimagining Women, Culture, and Development*. London: Zed Books.

"Big Mac Is Virtual, but Critics Are Real." 2002. *New York Times*, November 28, Circuits sec.

Bisnath, Savitri. 2002. "The WTO and the Liberalization of Trade in Services: Development, Equity, and Governance." Ph.D diss., Cornell University.

———. 2004. "The WTO, GATS, and TPRM: Serving Liberalization and Evading Equity Goals?" In *Global Tensions: Challenges and Opportunities in the Global Economy*, ed. Lourdes Benería and Savitri Bisnath, 155–71. New York: Routledge.

Bonilla, Adrián. 1992. "Conceptos, tradiciones y leyendas: Notas para pensar la cultura política en América Latina y Ecuador." Paper presented at the twenty-seventh meeting of the Latin American Studies Association, Los Angeles, California, September 24–27.

Boserup, Ester. 1970. *Woman's Role in Economic Development*. New York: St. Martin's Press.

Brodie, Janine. 1994. "Shifting the Boundaries: Gender and the Politics of Restructuring." In *The Strategic Silence: Gender and Economic Policy*, ed. Isabella Bakker, 46–60. London: Zed Books.

Buechler, Hans, Judith-Maria Buechler, Simone Buechler, and Stephanie Buechler. 1998. "Financing Small-Scale Enterprises in Bolivia." In *The Third Wave of Modernization in Latin America: Cultural Perspectives on Neoliberalism*, ed. Lynne Phillips, 83–108. Wilmington, Del.: Scholarly Resources Books.

Burawoy, Michael. 2000. "Reaching for the Global." Introduction to *Global Ethnography: Forces, Connections, and Imaginations in a Postmodern World*, ed. Michael Burawoy et al., 1–40. Berkeley and Los Angeles: University of California Press.

Burawoy, Michael, et al. 2000. *Global Ethnography: Forces, Connections, and Imaginations in a Postmodern World*. Berkeley and Los Angeles: University of California Press.

Burgos-Debray, Elisabeth. 1994. *I, Rigoberta Menchú: An Indian Woman in Guatemala*. New York: Verso.

Burt, Jo-Marie. 1997. "Political Violence and the Grassroots in Lima, Peru." In *The New Politics of Inequality in Latin America: Rethinking Participation and Representation*, ed. Douglas Chalmers et al., 281–309. London: Oxford University Press.

Burt, Jo-Marie, and Philip Mauceri, eds. 2004. *Politics in the Andes: Identity, Conflict, Reform*. Pittsburgh: University of Pittsburgh Press.

Butler, Judith. 1990. *Gender Trouble: Feminism and the Subversion of Identity*. New York: Routledge.

Butler, Judith, and Joan Scott, eds. 1992. *Feminists Theorize the Political*. New York: Routledge.

Buvinic, Mayra, Catherine Gwin, and Lisa M. Bates. 1996. *Investing in Women: Progress* and Prospects for the World Bank. Overseas Development Council in cooperation with the International Center for Research on Women. Baltimore: Johns Hopkins University Press.

Calderón, Fernando. 1988a. "Cómo vivir en la modernidad sin dejar de ser indio." In La modernidad en la encrucijada postmoderna, 71–78. Buenos Aires: Consejo Latinoamericano de Ciencias Sociales (CLACSO)

———. 1988b. La modernidad en la encrucijada postmoderna. Buenos Aires: Consejo Latinoamericano de Ciencias Sociales (CLACSO).

Calderón, Fernando, Alejandro Piscitelli, and José Luis Reyna. 1992. "Social Movements: Actors, Theories, Expectations." In The Making of Social Movements in Latin America: Identity, Strategy, Democracy, ed. Arturo Escobar and Sonia Alvarez, 19–36. Boulder, Colo.: Westview Press.

Calvimontes, Magda. 1997. Análisis de género, ordenanzas, resoluciones y reglamientos municipales de Tarma. Local Power series. La Paz, Bolivia: Sub-secretaría de Asuntos de Género.

Carrasco, Carlos Marx. 2001. Dolarización: Un camino de espinas y espejismos. Cuenca, Ecuador: Universidad de Cuenca.

Castells, Manuel. 1999. Interview. Television broadcast, April 23. Cochabamba, Bolivia.

Centro Ecuatoriano de Investigaciones Sociales (CEIS). 1984. "Problems That Concern Women and Their Consideration in Development Planning: The Case of Ecuador." Project report prepared for United Nations Educational, Scientific, and Cultural Organization (UNESCO), Quito.

Centro María Quilla. 1991. Protagonismo de las mujeres en el levantamiento indígena. Quito: Centro María Quilla.

Centro María Quilla/CEAAL. 1990. Mujeres, educación y conciencia de género en Ecuador. Quito: Centro María Quilla.

Chaney, Elsa. 1979. Supermadre: Women in Politics in Latin America. Austin: University of Texas Press.

Chang, Grace. 2000. Disposable Domestics: Immigrant Women Workers in the Global Economy. Boston: South End Press.

Chen, Martha. 1995. "A Matter of Survival: Women's Right to Employment in Bangladesh and India." In Women, Culture, and Development: A Study of Human Capabilities, ed. Martha Nussbaum and Jonathon Glover, 37–57. Oxford: Clarendon Press.

Chua, Peter, Kum-Kum Bhavnani, and John Foran. 2000. "Women, Culture, Development: A New Paradigm for Development Studies?" Ethnic and Racial Studies 23 (5): 820–41.

Clark, Kim. 2001. "Género, raza y nación: La protección a la infancia en el Ecuador (1910–1945)." In Estudios de género, ed. Gioconda Herrera, 183–210. Quito: Facultad Latinoamericana de Ciencias Sociales (FLACSO)/Instituto Latinoamericano de Investigaciones Sociales (ILDIS).

Cleaver, Frances, ed. 2002. Masculinities Matter! Men, Gender, and Development. London: Zed Books.

Cohen, Jean L., and Andrew Arato. 1992. Civil Society and Political Theory. Cambridge: MIT Press.

Comaroff, Jean, and John L. Comaroff. 2001. "Millenial Capitalism: First Thoughts on a Second Coming." In *Millenial Capitalism and the Culture of Neoliberalism*, ed. Jean Comaroff and John L. Comaroff, 1–56. Durham: Duke University Press.

———, eds. 2001. *Millenial Capitalism and the Culture of Neoliberalism*. Durham: Duke University Press.

Conaghan, Catherine. 1988. *Restructuring Domination: Industrialists and the State in Ecuador*. Pittsburgh: University of Pittsburgh Press.

Conaghan, Catherine M., and James Malloy. 1994. *Unsettling Statecraft: Democracy and Neoliberalism in the Central Andes*. Pittsburgh: University of Pittsburgh Press.

Condo-Riveros, Freddy. 1996. *Las Bartolinas: Sus orígenes, su historia y futuro*. La Paz, Bolivia: Federación Nacional de Mujeres Campesinas de Bolivia "Bartolina Sisa."

CONADE. 1993. *Agenda para el desarrollo: Plan de acción del gobierno 1993–1996*. Quito: CONADE.

CONADE/UNDP/UNESCO/UNICEF/Ministerio de Bienestar Social. 1991. "Informe General, Prueba Piloto de Evaluación de Impactos de los Proyectos de Acción del Ministerio de Bienestar Social en el Programa 'Red Comunitaria para el Desarrollo Infantil.'" Quito: CONADE/UNDP/UNESCO/UNICEF/Ministerio de Bienestar Social.

CONAIE. 1994. *Memorias de las jornadas del foro de la mujer indígena del Ecuador*. Quito: Confederación de Nacionalidades Indígenas del Ecuador (CONAIE)/United Nations Population Fund (UNFPA).

Corkill, David, and David Cubitt. 1988. *Ecuador: Fragile Democracy*. London: Latin American Bureau.

Cornejo Menacho, Diego. 2003. "En busca del rumbo perdido." *Hoy* (Quito), April 24, http://www.hoy.com.ec/especial/2003/e100dias.htm (accessed April 27, 2003).

Cornia, Giovanni Andrea, et al. 1987. *Adjustment with a Human Face*. Oxford: Clarendon Press.

Cowan, Paul. 1967. *The Making of an Un-American*, New York: Viking Press.

Crain, Mary M. 1996. "The Gendering of Ethnicity in the Ecuadorian Andes: Women's Self-Fashioning in the Urban Marketplace." In *Machos, Mistresses, Madonnas: Contesting the Power of Latin American Gender Imagery*, ed. Marit Melhuus and Kristi Anne Stølen, 134–58. London: Verso.

Craske, Nikke. 1999. *Women and Politics in Latin America*. Oxford: Polity Press.

Cueva, Agustín. 1988. *El proceso de dominación política en el Ecuador*. Quito: Editorial Planeta.

Cuvi, María. 1992. "Las mujeres en el discurso y la práctica estatal en los años 80." In *Entre los límites y las rupturas: Las mujeres ecuatorianas en la década de los 80*, ed. Centro de Planificación y Estudios Sociales (CEPLAES), 103–14. Quito: CEPLAES/CIDA (Canadian International Development Agency).

Daines, Victoria, and David Seddon. 1994. "Fighting for Survival: Women's Responses to Austerity Progams." In *Free Markets and Food Riots: The Politics of Global Adjustment*, by John Walton and David Seddon, 57–96. Cambridge, Mass.: Blackwell.

Dash, Robert, ed. 1997a. "Ecuador I: Politics and Rural Issues." Special issue, *Latin American Perspectives* 24 (3).

———. 1997b. "Ecuador II: Women and Popular Classes in Struggle." Special issue, *Latin American Perspectives* 24 (4).

Deere, Carmen Diana, and Magdalena León de Leal. 2001a. *Empowering Women: Land and Property Rights in Latin America*. Pittsburgh: University of Pittsburgh Press.

——. 2001b. "Institutional Reform of Agriculture Under Neoliberalism: The Impact of the Women's and Indigenous Movements." *Latin American Research Review* 36 (2): 31–63.

de Janvry, Alain, et al. 1994. *The Political Feasability of Adjustment in Ecuador and Venezuela*. Paris: Organization for Economic Cooperation and Development (OECD) Development Centre.

de Janvry, Alain, Elisabeth Sadoulet, and André Fargeix. 1991. *Adjustment and Equity in Ecuador*. Paris: OECD Development Centre.

de la Torre, Carlos. 2000. *Populist Seduction in Latin America: The Ecuadorian Experience*. Athens: Ohio University Press.

Delgado, Ernesto. 1992. "Ecuador: Balance de las políticas para pagar la deuda social 1987–1990, Programa 'Red Comunitaria para el Desarrollo Infantil."

Delgado Ribadeneira, Ernesto. 1992. "Programa Red Comunitaria para el Desarollo Infantil 1987–1990." In *Ecuador: Los costos sociales del ajuste, 1980–1990*. Vol. 2, *Informe de los consultores*, ed. Programa Regional de Empleo para America Latina y el Caribe (PREALC). Santiago de Chile: PREALC.

Delpino, Nena. 1991. "Las organizaciones femeninas por la alimentación: Un menú sazonado." In *La otra cara de la luna: Nuevos actores sociales en el Perú*, ed. Luís Pásara et al., 29–72. Buenos Aires: Centro de Estudios de Derecho y Sociedad (CEDYS).

DePalma, Anthony. 2000. "Latin America Decides, If You Can't Beat 'Em, Join 'Em." *New York Times*, January 23, http://www.nytimes.com/library/review/012300ecuador-dollar-review.html (accessed May 8, 2004).

de Soto, Hernando. 1989. *The Other Path*. New York: Harper and Row.

DINAMU. 1989. *Plan para la equidad de género 1988–1992*. Quito: DINAMU.

——. 1993. *Plan para la equidad de género 1993–1996*. Quito: DINAMU.

——. 1996. *Plan de igualdad de oportunidades 1996–2000*. Quito: DINAMU.

Dirmoser, Dietmar, ed. 2001. "La dolarización: Crisis o soluciones." Special issue, *Nueva Sociedad* 172 (March–April).

Dwyer, Daisy, and Judith Bruce, eds. 1988. *A Home Divided: Women and Income in the Third World*. Palo Alto: Stanford University Press.

Economist Intelligence Unit (EIU). 1995a. *Country Profile: Ecuador, 1994–1995*. London: Economist Intelligence Unit.

——. 1995b. *Country Report: Ecuador*, no. 1. London: EIU.

"El Salvador Learns to Love the Greenback." 2000. *Economist*, September 26, 2000, http://www.globalpolicy.org/nations/sovereign/statehood/dollar/2002/0926salvador.htm (accessed May 8, 2004).

Elson, Diane. 1992. "From Survival Strategies to Transformation Strategies: Women's Needs and Structural Adjustment." In *Unequal Burden: Economic Crises, Persistent Poverty, and Women's Work*, ed. Lourdes Benería and Shelley Feldman, 26–48. Boulder, Colo.: Westview Press.

——. 1995. "Male Bias in Macro-economics: The Case of Structural Adjustment." In *Male Bias in the Development Process*, ed. Diane Elson, 164–90. 2d ed. Manchester: Manchester University Press.

————. 1998. "Talking to the Boys: Gender and Economic Growth Models." In *Feminist Visions of Development: Gender Analysis and Policy,* ed. Cecile Jackson and Ruth Pearson, 155–70. New York: Routledge.

————. 2002. "Gender Justice, Human Rights, and Neo-liberal Economic Policies." In *Gender Justice, Development, and Rights,* ed. Maxine Molyneux and Shahra Razavi, 78–114. New York: Oxford University Press.

————, ed. 1995. *Male Bias in the Development Process.* 2d ed. Manchester: Manchester University Press.

Emeagwali, Gloria, ed. 1995. *Women Pay the Price: Structural Adjustment in Africa and the Caribbean.* Trenton, N.J.: Africa World Press.

Enloe, Cynthia. 1989. *Bananas, Beaches, and Bases: Making Feminist Sense of International Politics.* Berkeley and Los Angeles: University of California Press.

Escobar, Arturo. 1995. *Encountering Development: The Making and Unmaking of the Third World.* Princeton: Princeton University Press.

————. 2000. "Beyond the Search for a Paradigm? Post-development and Beyond." *Development* 43 (4): 11–14.

Escobar, Arturo, and Sonia Alvarez. 1992. "Theory and Protest in Latin America Today." Introduction to *The Making of Social Movements in Latin America: Identity, Strategy, Democracy,* ed. Arturo Escobar and Sonia Alvarez, 1–18. Boulder, Colo.: Westview Press.

————, eds. 1992. *The Making of Social Movements in Latin America: Identity, Strategy, Democracy.* Boulder, Colo.: Westview Press.

Esteva, Gustavo, and Madhu Suri Prakash. 1998. *Grassroots Post-modernism: Remaking the Soil of Cultures.* London: Zed Books.

Feijoo, María del Carmen. 1994. "La trampa del efecto: Mujer y democracia en Argentina." In *Mujeres y participación política: Avances y desafíos en América Latina,* ed. Magdalena León, 319–47. Bogotá: Tercer Mundo Ediciones.

Ferber, Marianne, and Julie Nelson, eds. 1993. *Beyond Economic Man: Feminist Theory and Economics.* Chicago: University of Chicago Press.

Ferguson, James. 1994. *The Anti-politics Machine: "Development," Depoliticization, and Bureaucratic Power in Lesotho.* Minneapolis: University of Minnesota Press.

Fernández-Alemany, Manuel. 2000. "Negotiating Gay Identities: The Neoliberalization of Sexual Politics in Honduras." Paper presented at the twenty-eighth meeting of the Latin American Studies Association, Miami, Florida, March.

Fine, Kathleen Sue. 1991. *Cotocollao: Ideología, historia y acción en un barrio de Quito.* Quito: Ediciones Abya-Yala.

Fiol-Matta, Licia. 2002. *A Queer Mother for the Nation: The State and Gabriela Mistral.* Minneapolis: University of Minnesota Press.

Fisher, Robert, and Jo Kling, eds. 1993. *Mobilizing the Community: Local Politics in the Era of the Global City.* Beverley Hills, Calif.: Sage.

Floro, Maria. 2001. "The Gender Dimensions of the Financing for Development Agenda." United Nations Development Fund for Women (UNIFEM), New York, April.

Folbre, Nancy. 1988. "The Black Four of Hearts: Toward a New Paradigm of Household Economics." In *A Home Divided: Women and Income in the Third World,* ed. Daisy Dwyer and Judith Bruce, 248–62. Palo Alto: Stanford University Press.

———. 1994. *Who Pays for the Kids? Gender and the Structures of Constraint.* New York: Routledge.

Folbre, Nancy, and Michael Bittman, eds. 2004. *Family Time: The Social Organization of Care.* New York: Routledge.

Foucault, Michel. 1980. *Power/Knowledge: Selected Interviews and Other Writings 1972– 1977.* New York: Pantheon Books.

Franco, Jean. 1989. *Plotting Women: Gender and Representation in Mexico.* New York: Columbia University Press.

———. 1996. "The Gender Wars." NACLA Report on the Americas 29 (4): 6–9.

———. 1999. "Globalization and the Crisis of the Popular." In *Critical Passions: Selected Essays by Jean Franco,* ed. Mary Louise Pratt and Kathleen Newman, 208–20. Durham: Duke University Press.

Frankenberg, Ruth. 1993. *White Women, Race Matters: The Social Construction of Whiteness.* Minneapolis: University of Minnesota Press.

Fraser, Nancy. 1989. *Unruly Practices: Power, Discourse, and Gender in Contemporary Social Theory.* Minneapolis: University of Minnesota Press.

———. 1997. "Rethinking the Public Sphere: A Contribution to the Critique of 'Actually Existing Democracy.'" In *Justice Interruptus: Critical Reflections on the "Post-Socialist" Condition,* 69–98. New York: Routledge.

Fraser, Nancy, and Linda Gordon. 1994. "A Genealogy of Dependency: Tracing a Keyword of the U.S. Welfare State." *Signs* 19 (2): 303–37.

Freeman, Carla. 2001. "Is Local : Global as Feminine : Masculine? Rethinking the Gender of Globalization." *Signs* 26 (4): 1007–37.

Friedland, Lewis A. 2000. "Covering the World." *The Globalization Reader,* ed. Frank Lechner and John Boli, 293–300. Malden, Mass.: Blackwell.

Friedman, Elisabeth. 1999. "The Effects of 'Transnationalism Reversed' in Venezuela: Assessing the Impact of UN Global Conferences on the Women's Movement." *International Feminist Journal of Politics* 1 (3): 357–81.

———. 2000. *Unfinished Transitions: Women and the Gendered Development of Democracy in Venezuela, 1936–1996.* University Park: Pennsylvania State University Press.

Fuller, Norma. 2001. "The Social Construction of Gender Identity Among Peruvian Men." *Men and Masculinities* 3 (3): 316–31.

Fuss, Diana. 1989. *Essentially Speaking: Feminism, Nature, and Difference.* New York: Routledge.

Garcés, Miriam. 1999. "Ética y equidad: Perspectiva." In *Ecuador: Los desafíos éticos del presente,* ed. Luis Mella, 125–35. Quito: Santillana.

García Canclini, Nestor. 1993. *Transforming Modernity: Popular Culture in Mexico.* Austin: University of Texas Press.

———. 2001. *Consumers and Citizens: Globalization and Multicultural Conflicts.* Minneapolis: University of Minnesota Press.

George, Susan. 1997. "How the Poor Develop the Rich." In *The Post-development Reader,* ed. Majid Rahnema with Victoria Bawtree, 207–13. London: Zed Press.

Gerlach, Allen. 2003. *Indians, Oil, and Politics: A Recent History of Ecuador.* Wilmington, Del.: Scholarly Resources.

Gibson Graham, J. K. 1996. *The End of Capitalism (As We Knew It): A Feminist Critique of Political Economy.* Cambridge, Mass.: Basil Blackwell.

Gill, Lesley. 2000. *Teetering on the Rim: Global Restructuring, Daily Life, and the Armed Retreat of the Bolivian State*. New York: Columbia University Press.

Goetschel, Ana María. 1999. *Mujeres e imaginarios: Quito en los inicios de la modernidad*. Quito: Abya-Yala Ediciones.

Goetz, Anne Marie, ed. 1997. *Getting Institutions Right for Women in Development*. London: Zed Press.

Gómez, Rosario. 1993. "Logros y dificultades de la Dirección Nacional de la Mujer: Ministerio de Bienestar Social (DINAMU)." In *Políticas sociales para la mujer: Memorias del seminario internacional*, ed. Organismo Nacional del Menor, Mujer y Familia (ONAMFA), 59–74. La Paz, Bolivia: ONAMFA.

Gowan, Teresa, and Seán Ó Riain. 2000. Preface to *Global Ethnography: Forces, Connections, and Imaginations in a Postmodern World*, ed. Michael Burawoy et al., ix–xv. Berkeley and Los Angeles: University of California Press.

Green, Linda 1998. "The Localization of the Global: Contemporary Production Practices in a Mayan Community in Guatemala." In *The Third Wave of Modernization in Latin America: Cultural Perspectives on Neoliberalism*, ed. Lynne Phillips, 51–61. Wilmington, Del.: Scholarly Resources Books.

Grewal, Inderpal, and Caren Kaplan, eds. 1994. *Scattered Hegemonies: Postmodernity and Transnational Feminist Practices*. Minneapolis: University of Minnesota Press.

Guy, Donna. 1991. *Sex and Danger in Buenos Aires: Prostitution, Family, and Nation in Argentina*. Lincoln: University of Nebraska Press.

Handelman, Howard. 1992. "The Origins of the Ecuadorian Bourgeoisie: A Generational Transformation." Paper presented at the twenty-seventh meeting of the Latin American Studies Association, Los Angeles, California, September 24–27.

Harcourt, Wendy. 1993/4. "Women, Sexuality, and the Family." *Development*: 25–27.

———, ed. 2000. Special issue (on postdevelopment), *Development* 43 (4).

Harris, Olivia. 1978. "Complementarity and Conflict: An Andean View of Women and Men." In *Sex and Age as Principles of Social Differentiation*, ed. J. LaFontaine. London: Academic Press.

———. 2000. *To Make the Earth Bear Fruit: Ethnographic Essays on Fertility, Work, and Gender in Highland Bolivia*. London: Institute of Latin American Studies, University of London.

Herdt, Gilbert, ed. 1994. *Third Sex, Third Gender: Beyond Sexual Dimorphism in Culture and History*. New York: Zone Books.

Herrera, Gioconda, ed. 2000. *Las fisuras del patriarcado: Reflexiones sobre feminismo y derecho*. Quito: Facultad Latinoamericana de Ciencias Sociales (FLACSO).

———, ed. 2001. *Estudios de género*. Quito: Facultad Latinoamericana de Ciencias Sociales (FLACSO)/Instituto Latinoamericano de Investigaciones Sociales (ILDIS).

Herzfeld, Michael. 1992. *The Social Production of Indifference: Exploring the Symbolic Roots of Western Bureaucracy*. Chicago: University of Chicago Press.

Heyzer, Noeleen, ed. 1995. *A Commitment to the World's Women: Perspectives on Development for Beijing and Beyond*. New York: United Nations Development Fund for Women (UNIFEM).

Hidrobo, Jorge A. 1992. *Power and Industrialization in Ecuador*. Boulder, Colo.: Westview Press.

Hondagneu-Sotelo, Pierrette. 2001. *Doméstica: Immigrant Workers Cleaning and Caring in the Shadows of Affluence.* Berkeley and Los Angeles: University of California Press.

Howe, Alyssa Cymene. 2000. "Undressing the Universal Queer Subject: Nicaraguan Activists and Transnational Identities." Paper presented at the eighteenth meeting of the Latin American Studies Association (LASA), Miami, Florida, March 16–18.

Htun, Mala. 2003. *Sex and the State: Abortion, Divorce, and the Family Under Latin American Dictatorships and Democracies.* New York: Cambridge University Press.

Hurtado, Osvaldo. 1997. *El poder político en el Ecuador.* Quito: Pontificia Universidad Católica del Ecuador.

Illich, Ivan. 1969. *Celebration of Awareness.* New York: Pantheon Books.

ILDIS (Instituto Latinoamericano de Investigaciones Sociales). 1993. *Informe social Ecuador: Ajuste y situación social.* Quito: ILDIS.

IADB (Inter-American Development Bank). 1994. *Economic and Social Progress in Latin America: 1994 Report.* Washington, D.C.: IADB.

IULA (International Union of Local Authorities)/CELCADEL (Centro Latinoamericano de Capacitación y Desarrollo de los Gobiernos Locales)/RHUDO-USAID (Regional Housing and Urban Development Unit–United States Agency for International Development). 1992. *De la mujer al género: Democratización municipal y nuevas perspectivas de desarrollo local.* Quito: United States Agency for International Development.

———. 1996. *Local Governments and Gender Equity: New Perspectives and Responsibilities.* Quito: United States Agency for International Development.

———. 1997. *Los procesos de reforma del estado a la luz de las teorías de género.* Quito: USAID.

Isbell, Billie Jean. 1978. *To Defend Ourselves: Ecology and Ritual in an Andean Village.* Prospect Heights, Ill.: Waveland Press.

Jackson, Cecile, and Ruth Pearson, eds. 1998. *Feminist Visions of Development: Gender Analysis and Policy.* New York: Routledge.

James, Joy. 1996. *Resisting State Violence: Radicalism, Gender, and Race in U.S. Culture.* Minneapolis: University of Minnesota Press.

Jameson, Fredric, and Masao Miyoshi, eds. 1998. *The Cultures of Globalization.* Durham: Duke University Press.

Jaquette, Jane. ed. 1994. *The Women's Movement in Latin America: Participation and Democracy.* Boulder, Colo.: Westview Press.

Jetter, Alexis, Annelise Orleck, and Diana Taylor, eds. 1997. *The Politics of Motherhood: Activist Voices from Left to Right.* Lebanon: University Press of New England.

Jelin, Elizabeth, ed. 1990. *Women and Social Change in Latin America.* London: Zed Books/United Nations Research Institute for Social Development (UNRISD).

Jochnick, Chris. 1999. "Economic, Social, and Cultural Rights in Ecuador." Research report, Centro de Derechos Económicos y Sociales (CDES), Quito.

Joseph, Gilbert, and Daniel Nugent, eds. 1994. *Everyday Forms of State Formation: Revolution and Negotiation of Rule in Modern Mexico.* Durham: Duke University Press.

Kabeer, Naila. 1994. *Reversed Realities: Gender Hierarchies in Development Thought.* New York: Verso.

Kaplan, Caren. 1996. *Questions of Travel: Postmodern Discourses of Displacement.* Durham: Duke University Press.

Kaplan, Caren, Norma Alarcón, and Minoo Moallem, eds. 1999. *Between Woman and Nation: Nationalisms, Transnational Feminisms, and the State.* Durham: Duke University Press.

Kayatekin, Serap, and David Ruccio. 1998. "Global Fragments: Subjectivity and Class Politics in Discourses of Globalization." *Economy and Society* 27 (1): 74–96.

Keck, Margaret E., and Kathryn Sikkink. 1998. *Activists Beyond Borders: Advocacy Networks in International Politics.* Ithaca, N.Y.: Cornell University Press.

Kirk, Robin. 1993. *Grabado en piedra: Las mujeres de Sendero Luminoso.* Lima: Instituto de Estudios Peruanos.

Kirkwood, Julieta. "Feministas y políticas." In *Mujeres latinoamericanas: Diez ensayos y una historia colectiva,* ed. Centro de la Mujer Peruana Flora Tristan, 17–28. Lima: Ediciones Flora Tristan, 1988.

Klor de Alva, J. Jorge. 1995. "The Postcolonization of the (Latin) American Experience: A Reconsideration of 'Colonialism,' 'Postcolonialism,' and 'Mestizaje.'" In *After Colonialism: Imperial Histories and Postcolonial Displacements,* ed. Gyan Prakash, 241–78. Princeton: Princeton University Press.

Kondo, Dorinne. 1990. *Crafting Selves: Power, Gender, and Discourses of Identity in a Japanese Workplace.* Chicago: University of Chicago Press.

Kruze, Thomas. 1999. "Mujeres Creando Paints Bolivia." http://www.americas.org/news/ Features . . . ights/bolivias_mujeres_creando.htm (accessed May 7, 2003).

Kuczunski, Pedro Pablo. 1988. *Latin American Debt.* Baltimore: Johns Hopkins University Press.

Larson, Brooke, and Olivia Harris, eds. 1995. *Ethnicity, Markets, and Migration in the Andes.* Durham: Duke University Press.

Lechner, Franck, and John Boli, eds. 2001. *The Globalization Reader.* Malden, Mass: Blackwell.

Lechner, Norbert. 1990. *Los patios interiores de la democracía.* Mexico City: Fondo de Cultura Económica.

Lefeber, Louis. 2330. "Problems of Contemporary Development: Neoliberalism and Its Consequences." In *Rural Progress: Rural Decay,* ed. Liisa North and John D. Cameron, 25–45. Bloomfield, Conn.: Kumarian Press.

León Trujillo, Magdalena. 1992. "Políticas neoliberales frente al trabajo femenino, Ecuador 1984–1988." In *Tiempo y espacio: Las luchas sociales de las mujeres latinoamericanas,* ed. María del Carmen Feijoó. Buenos Aires: Consejo Latinoamericano de Ciencias Sociales (CLACSO).

———, ed. 1996. *Agenda política: Coordinadora Política Nacional de Mujeres.* Quito: Coordinadora Política Nacional de las Mujeres.

Lim, Linda. 1997. "Capitalism, Imperialism, and Patriarchy: The Dilemma of Third World Women Workers in Multinational Factories." In *The Women, Gender, and Development Reader,* ed. Nalini Visvanathan, Lynn Duggan, Laurie Nisonoff, and Nan Wiegersma, 216–29. London: Zed Press.

Lind, Amy. 1990. *Economic Crisis, Women's Work, and the Reproduction of Gender Ideology: Popular Women's Organizations in Quito, Ecuador.* M.R.P. thesis, Cornell University.

———. 1992. "Gender, Power, and Development: Popular Women's Organizations and the Politics of Needs in Ecuador." In *The Making of Social Movements in Latin*

America: Identity, Strategy, Democracy, ed. Arturo Escobar and Sonia Alvarez, 134–49. Boulder, Colo.: Westview Press.

———. 1995. *Gender, Development, and Women's Political Practices in Ecuador*. Ph.D. diss., Cornell University.

———. 1997. "Gender, Development, and Urban Social Change: Women's Community Action in Global Cities." *World Development* 25 (8): 1205–24.

———. 2000. "Negotiating Boundaries: Women's Organizations and the Politics of Development in Ecuador." In *Gender and Global Restructuring: Sightings, Sites, and Resistances*, ed. Marianne Marchand and Anne Sisson Runyan, 161–75. New York: Routledge.

———. 2002. "Making Feminist Sense of Neoliberalism: The Institutionalization of Women's Struggles for Survival in Ecuador and Bolivia." *Journal of Developing Societies* 18 (2–3): 228–58.

———. 2003a. "Feminist Post-development Thought: 'Women in Development' and the Gendered Paradoxes of Survival in Bolivia." *Women's Studies Quarterly* 31 (3–4): 227–46.

———. 2003b. "Gender and Neoliberal States: Feminists Remake the Nation in Ecuador." *Latin American Perspectives* 30 (1): 181–207.

———. 2004. "Engendering Andean Politics: The Paradoxes of Women's Movements in Neoliberal Ecuador and Bolivia." In *Politics in the Andes: Identity, Conflict, Reform*, ed. Jo-Marie Burt and Philip Mauceri, 58–78, Pittsburgh: University of Pittsburgh Press.

Lind, Amy, and Jessica Share. 2003. "Queering Development: Institutionalized Heterosexuality in Development Theory, Practice, and Politics in Latin America." In *Feminist Futures: Re-imagining Women, Culture, and Development*, ed. Kum-Kum Bhavnani, John Foran, and Priya Kurian, 55–73. London: Zed Books.

Loayza Castro, Natasha. 1997. *El trabajo de las mujeres en el mundo global: paradojas y promesas*. El Alto, Bolivia: Centro de Promoción de la Mujer "Gregoria Apaza."

McDowell Santos, Cecilia. 1998. "Feminists in/Against the State: Women's Police Stations in Brazil." Paper presented at the conference "Feminism(s) in Latin America and the Caribbean: Prospects and Challenges on the Eve of the Twenty-first Century," University of California at Berkeley, April.

McFarren, Wendy. 1992. "The Politics of Bolivia's Economic Crisis: Survival Strategies of Displaced Tin-Mining Households." In *Unequal Burden: Economic Crises, Persistent Poverty, and Women's Work*, ed. Lourdes Benería and Shelley Feldman, 131–58. Boulder, Colo.: Westview Press.

Marchand, Marianne, and Jane Parpart, eds. 1995. *Feminism/Postmodernism/Development*. London: Routledge.

Marchand, Marianne, and Anne Sisson Runyan. 2000. "Feminist Sightings of Global Restructuring: Conceptualizations and Reconceptualizations." Introduction to *Gender and Global Restructuring: Sightings, Sites, and Resistances*, ed. Marianne Marchand and Anne Sisson Runyan, 1–22. New York: Routledge.

———, eds. 2000. *Gender and Global Restructuring: Sightings, Sites, and Resistances*. New York: Routledge.

Marshall, T. H. 1964. *Class, Citizenship, and Social Development*. Chicago: University of Chicago Press.

Martz, John. 1987. *Politics and Petroleum in Ecuador*. New Brunswick, N.J.: Transaction.

Meisch, Lynn A. 200. "Crisis and Coup in Ecuador." *Against the Current* 15 (3): 14–16.

Menéndez-Carrión, Amparo. 1986. *La conquista del voto: De Velasco a Roldós*. Quito: Facultad Latinoamericana de Ciencias Sociales (FLACSO).

———. 1989. "Mujer y participación política en el Ecuador: Elementos para la configuración de una temática." Working paper, Facultad Latinoamericana de Ciencias Sociales (FLACSO), Quito, November.

———. 1994. "Ciudadanía." In "Léxico político ecuatoriano," ed. Alberto Acosta, n.p. Instituto Latinoamericano de Investigaciones Sociales (ILDIS), Quito. Photocopy.

Menjívar, Cecilia, ed. 2002. "Structural Changes and Gender Relations in Latin America and the Caribbean." Special issue, *Journal of Developing Societies* 18, nos. 2–3.

Meyer, Mary K., and Elisabeth Prügl, eds. 1999. *Gender Politics in Global Governance*. New York: Rowman and Littlefield.

Mikell, Gwendolyn, ed. 1997. *African Feminisms: The Politics of Survival in Sub-Saharan Africa*. Philadelphia: University of Pennsylvania Press.

Miller, Francesca. 1991. *Latin American Women and the Search for Social Justice*. Lebanon, N.H.: University Press of New England.

"Mixed Blessing: Can Dollarized Ecuador Avoid the Argentine Trap?" 2002. *Financial Times*, January 24, http://www.globalpolicy.org/nations/dollar/0124ecuador.htm (accessed May 8, 2004).

Moallem, Minoo. 1999. "Transnationalism, Feminism, and Fundamentalism." In *Between Woman and Nation: Nationalisms, Transnational Feminisms, and the State*, ed. Caren Kaplan, Norma Alarcón, and Minoo Moallem, 320–48. Durham: Duke University Press.

Moallem, Minoo, and Iain A. Boal. 1999. "Multicultural Nationalism and the Poetics of Inauguration." In *Between Woman and Nation: Nationalisms, Transnational Feminisms, and the State*, ed. Caren Kaplan, Norma Alarcón, and Minoo Moallem, 243–63. Durham: Duke University Press.

Mohanty, Chandra Talpade. 1991. "Under Western Eyes: Feminist Scholarship and Colonial Discourses." In *Third World Women and the Politics of Feminism*, ed. Chandra Talpade Mohanty, Ann Russo, and Lourdes Torres, 1–50. Bloomington: Indiana University Press.

———. 2003. *Feminism Without Borders: Decolonizing Theory, Practicing Solidarity*. Durham: Duke University Press.

Molyneux, Maxine. 1985. "Mobilisation Without Emancipation? Women's Interests, the State, and Revolution in Nicaragua." *Feminist Review* 11:227–54.

———. 1998. "Analyzing Women's Movements." In *Feminist Visions of Development: Gender Analysis and Policy*, ed. Cecile Jackson and Ruth Pearson, 65–88. New York: Routledge.

Molyneux, Maxine, and Elisabeth Dore, eds. 2000. *Hidden Histories of Gender and the State in Latin America*. Durham: Duke University Press.

Montaño, Sonia. 1993. "Programa de la Mujer: Un esfuerzo por mirar de diferente manera el problema." In *Políticas sociales para la mujer: Memorias del Seminario Internacional*, ed. ONAMFA (Organismo Nacional del Menor, Mujer y Familia), 25–44. La Paz, Bolivia: ONAMFA.

———. 1996. "La construcción de una agenda de género en el gobierno de Bolivia de 1989–1995." La Paz, Bolivia: Proyecto de Recursos Humanos para el Desarrollo.

————. 1997. "Género, cultura y poder local." In *Los procesos de reforma del estado a la luz de las teorías de género*, ed. IULA/CELCADEL/RHUDO-USAID, 55–68. Quito: IULA.

Morris, Aldon D., and Carol McClurg Mueller, eds. 1992. *Frontiers in Social Movement Theory*. New Haven: Yale University Press.

Moser, Caroline. 1989a. "Gender Planning in the Third World: Meeting Practical and Strategic Gender Needs." *World Development* 17 (11): 1799–825.

————. 1989b. "The Impact of Recession and Structural Adjustment Policies at the Micro-level: Low-Income Women and Their Households in Guayaquil, Ecuador." UNICEF-Ecuador, January.

————. 1993. *Gender Planning and Development*. New York: Routledge.

Mueller, Adele. 1985. "The Bureaucratization of Feminist Knowledge: The Case of Women and Development." *Resources for Feminist Research/Documentation sur la Recherche Feministe* 15 (1): 49–51.

————. 1991. "Women in and Against Development."

Muñoz Jaramillo, Francisco, ed. 1998. *Asamblea: Análisis y propuestas*. Quito: Tramasocial Editorial.

Muteba Rahier, Jean. 2003. "Racist Stereotypes and the Embodiment of Blackness: Some Narratives of Female Sexuality in Quito." In *Millenial Ecuador: Critical Essays on Cultural Transformations and Social Dynamics*, ed. Norman Whitten, 296–324. Iowa City: University of Iowa Press.

Nandy, Ashis. 1998. "Colonization of the Mind." In *The Post-development Reader*, ed. R. Rahnema with V. Bawtree, 168–78. London: Zed Books.

Naples, Nancy, ed. 1998. *Community Activism and Feminist Politics: Organizing Across Race, Class, and Gender*. New York: Routledge.

Naples, Nancy, and Manisha Desai, eds. 2002. *Women's Activism and Globalization: Linking Local Struggles and Transnational Politics*. New York: Routledge.

Navarro, Marysa. 1989. "The Person Is Political: Las Madres de Plaza de Mayo." In *Power and Popular Protest: Latin American Social Movements*, ed. Susan Eckstein, 241–58. Berkeley and Los Angeles: University of California Press.

North, Liisa. 1999. "Austerity and Disorder in the Andes." NACLA Report on the Americas 33 (1): 6–9.

————. 2004. "Static Building, State Dismantling, and Financial Crises in Ecuador." In *Politics in the Andes: Identity, Conflict, Reform*, ed. Jo-Marie Burt and Philip Mauceri, 187–206. Pittsburgh: University of Pittsburgh Press.

North, Liisa, and John D. Cameron. 2003. *Rural Progress, Rural Decay*. Bloomfield, Conn.: Kumarian Press.

Ochsendorf, A. 1998. *Constructing Power Through Food-for-Work Projects in El Alto, Bolivia*. Bachelor's thesis, Wellesley College.

Ojeda Segovia, Lautaro. 1993. *El descrédito de lo social: Las políticas sociales en el Ecuador*. Quito: Centro para el Desarrollo Social (CDS).

————. 1998. *Encrucijadas y perspectivas de la descentralización en el Ecuador*. Quito: Ediciones Abya-Yala.

Olea, Raquel. 1995. "Feminism: Modern or Postmodern?" In *The Postmodernism Debate in Latin America*, ed. J. Beverley, J. Oviedo, and M. Aronna, 195–200. Durham: Duke University Press.

Olea Mauleón, Cecilia, ed. 1998. *Encuentros, (des)encuentros y búsquedas: El movimiento feminista en América Latina*. Lima: Centro Flora Tristán.

Ong, Aihwa. 1987. *Spirits of Resistance and Capitalist Discipline*. Albany: State University of New York Press.

Oyĕwùmí, Oyèrónké. 1997. *The Invention of Women: Making an African Sense of Western Gender Discourses*. Minneapolis: University of Minnesota Press.

Narayan, Uma. 1997. *Dislocating Cultures: Identities, Traditions, and Third World Feminism*. New York: Routledge.

Pachano, Simón. 1996. *Democracia sin sociedad*. Quito: Instituto Latinoamericano de Investigaciones (ILDIS).

Paulson, Susan, and Pamela Calla. 2000. "Gender and Ethnicity in Bolivian Politics: Transformation or Paternalism?" *Journal of Latin American Anthropology* 5 (2): 112–49.

Pearson, Ruth. 1998. "'Nimble Fingers' Revisited: Reflections on Women and Third World Industrialization in the Late Twentieth Century." In *Feminist Visions of Development: Gender Analysis and Policy*, ed. C. Jackson and R. Pearson, 171–88. New York: Routledge.

Peet, Richard, ed. 1987. *International Capitalism and Industrial Restructuring*. Boston: Allen and Unwin.

Peters, Julie, and Andrea Wolper, eds. 1995. *Women's Rights, Human Rights: International Feminist Perspectives*. New York: Routledge.

Peterson, V. Spike. 1996. "Shifting Ground(s): Epistemological and Territorial Remapping in the Context of Globalization(s)." In *Globalization: Theory and Practice*, ed. E. Kofman and G. Youngs. London: Pinter.

———. 2003. *A Critical Rewriting of Global Political Economy*. New York: Routledge.

Petras, James, and Morris Morley. 1992. *Latin America in the Time of Cholera: Electoral Politics, Market Economics, and Permanent Crisis*. New York: Routledge.

Phillips, Lynne. 1987. "Women, Development, and the State in Rural Ecuador." In *Rural Women and State Policy: Feminist Perspectives on Latin American Agricultural Development*, ed. C. D. Deere and M. León, 105–23. Boulder, Colo.: Westview Press.

———, ed. 1998. *The Third Wave of Modernization in Latin America: Cultural Perspectives on Neoliberalism*. Wilmington, Del: Scholarly Resources Books.

Pietela, Hilkka, and Jeanne Vickers. 1990. *Making Women Matter: The Role of the United Nations*. London: Zed Press.

Pion-Berlin, David. 1989. *The Ideology of State Terror: Economic Doctrine and Political Repression in Argentina and Peru*. Boulder, Colo.: Lynne Reinner.

Piore, Michael, and Charles F. Sabel. 1984. *The Second Industrial Divide: Possibilities for Prosperity*. New York: Basic Books.

Placencia, Mercedes, and Elvia Caro. 1998. "Institucionalidad para mujer y género en América Latina y el Caribe." Regional report, Inter-American Development Bank, Quito.

Power, Margaret. 2002. *Right-Wing Women in Chile: Feminine Power and the Struggle Against Allende, 1964–1973*. University Park: Pennsylvania State University Press.

Pratt, Minnie Bruce. 1995. "Gender Quiz." In *S/he*, 11–22. Ithaca, N.Y.: Firebrand Books.

Prieto, Mercedes. 1987. "Notas sobre el movimiento de mujeres en el Ecuador." In *Movi-*

mientos sociales en el Ecuador, ed. Luis Verdesoto Custode. Quito: Centro de Planificación y Estudios Sociales (CEPLAES)/Consejo Latinoamericano de Ciencias Sociales (CLACSO)/ Centro de Documentación e Información de los Movimientos Sociales del Ecuador (CEDIME).

Radcliffe, Sarah. 2001. "Decentralized Boundaries Around Urban Politics in an Era of Transnationalism and Neoliberalism: Indigenous Municipalities in Andean Latin America." Paper presented at the conference "Urban Informality in the Era of Liberalization: A Transnational Perspective," University of California at Berkeley, January 26–27.

Radcliffe, Sarah, Nina Laurie, and Robert Andolina. 2004. "The Transnationalization of Gender and Reimagining Andean Indigenous Development," *Signs* 29 (2): 387–416.

Radcliffe, Sarah, and Sallie Westwood. 1996. *Remaking the Nation: Place, Identity, and Politics in Latin America*. New York: Routledge.

Rahnema, Majid, and Victoria Bawtree, eds. 1997. *The Post-development Reader*. London: Zed Press.

Rathgeber, Eva. 1990. "WID, WAD, GAD: Trends in Research and Practice." *Journal of Developing Areas* 24 (July): 489–502.

Reed, Carolina, Carlos Larrea, and Mercedes Prieto. 1997. *Indicadores Sociales para el análisis de las desigualdades de género: Educación y empleo en el Ecuador*. Quito: DINAMU/Secretaría Técnica del Frente Social/UNICEF.

Ríos, Marcela, ed. 1998. *Reflexiones teóricas y comparativas sobre los feminismos en Chile y America Latina*. Santiago: Universidad de Chile.

Rist, Gilbert. 1990. "'Development' as a Part of the Modern Myth: The Western Sociocultural Dimension of 'Development.'" *European Journal of Development Research* 2 (1): 10–19.

Ritzer, George. 1993. *The McDonaldization of Society*. Thousand Oaks, Calif.: Pine Ridge Press.

Rivera Cusicanqui, Silvia, Denise Arnold, Zulema Lehm, Susan Paulson, and Juan de Díos Yapita, eds. 1996. *Ser mujer indígena, chola o birlocha en la Bolivia postcolonial de los años 90*. La Paz, Bolivia: Ministerio de Desarrollo Humano/Secretaría Nacional de Asuntos Etnicos, de Género y Generacionales/Subsecretaría de Asuntos de Género.

Rodas, Raquel. N.d. *Tránsito amaguaña: Su testimonio*. Quito: Centro de Documentación e Información de los Movimientos Sociales del Ecuador (CEDIME).

———. "Muchas voces, demasiados silencias: Los discursos de las lideresas del movimiento de mujeres del Ecuador." Working paper no. 4, Canadian International Development Agency, Quito.

Rodríguez, Ileana, ed. 2001. *The Latin American Subaltern Studies Reader*. Durham: Duke University Press.

Rodríguez, Lilia. 1986. "Ecuador: Women and Legal Services." In *Empowerment and the Law: Strategies of Third World Women*, ed. Margaret Schuler, 323–26. Washington, D.C.: Overseas Education Fund International.

———. 1990. *Directorio Ecuatoriano de Centros de Mujeres*. Quito: Centro Ecuatoriano para la Promoción y Acción de la Mujer (CEPAM)/Instituto Latinoamericano de Investigaciónes Sociales (ILDIS).

————. 1993. *Género y desarrollo: Nudos y desafíos en el trabajo no-gubernmental en el Ecuador.* Quito: Centro Ecuatoriano para la Promoción y Acción de la Mujer (CEPAM).

————. 1994. "Barrio Women: Between the Urban and the Feminist Movement." *Latin American Perspectives* 21 (3): 32–48.

————, ed. 1996. *Mujeres del barrio.* Quito: Centro Ecuatoriano para la Promoción y Acción de la Mujer (CEPAM).

Romo-Leroux, Ketty. 1997. *Movimiento de mujeres en el Ecuador.* Guayaquil: Editorial de la Universidad de Guayaquil.

Roos, Wilma, and Omer van Reuterghem. 1997. *Ecuador in Focus.* New York: Interlink Books.

Roper, J. Montgomery, Thomas Perreault, and Patrick Wilson. 2003. "New Indigenous Transformational Movements in Latin America." Introduction to *Latin American Perspectives* 30 (1): 5–22.

Rosero, Rocío. 1983. "Situación de las mujeres y perspectivas del movimiento femenino organizado." Research report, Centro Ecuatoriano para la Promoción y Acción de la Mujer (CEPAM), Quito.

————. 1988. "Balance y perspectiva del movimiento de mujeres." In *Mujeres, Crisis y Movimiento: America Latina y el Caribe,* ed. ISIS International, 125–32. Santiago de Chile: ISIS International.

————. 1997. "El despertar del ser social hacia la identidad ecuatoriana." In *¿Y ahora qué? Una contribución al análisis político-histórico actual,* ed. R. Baéz, 173–95. Quito: Eskeletra Editorial.

————. 2000. Personal e-mail communication. February 21.

Rosero, Rocío, and Amparo Armas. 1990. "La Organización de la Unión Popular de Mujeres de Loja, Ecuador." Report prepared for the Food and Agriculture Organization (FAO). Centro María Quilla, Quito.

Rosero, Rocío, Cecilia Miño, Jimena Jijón, Consuelo Obando, and Marcia Vallejo. 1991. "Protagonismo de las mujeres en el levantamiento indígena." Centro María Quilla, Quito.

Rosero, Rocío, María Pilar Vega, and Ariadna Reyes Ávila. 2000. *De las demandas a los derechos: Las mujeres en la constitución de 1998.* Quito: Foro Nacional Permanente de la Mujer Ecuatoriana/Consejo Nacional de las Mujeres/Embajada Real de los Países Bajos.

Rubin, Jeffrey. 1997. *Decentering the Regime: Ethnicity, Radicalism, and Democracy in Juchitan, Mexico.* Durham: Duke University Press.

Ruíz, Carmen Beatriz. 1996. *Mujer, género y desarrollo local urbano.* El Alto, Bolivia: Centro de Promoción de la Mujer Gregoria Apaza.

Sachs, Jeffrey, ed. 1992. *The Development Dictionary: A Guide to Knowledge as Power.* London: Zed Press.

Safa, Helen. 1995. *The Myth of the Male Breadwinner: Women and Industrialization in the Caribbean.* Boulder, Colo.: Westview Press.

Said, Edward. 1978. *Orientalism.* New York: Random House.

Salinas Mulder, S., et al. 1994. "Una protesta sin propuesta: Situación de la mujer en Bolivia: 1976–1994." La Paz, Bolivia.

Sampson, Gary, ed. 2001. *The Role of the World Trade Organization in Global Governance.* Hong Kong: United Nations University Press.

Sandercock, Leonie. 1998a. "Framing Insurgent Historiographies for Planning." Introduction to *Making the Invisible Visible: A Multicultural Planning History*, ed. Leonie Sandercock, 1–33. Berkeley and Los Angeles: University of California Press.
———, ed. 1998b. *Making the Invisible Visible: A Multicultural Planning History*. Berkeley and Los Angeles: University of California Press.
Saporta Sternbach, Nancy, et al. 1992. "Feminisms in Latin America: From Bogotá to
San Bernardo." *Signs* 17 (2): 393–434.
Sara-Lafosse, Violeta. 1984. *Comedores comunales: La mujer frente a la crisis*. Lima: Ser-
vicios Urbanos para Mujeres de Bajos Ingresos (SUMBI).
———. 1986. "Communal Kitchens in Lima." In *Learning About Women and Urban
Services in Latin America and the Caribbean*, ed. Marianne Schmink et. al. New
York: Population Council.
Sassen, Saskia. 1998. *Globalization and Its Discontents*. New York: New Press.
Sawyer, Suzana. 1997. "The 1992 Indian Mobilization in Lowland Ecuador." *Latin
American Perspectives* 24 (3): 65–82.
———. 2004. *Crude Chronicles: Indigenous Politics, Multinational Oil, and Neoliberalism in Ecuador*. Durham: Duke University Press.
Schild, Verónica. 1998. "New Subjects of Rights? Women's Movements and the Construction of Citizenship in the 'New Democracies.'" In *Cultures of Politics/Politics
of Cultures: Re-visioning Latin American Social Movements*, ed. Sonia Alvarez,
Evelina Dagnino, and Arturo Escobar, 93–117. Boulder, Colo.: Westview Press.
———. 2000. "Neo-liberalism's New Gendered Market Citizens: The 'Civilizing' Dimension of Social Programmes in Chile." *Citizenship Studies* 4 (3): 275–305.
———. 2002. "Engendering the New Social Citizenship in Chile: NGOs and Social
Provisioning Under Neo-liberalism." In *Gender Justice, Development, and Rights*,
ed. Maxine Molyneux and Shahra Razavi, 170–203. Oxford: Oxford University
Press.
Schodt, David. 1987. *Ecuador: An Andean Enigma*. Boulder, Colo.: Westview Press.
Scott, Allen J., and Michael Storper, eds. 1986. *Production, Work, and Territory: The
Geographical Anatomy of Industrial Capitalism*. Boston: Allen and Unwin.
Segarra, Monique. 1996. "Redefining the Public/Private Mix: NGOs and the Emergency
Social Investment Fund in Ecuador." In *The New Politics of Inequality in Latin
America: Rethinking Participation and Representation*, ed. Douglas A. Chalmers,
Carlos M. Vilas, Katherine Hite, Scott B. Martin, Kerri Piester, and Monique
Segarra, 489–515. Oxford: Oxford University Press.
Selverston-Scher, Melina. 2001. *Ethnopolitics in Ecuador: Indigenous Rights and the
Strengthening of Democracy*. Miami: University of Miami North South Center.
Sen, Amartya. 1990. "Gender and Cooperative Conflicts." In *Persistent Inequalities:
Women and World Development*, ed. Irene Tinker, 123–49. Oxford: Oxford Univer-
sity Press.
Sen, Gita, and Caren Grown. 1987. *Development, Crises, and Alternative Visions: Third
World Women's Perspectives*. New York: Monthly Review Press.
Shachar, Ayelet. 2001. *Multicultural Jurisdictions: Cultural Differences and Women's
Rights*. Cambridge: Cambridge University Press.
Shiva, Vandana. 1989. *Staying Alive: Women, Ecology, and Development*. London: Zed
Books.

Shore, Cris, and Susan Wright. 1997a. "Policy: A New Field of Anthropology." In *Anthropology of Policy: Critical Perspectives on Governance and Power*, ed. Cris Shore and Susan Wright, 3–39. New York: Routledge.

———, eds. 1997b. *Anthropology of Policy: Critical Perspectives on Governance and Power*. New York: Routledge.

Sieder, Rachel. 2002. Introduction to *Multiculturalism in Latin America: Indigenous Rights, Diversity, and Democracy*, ed. Rachel Sieder, 1–23. London: Palgrave Macmillan.

Silverblatt, Irene. 1987. *Moon, Sun, and Witches: Gender Ideologies and Class in Inca and Colonial Peru*. Princeton: Princeton University Press.

Simmons, Pam. 1997. "'Women in Development': A Threat to Liberation." In *The Post-development Reader*, ed. Majid Rahnema, 244–55. London: Zed Press.

Slater, David. 1985. *New Social Movements and the State in Latin America*. Amsterdam: Centre for Latin American Research and Documentation (CEDLA).

Smith, Jackie, Charles Chatfield, and Ron Pagnucco, eds. 1997. *Transnational Social Movements and Global Politics*. Syracuse: Syracuse University Press.

Smith, William, Carlos Acuña, and Eduardo Gamarra, eds. 1994. *Latin American Political Economy in the Age of Neoliberal Reform*. New Brunswick, N.J.: Transaction.

Smyth, Ines. 1991. "NGOs in a Post-feminist Era." In *Feminists Doing Development: A Practical Critique*, ed. M. Porter and E. Judd, 17–28. London: Zed Books.

Solimano, Andrés. 1999. "Globalization and National Development at the End of the 20th Century: Tensions and Challenges." Paper prepared for the conference "Globalization and Problems of Development," Havana, Cuba, January.

Sparr, Pamela, ed. 1994. *Mortgaging Women's Lives: Feminist Critiques of Structural Adjustment*. London: Zed Books.

Starn, Orin. 1991. "Missing the Revolution: Anthropologists and the War in Peru." *Cultural Anthropology* 6 (3): 63–91.

———. 1999. *Nightwatch: The Politics of Protest in the Andes*. Durham: Duke University Press.

Stephen, Lynn. 1997. *Women and Social Movements in Latin America: Power from Below*. Austin: University of Texas Press.

Stephenson, Marcia. 1999. *Gender and Modernity in Andean Bolivia*. Austin: University of Texas Press.

Stern, Steven, ed. 1998. *Shining and Other Paths: War and Society in Peru, 1980–1995*. Durham: Duke University Press.

Stølen, Kristi Anne. 1987. *A Media Voz: Relaciones de Género en la Sierra Ecuatoriana*. Quito: CEPLAES.

Stoler, Ann Laura. 1995. *Race and the Education of Desire: Foucault's History of Sexuality and the Colonial Order of Things*. Durham: Duke University Press.

Striffler, Steve. 2002. *In the Shadows of State and Capital: The United Fruit Company, Popular Struggle, and Agrarian Restructuring in Ecuador, 1900–1995*. Durham: Duke University Press.

Sunder Rajan, Rajeswari. 2003. *The Scandal of the State: Women, Law, and Citizenship in Postcolonial India*. Durham: Duke University Press.

Taylor, Diana. 1997. *Disappearing Acts: Spectacles of Gender and Nationalism in Argentina's "Dirty War."* Durham: Duke University Press.

Thayer, Millie. 2000. "Traveling Feminisms: From Embodied Women to Gendered Citizenship." In *Global Ethnography: Forces, Connections, and Imaginations in a Postmodern World*, ed. Michael Burawoy et al., 203–33. Berkeley and Los Angeles: University of California Press.

Tiano, Susan. 1994. *Patriarchy on the Line: Labor, Gender, and Ideology in the Mexican Maquila Industry*. Philadelphia: Temple University Press.

Tinker, Irene. 1990. "The Making of a Field: Advocates, Practitioners, and Scholars." In *Persistent Inequalities: Women and World Development*, ed. Irene Tinker, 27–53. Oxford: Oxford University Press.

———, ed. 1990. *Persistent Inequalities: Women and World Development*. Oxford: Oxford University Press.

UNDP (United Nations Development Program)/Alternativa. 1992. *Directorio de ONGs: Organizaciones no gubernmentales dedicadas al desarrollo en el Ecuador*. Quito: Alternativa.

UNICEF (United Nations Children's Fund). 1987. *The Invisible Adjustment: Poor Women and the Economic Crisis*. Santiago de Chile: The Americas and the Caribbean Regional Office.

Valdés, Teresa. 1994. "Movimiento de mujeres y producción de conocimiento de género: Chile, 1978–1989." In *Mujeres y participación política: Avances y desafíos en América Latina*, ed. Magdalena León, 291–318. Bogotá: Tercer Mundo Ediciones.

Valenzuela, María Elena. 1998. "Las mujeres y el poder: La acción estatal desde una perspectiva de género en Chile." In *Reflexiones teóricas y comparativas sobre los feminismos en Chile y América Latina*, ed. Marcela Ríus, 36–49. Santiago de Chile: Facultad Latinoamericana de Ciencias Sociales (FLACSO-Chile).

Van Cott, Donna Lee. 2002. "Constitutional Reform in the Andes: Redefining Indigenous-State Relations." In *Multiculturalism in Latin America: Indigenous Rights, Diversity, and Democracy*, ed. Rachel Sieder, 45–73. New York: Palgrave Macmillan.

Vargas, Virginia.1992. *Cómo cambiar el mundo sin perdernos: El movimiento de mujeres en el Peru y America Latina*. Lima: Centro Flora Tristan.

———. 1999. Paper presented at the conference "Rethinking Feminisms in the Americas," Cornell University, Ithaca, New York, April.

Vega, Silvia. 1997. "Las mujeres y la caída de Bucaram." Quito.

———. 1998. *Asamblea nacional: Balance de la participacion de las mujeres y reflexiones para el futuro*. Quito: Coordinadora Política de Mujeres Ecuatorianas (CPME)/ United Nations Development Program (UNDP).

———. 2004. "Movimiento de mujeres: ¿Cuál es el 'nuevo momento'?" *Tendencia: Revista Ideológica Política*, no. 1 (March): 68–75.

Visvanathan, Nalini, Lynn Duggan, Laurie Nisonoff, and Nan Wiegersma, eds. 1997. *The Women, Gender, and Development Reader*. London: Zed Books.

Walton, John, and David Seddon. 1994. *Free Markets and Food Riots: The Politics of Global Adjustment*. Cambridge, Mass.: Blackwell.

Wappenstein, Susana. 1992. "Women, Violence, and the Politics of Daily Survival: The Formation of a Gender-Based Culture of Resistance in Lima, Perú." Master's thesis, Cornell University.

Ward, Kathryn, ed. 1990. *Women Workers and Global Restructuring*, Ithaca, N.Y.: Cornell University Industrial and Labor Relations (ILR) Press.

Weismantel, Mary. 1988. *Food, Gender, and Poverty in the Ecuadorian Andes.* Philadelphia: University of Pennsylvania Press.

———. 2001. *Cholas and Pishtacos: Stories of Race and Sex in the Andes.* Chicago: University of Chicago Press.

———. 2003. "Mothers of the *Patria*: La Chola Cuencana and la Mama Negra." In *Millenial Ecuador: Critical Essays on Cultural Transformations and Social Dynamics,* ed. Norman Whitten, 325–54. Iowa City: University of Iowa Press.

Westwood, Sallie, and Anne Phizacklea, eds. 2000. *Trans-nationalism and the Politics of Belonging.* New York: Routledge.

Whitton, Norman E., Jr. 2003a. Introduction to *Millenial Ecuador: Critical Essays on Cultural Transformations and Social Dynamics,* ed. Norman E. Whitton, Jr., 1–45. Iowa City: University of Iowa Press.

———, ed. 2003b. *Millenial Ecuador: Critical Essays on Cultural Transformations and Social Dynamics.* Iowa City: University of Iowa Press.

"Women's Protest in Brazil." 2001. *Arizona Republic,* March 9.

World Bank. 1984. *Ecuador: An Agenda for Recovery and Sustained Growth.* Washington, D.C.: World Bank.

———. 2001. *Engendering Development: Through Gender Equality in Rights, Resources, and Voice.* Washington, D.C.: World Bank/New York: Oxford University Press.

———. 2003a. "Distribution of Income or Consumption." http://www.worldbank.org/poverty/data/2_8wdi2002.pdf (accessed May 8, 2004).

———. 2003b. "Ecuador: Country Brief." http://devdata.worldbank.org/external/CP-Profile.asp?SelectedCountry = ECU&CCOD   E = ECU&CNAME = Ecuador& PTYPE = CP (accessed May 8, 2004).

———. 2003c. "Ecuador: Overview." http://lnweb18.worldbank.org/External/lac/lac.nsf/093e74928c454fb852567d6006b0 cda/. . . . April 17.

———. 2003d. "Ecuador at a Glance." http://wbln0018.worldbank.org/external/lac/lac.-nsf, May 8, 2004.

———. 2003e. "Global Poverty Monitoring: Latin America." http://www.worldbank.org/research/povmonitor/regional/Latin%20America.htm. April 17.

———. 2003f. "Women and Development." http://worldbank.org/genderstats (accessed May 8, 2004).

Wrigt, Natalia ed. 1991. *Mujer y políticas de desarrollo social.* Quito: United Nations Children's Fund (UNICEF)/Consejo Nacional de Desarrollo (CONADE)/Dirección Nacional de las Mujeres (DINAMU).

Zabala, María Lourdes. 1995. *Nos/otras en democracia: Mineras, cholas, y feministas (1976–1994).* La Paz, Bolivia: Instituto Latinoamericano de Investigaciones Sociales (ILDIS).

———. 1999. *Mujeres, cuotas y ciudadania en Bolivia.* La Paz, Bolivia: Coordinadora de la Mujer/UNICEF.

Newspapers, Newsletters, Bulletins, Serials

La Abeja
Boletín (Coordinadora Política de Mujeres del Ecuador [CPME])
El Comercio

Fempress
Diario Hoy
La Mujer
NACLA *Report on the Americas*
New York Times
Nuestra Voz
Punto de Vista

Interviews

All interviews were conducted by the author in Quito, unless otherwise noted. Interviewees: fifty-five members of eight community women's organizations, Quito, June–August 1989; fifteen members of eight community women's organizations, Quito, October 1992–February 1993.

María Arboleda, July 1989; February 17, 1993
Pablo Better, August 19, 1993
Diego Carrión, July 26, 1993
Tatiana Cisneros, August 5, 1989
Ernesto Delgado Ribadaneira, December 8, 1993
Rosario Gomez, February 11, 1993
Gioconda Herrera, April 21, 1998
Hernan Ibarra, July 6, 1993
Magdalena León Trujillo, June 17, 1993
Nela Martinez, September 15, 1993
Amparo Menéndez-Carrión, October 14, 1992
Nela Meriguet, July 23, 1989
Lautaro Ojeda Segovia, October 28, 1993
Martha Ordoñez, April 25, 1998
Simón Pachano, July 6, 1993
Dolores Padilla, September 30, 1993; December 14, 1993
Patricia Palacios, June 2,1993
Rodrigo Paz, August 2, 1993
Mercedes Prieto, June 5, 1993
Lilia Rodríguez, October 29, 1993
Rocío Rosero, October 27, 1993; April 21, 1998; August 3, 2000
Mario Unda, July 28, 1993
Silvia Vega, July 15, 1989; December 7, 1993
Lola Villaquirán, April 22, 1998
María Lourdes Zabala, April 15, 1999 (Cochabamba, Bolivia)

INDEX